U0647723

Foreign Language
Culture
Teaching

外语·文化·教学论丛

浙江工商大学外国语言文学一级学科资助出版

A Study of Teachers' Perspectives on the Role of Teacher Autonomy
in English Classrooms in Chinese Secondary Schools

英语基础教育中
教师自主性实证研究

孔佩佩 ◎ 著

by Peipei KONG

ZHEJIANG UNIVERSITY PRESS
浙江大学出版社

PREFACE

This book is an attempt to look inside the teaching and learning of English language in Chinese secondary schools. It is a product of the work done as part of my doctoral studies at the University of Sheffield in the UK. In the past, many researchers have identified a variety of problems militating against the effective teaching and learning of English in Chinese secondary schools. However, very few of them explored recent changes and developments in English Language Teaching (ELT) in China. I was motivated to embark on this work by the lack of research that explicitly focused on the teaching of English in both private and public Chinese secondary schools. My objective is to bring to light the teacher's role in the English language teaching and learning process and to highlight some of the factors bedevilling the effective teaching and learning of English within the Chinese secondary schools' context. Apart from identifying the problems and finding out the changes in the field, I believe that it is also important to find a way to address these problems in order to further develop the ELT curriculum.

I have organised the book into clear chapters to make it easy for the readers to follow the development of the full story. For those of you who are interested in academic research, apart from exploring the conceptual under-standing of issues around ELT, the book also illuminates key theoretical and practical issues in educational research. For instance, it articulates the use of qualitative research design, the use of a multiple case study approach as well as the triangulation of data collection methods. The study findings are reported in an honest manner making connections with the existing literature within the field of ELT. An effort is made to demonstrate how to conduct research in an ethically sound manner. In addition, the book discusses key concepts such as learner autonomy and teacher autonomy, making explicit connections between the two concepts and how they play a pivotal role in the improvement of English language teaching and learning.

I would like to acknowledge the help of all the people who gave their time for interviews and who collaborated with me for all the English lesson observations in schools as well as those who provided me with valuable feedback in the process of compiling this book. For ethical reasons, I cannot name any of my participants, but they may recognise their voices and their contributions if they read this book. However, I would like to single out my PhD supervisor, Professor Terry Lamb, to thank him for his advice and guidance throughout my research, which led to this book.

In a nutshell, this book explores the teaching and learning of English in Chinese secondary schools. It provides contextualised experiences of English teachers and identifies problems and ways of addressing them with a view to improving the teaching and learning of English language in schools. It is my cherished hope that readers will find the book interesting and useful. If you have any constructive criticism, praise or pleasant comments, please tell me at: kongpeipei1985@hotmail.com. For any other comments, please send them to the publisher.

CONTENTS

List of Tables

Abbreviations

ELT	English Language Teaching
CLT	Communicative Language Teaching
TESOL	Teaching English to Speakers of Other Languages
SDPD	Self-directed Professional Development
TBLT	Task-based Language Teaching
CET4	College English Test Band 4

CHAPTER 1

Introduction

English language is an important foreign language in China, playing a pivotal role in the country's economic life. Wang and Ma (2009) state that English language is serving the state's priority of driving economic growth. In the last three decades, the teaching and learning of English language in Chinese schools has received considerable attention with a number of theories and ideologies being introduced. Autonomous learning is one of the concepts that have been embraced in the education system in general, and in the teaching and learning of English language in particular. My study is focused on teachers' perspectives on the teaching and learning of English language, which also includes but is not limited to the teachers' perspectives on the development of learner autonomy. I will look at the connection between teacher autonomy and learner autonomy. The Chinese education system was predominantly teacher-centred and the need of a transition to student-centred approaches which was aimed at improving the quality of students was felt (Hu, 2003). The changes that were taking place elsewhere and in the society impacted on the opinion of the government departments, in particular, the Ministry of Education and led to the redefining of the education goals. As observed by Yong commenting on the development of learner autonomy in China, 'developments in technology and society have made an undeniable contribution to the spread of autonomy' (Yong, 2015: 216). An important question that can be asked is, 'to what extent was the Chinese education system prepared to embrace all these changes?' Reflecting on the situation in China, when the idea of autonomous learning was brought into the teaching and learning of English as a foreign language in the early 1990s, some Chinese scholars accepted the concept without any critical reflection on its appropriate application in a Chinese context.

1

Surely, this underscores the need to understand from the teachers' perspective how innovative ideas like autonomous learning, teacher autonomy and so on have been developed within the Chinese education system. The last decade has also seen a lot of attention being given to teacher autonomy. It has been shown that teacher autonomy is an important ingredient in the development of learner autonomy (Feryok, 2013). As indicated earlier, the goal of current education is to enhance learner autonomy to help students survive in the society. There was the realisation that a teacher-dominated system did not help students to develop fully in the learning process. It is therefore important to ensure that teachers are made aware of the need to promote autonomous learning by being more autonomous and reflective in their teaching. Building on previous studies, the present study seeks to understand the role played by teachers in the teaching of English language in Chinese schools, that is, an exploration of the concept of teacher autonomy in the teaching and learning of English language. The book presented here is the result of the research undertaken towards a PhD degree qualification. In this section, a discussion of the background and context of the study is to be made. In addition, the problem statement of the study, the research questions and researcher positionality are to be presented.

1.1　Background of the study

My study is focused on teachers' perceptions on how to improve the teaching and learning of English language in Chinese secondary schools. In this section I will explain briefly the Chinese school system and why I am interested in the topic at hand. Furthermore, I will present the background of the English Language Teaching (ELT) in China, high-lighting both my personal learning experience and previous research.

1.1.1　Chinese school system

China has the largest education system in the world. The education system is divided into different levels, including pre-school education, primary and secondary education and the higher education sector which includes colleges and universities. Pre-school education is mainly for the three-year-olds whereas primary school is attended for five or six years by students aged between 6 and 7 years on admission. The language of instruction in most of the primary schools except those schools that mainly admit ethnic minority students and some private schools is Mandarin Chinese. A total of nine subjects are studied by children during their time at primary school level.

Children aged between 12 and 15 enter into secondary school level and this junior level takes up to three years. At this level, foreign languages are examined at school level with examinations set under the guidance of local education authorities. Students should also satisfy minimum expectations in physical education. As indicated above, the individual schools are responsible for setting the examinations undertaken by students but clear guidelines are provided by the local authorities. Apart from a foreign language, students take examinations in five other subjects which include moral education, mathematics, Chinese language, physics and chemistry. In China, there is a nine-year compulsory education programme which means students should at least go through six years of primary education and three years of junior secondary education. This law was enacted in 1986 and the government takes full responsibility for the funding of this nine-year compulsory education programme.

There are two possible routes that students can take once they complete the compulsory education programme. At the end of the junior secondary education, students can proceed to enroll on an academic route, that is, they can join the senior secondary school. Usually, the senior secondary education programme takes up to four years. All students interested to pursue the academic education should attend entrance examinations set by the provincial education authorities. The subjects taken by students in the junior secondary education programme are examined, including a foreign language which is usually English language. Similarly, upon completion of the senior secondary education, if students are interested to pursue higher education, they have to attend the National College Entrance Examination.

On the other hand, students who choose not to continue with academic education programme at senior secondary school level can opt for vocational education. Currently, in China vocational education is provided at both senior secondary and higher education levels. This type of education is focused on equipping students with job-related skills. After senior secondary education, students can enter into the job industry or pursue further studies in higher education if they want. Effected from 2000, the government opened up the opportunity for students in the vocational fields to attend National College Entrance Examinations so they can enroll in higher education institutions like their counterparts from the academic pathway. Different higher education institutions are available in China to cater for the diverse needs of students from senior secondary schools; however, it is a prerequisite that students should pass the entrance examinations.

There are primarily two types of schools in China, namely public and private schools. These two types of schools differ in relation to the source of funding with public schools being funded by the government, while private schools are funded by private organisations or individuals. In addition, the types of curricula provided to students in each group of schools are different. In private schools there is more emphasis on English language learning and computer skills. Moreover, private schools are generally well-resourced, providing excellent learning and living conditions and a low teacher–student ratio (Lin, 1999). According to Lin (1999), public schools follow a centralised curriculum designed by the state education commission, which means in public schools, the same set of textbooks and teaching guidelines are used.

1.1.2 ELT in China

English language is taught at different levels. Since it is believed that a foreign language should be learnt as early as possible so as to establish a solid foundation in that language, English language is considered one of the three major subjects in secondary schools and in some primary schools. English has become a major part of the matriculation examinations and counts heavily in entrance examinations for college and university students. In colleges and universities English as a foreign language is a compulsory course. Without passing the English language examination, students cannot obtain their graduate diplomas or become postgraduate students. Furthermore, after graduation, English language is required for promotion in many work areas.

Crystal (2003) makes an observation that English is the most widely taught foreign language in the 21st century. There are more than one hundred countries which have designated English as a primary foreign language, in which China is one of the countries prioritising the teaching of the language. Crystal (2003) used the term 'global language' to refer to English and further defines the term 'global language' as a language that achieves a genuinely global status when it develops a special role that is recognised in every country. Following the economic reformation in China in the late 1970s, foreign language education, especially English education, has become increasingly important for Chinese learners at all levels of education over the last 30 years (Cheng, 2008). With the rapid development of its tourism, foreign trade and internationalisation of education, China has experienced the most exponential increase in the demand for English-speaking bilinguals. From international mega-events such as the 2008 Beijing Summer Olympics and the Expo 2010 Shanghai China, the demand for English can hardly be underestimated. Studying English has become a 'whole-nation movement in the 21st century' in China.

Enthusiasm for English language learning in China has been growing at an astounding rate over the past few years and with it grows a new disposition to engaging foreign teachers of English to support in the mission of making China part of the global English-speaking community. In China, it is widely believed that high English proficiency is the key to acquire success in many areas such as governmental, educational, scientific research, financial, business and other government-supported institutions (Cheng, 2008). Morrison and Lui (2000) assert that Chinese people seek and use English for various economic, sociocultural and political reasons. The societal and individual need to use English has increased to an unparalleled level in China. If we take all these perspectives into account, it can be found that the need to use English in societies across China has increased exponentially in the past decades. Hence, the term ELT has become prominent over the last few decades. This has been attributed to the 'strong and growing conviction of the Chinese government that English competence and computer skills are a must for the younger generations in the 21st century' (Luo, 2007: 12). The importance of English for the region and for individuals has increased dramatically, partly because of the regional government policies to promote English language education. English has only been obligatory for secondary school students two decades ago. In the mid-1990s, English was extended to Primary 5 and Primary 6 school children. In the last decade, however, children in all major cities are taught English from Primary 1 to university. Most of the people in the country perceive the importance of the English language and are, therefore, engaging enthusiastically in its learning. There is no sign that English learning 'fever' is cooling down. Indeed, English continues to enjoy supreme position against other languages.

The development of teaching and learning of English in China is still having problems. Some of the challenges faced, for example, relate to the issue that a large number of teachers and students in China focus on reading and listening but ignore speaking and writing competency in English (Xie, 2010; Zhang and Head, 2010). This may imply that, although students begin to study English from an early age of six when they enter primary school and have had 15 years of English instruction by the time they graduate from university, many of them lack the competence to use the language to communicate with others in everyday situations. In addition, there are not many opportunities to use English for communication purposes so they lack English proficiency and confidence (Jackson, 2002; Liu and Littlewood, 1997).

In recent years, many scholars have started to notice the problem and seek to improve the communicative competence of students (Xie, 2010; Hu, 2005; Liao, 2004; Li, 2003; Nunan, 1989, 1999). However, this can be very difficult to achieve. According to my learning experience and the research conducted, the difficulties may be attributed to five key factors: the examination-oriented system (Lau and Lee, 2008; Preus, 2007); the traditional grammar-oriented method and materials (Arndt et al., 2000); the traditional role of teacher and learner (Zhou et al., 2009); the learning motivation (Ruan et al., 2015); and the limited number of facilities in rural areas (large class sizes) (Hu, 2005). All of these factors make the ELT educational reform quite difficult. Although changes cannot be made immediately, there is room for improvement. Some avenues for improvement include: teacher autonomy (Lamb, 2008), revised teaching approach (Bax, 2003; Nunan, 1991), curriculum design (Van Lier, 1996), and testing system reformation (Qi, 2007; Tomlinson, 2005). These studies look at, among other things, the problems in Chinese secondary schools from teachers' perspectives and also explores teachers' beliefs about their roles in ELT education. Therefore, this research will focus on improving teacher autonomy as a potential alternative way of reforming the learning and teaching of English. Vieira (2003) considers teacher autonomy to be the willing-ness and ability to manage constraints within the frame-work of education as liberation and empowerment. Here, teacher autonomy refers to teacher's Self-directed Professional Development (SDPD) as well as willingness and ability to manage constraints, which is very important in current education. It is hoped that academic performance in the learning and teaching of English in Chinese secondary schools will improve through exploration of teacher autonomy.

1.1.3　My learning experience

In October 2010, I started working on a PhD course as a full time student in the School of Education at the University of Sheffield. My previous learning experience inspired me to conduct this research. I have never thought that I would come to the UK to study the use of the English language. Before coming to the United Kingdom to do my first master's degree course, I identified myself as a non-English speaker with a very low spoken and written English level. I could not, for example, pass a one-hundred-word writing test or discern when to use past tense or present tense. I could not even make sure whether each sentence should have only one verb or when to use the third person singular. Further, having no background in business studies, it was hard for me to write in English as well as to give presentations. However, when I came to the UK to study for a MSc in University of Hull, I realised the urgency to improve my speaking as well as writing in English. Over the past four years, I have learnt that having self-determination is very important for a learner. Based on my learning experience, I believe that self-direction and self-determination have great power over learning.

In addition, I have discovered that teachers have a great influence on learning. In my own learning experience, I have always come across good teachers who have given me a lot of encouragement and inspiration. Their positive attitude towards me and my colleagues has helped to increase my motivation for learning. I observed how my high school class tutor stimulated students' interest and improved their self-awareness to study. The average aptitude of our class was amongst the lowest in our year group; however, during the university entrance examination our class achieved the highest. From this, I felt that teachers could help learners to take responsibility for their own learning. So while it is impossible to reform the educational system in China immediately, it is still possible for teachers to enhance their impact on students' learning and teaching.

1.1.4 Prior research

In July 2009, I travelled back to China to do data collection for my second master's (TESOL with translation studies, TESOL—Teaching English to Speakers of Other Languages) dissertation research work that focused on Communicative Language Teaching (CLT) approaches in Chinese secondary schools' English classes. I visited two different classrooms and interviewed three teachers. From my research, I found that these teachers held a very positive attitude towards the CLT approach and expressed their willingness and desire to change the traditional approach to teaching in their own language classrooms. Although it is difficult to implement the CLT approach in secondary schools, the teachers interviewed did not reject this approach entirely and they often tried to apply it in their teaching. Amongst the responses from some of the teachers, they felt that any communicative activity design should be fresh and creative and be based on students' interests (Kong, 2009).

The outcome of my dissertation suggests that, although some teachers would like to implement CLT practices, they still face many systemic constraints, the examination system, the traditional role of teachers and students, the negative motivation to learning and the constraints by underdeveloped rural areas where many schools locate in (Kong, 2009).

1.1.5　Teacher education in China

Teacher education constitutes an important part of the education system in China. The country has in place a teacher education system that is designed to meet the needs of basic education of different types and at different levels. Basically, teacher education consists of two pathways, namely pre-service and in-service teacher education. There are different educational institutions that provide teacher education in China, including universities and colleges. However, it must be noted that in China majoring in teacher education is not necessary for becoming a teacher. In normal universities[①] teacher education programmes are provided. However, students who study in other multi-disciplinary universities and who do not major in education may also become school teachers. So if students have a degree they can become teachers and access in-service teacher training. In the case of English teachers, graduates of English language can do a language teaching course to work as a qualified English teacher. Such professional qualifications can be done online or face to face, coordinated by institutions like TEFL or TESOL.

1.2　Problem statement

As stated above, the learning and teaching of English language in China is confronted

---

① Universities that provide teacher education programmes in China. Some normal universities are under the Ministry of Education and some under the local education authorities. Both are dedicated to educating prospective school teachers.

with a number of difficulties. Many research projects have identified these problems in China. However, very few of them explored recent changes and developments in ELT in China. After 1978, there have been numerous changes made to the Chinese education system, particularly in the 21st century. The speed of development may go beyond the estimation of many countries. There is a need to explore more aspects of the ELT at secondary school level. Apart from only identifying the problems and finding out the changes, I feel that it is also important to find a way to address these problems in order to further develop the ELT curriculum. I therefore have chosen to work with teachers because they work directly with students and would have ideas related to my interests.

1.3   Aim of the study

The aim of this research is to increase understanding of the ELT situation in Chinese secondary schools, including changes and problems from the perspective of teachers. Furthermore, to explore teachers' willingness and ability to improve their teaching approaches in order to further develop the teaching and learning of the English language.

1.4   Research questions

The key question is how the secondary school teachers can have an impact on the five issues raised previously about ELT in order to impact the learning of the language in China. In order to address this, below is a set of research questions that will be explored in this study. These are divided into two points of view, one focusing on the teachers' perspectives on ELT and another focusing on the teachers' perspectives on their role as agents of change in ELT.

1. What are the teachers' perspectives on the content[①] of the ELT curriculum?
2. What are the teachers' perspectives regarding how they design and teach the ELT curriculum?
3. What are the teachers' perspectives on the key problems being faced in the

---

① Content here refers to the subject matter being taught in English language classrooms.

teaching and learning of the English language in schools?

4. From the teachers' perspectives, what can be done to ensure effective teaching of the English language in schools?

5. What opportunities exist for teachers to develop professionally in schools?

6. From the teachers' perspectives, what role does SDPD play in the learning and teaching of the English language?

1.5　Significance of the study

The value of this research is to explore the current situation of the learning and teaching of English in Chinese secondary schools, which has not yet been sufficiently brought to light. Research outcomes may help to create more opportunities for teachers to improve their willingness and ability to enhance language teaching in order to improve teaching approaches and, among other things, to discover ways of motivating learners' language learning. I hope that this study will make contributions to the current learning and teaching of English.

1.6　Structure of the study

Chapter 1　Introduction

This chapter presents the background to this study, its aims, the problem statement, research questions and the significance of this study, and explains my positionality, including my educational background, work experience, learning experience, as well as ontological and epistemological assumptions.

Chapter 2　Literature Review

This chapter focuses on the theoretical framework of this research. It discusses the relevant research in this area and attempts to find ways which might contribute to my research. The chapter includes themes addressed in my study and helps to discuss the findings of my study effectively.

Chapter 3　Research Methodology and Ethical Considerations

This chapter describes and analyses what kind of research approach will be applied to this study. It will also address the procedure of data collection, that is, how to prepare and design the plan before collecting data.

Chapter 4　Data Presentation and Analysis

This chapter presents the data generated from the teachers involved in this research. It aims to reflect their views to enable transparent interpretation and analysis of data.

Chapter 5　Discussion of Findings

The chapter focuses on the discussion of findings from three schools and suggests strategies emerging from this analysis.

Chapter 6　Conclusion and Recommendations

The chapter presents the conclusion and some recommendations for further research. In addition, the limitations of the study, including some personal reflections on the research, are discussed.

1.7　Positionality

In social science there is an understanding and acceptance that research is not value free. It is widely accepted that the researcher influences the research process at many stages; hence, positionality has become a very popular concept in the conduct of research. In this section, I will discuss the definition of positionality as it is understood in social science research and explain how it influences the choice of my research topic, methodology and practice. Reflecting on positionality, Sikes (2004: 18) considers that

> ...the most significant factor that influences the choice and use of methodology and procedures is 'where the researcher is coming from' in terms of their philosophical position and their fundamental assumptions concerning social reality (ontological assumptions), the nature of knowledge (epistemological assumptions) and human nature and agency.

The researcher's fundamental assumptions are influenced by a host of factors including social class, ethnicity, gender, historical and geographical location. This view is consistent with observations made by Wellington et al. (2005: 99) who posit that 'the methodology and methods selected will be influenced by a variety of factors, including the personal predilections, interests and disciplinary background of the researcher...' I will focus on my educational background and learning experience for these are important in terms of making my positionality explicit.

From a very early age, I wanted to become a teacher. I went on to pursue under-graduate studies and graduated with a bachelor's degree in Chinese Literature and Education. Interestingly, after this I embarked on postgraduate studies in the UK in a discipline not related to education, but I welcomed the opportunity to study in an English speaking environment to improve my English language skills, thinking that after the studies I could still be a teacher. In 2007, I enrolled at one of the UK universities and studied for a master's degree in Business Management. This was the first time that I was in an English education system, using English for all my studies. During group studies for the MSc programme, I found it difficult to communicate effectively in English and to understand other people's ideas. This environment stimulated my motivation to learn English and made me realise the importance of oral communication. Although I have learned English for ten years before coming to the UK, I still lacked effective English communication skills. This made me realise that the learning and teaching of English in China did not place enough emphasis on oral skills, and it also made me want to pursue teaching English as a second language. Thus in 2008, I went on to study for another master's degree in TESOL with translation studies, in order to expand my knowledge and interest in this area. During this period, I experienced different teaching approaches and different social relationships between learners and teachers. I think this programme helped me to develop great interest and enthusiasm for teaching English as a second language in secondary schools.

In June 2010, I went back to China and took a two-month teaching job at a local English language training centre. My task was to teach English as a second language to Chinese secondary school students with a view to developing their English language communication skills. While working as a teacher, I realised that students not only lacked communication skills and confidence but also lacked intrinsic motivation to study English language. In line with my experience, I also observed that teachers have significant impact on learning. Therefore, I wanted to carry out research from the perspectives of teachers.

CHAPTER 2

Literature Review

2.1 Introduction

This chapter presents a review of the literature related to the topics under consideration in my study. As highlighted in the previous chapter, the focus of my study is to explore ways to enhance ELT in Chinese secondary schools and in particular teachers' perspectives[①], including an examination of the role of teacher autonomy in ELT. To focus on the aims and objectives of my study, the exclusion criteria during the literature survey included the following:

- The study focused on ELT
- The study focused on teachers' perspectives on learner autonomy in ELT
- The study focused on ELT in China
- The study focused on teacher autonomy in ELT

I managed to retrieve relevant papers identified from different types of publications, including papers from empirical studies, editorial reviews and grey literature. Several themes emerged and the following themes that are closely related to the topic under consideration were prioritised:

- ELT in China
- Learner autonomy in language learning
- Teacher development/Professional development
- Teacher autonomy

The above themes have been selected for a deep understanding of the different

---

① 'Perspectives' here is being used to refer to the views held by teachers, that is, what they think about the teaching and learning of English language in schools.

issues included in my study. Firstly there is a section on English teaching in China, which provides an overview of the condition of language teaching, including problems and constraints. I then take a look at the concept of learner autonomy being developed across the globe and in China. Given that my study is focusing on teacher development, I will look at how teacher development is conducted in different countries and particularly in China. Teacher autonomy focuses on defining the concept and exploring what is being done to promote teacher autonomy in China and other countries. A strong link has been established between learner autonomy and teacher autonomy and this will be used in discussing the overall findings of my study.

The following section focuses on ELT in China.

2.2　ELT in China

More than a decade ago, ELT in China was described as a bridge to the future (Jin and Cortazzi, 2002). This underscores the importance attached to the teaching and learning of English language in the country, a trend that has continued up to the present day. One of the aspects I focused on in my literature review is the overview of the teaching and learning of English language in Chinese secondary schools. I sought to understand the factors that contributed to the learning of English language, including the problems and challenges faced by both teachers and students. In this section I will also discuss teacher perceptions regarding the effective teaching and learning of English language in Chinese schools.

Jin and Cortazzi (2002: 53) observe that 'ELT in China [was] characterised by scale and enthusiasm.' Many people chose to learn the English language in both formal and informal contexts because acquiring the language opened doors to academic, professional and business success. This remains true even today, about two decades later, where many students continue to learn the language either to travel, study abroad or to enhance their chances of employment. The learning of English language now starts as early as the kindergarten level attended by children aged between 2 and 6. At this level, the lessons use oral approaches focusing on activities such as songs, rhymes, games and movement, presenting an active use of pictures and objects.

At primary school level where children enter at the age of 6 or 7, the study of English language continues. National textbooks published jointly with international publishers such as Longman are used. These primary English textbooks and classes include the use of phonetics to teach pronunciation. Some schools, especially private schools, are employing native English speakers to improve teaching outcomes. Furthermore, some schools are developing links and engaging in pupils exchange programmes with schools in the western countries (Jin and Cortazzi, 2002).

As stated in the preceding section, at junior secondary school level, the learning of a foreign language is compulsory and students have to pass the subject in the entrance examinations. In these schools, national textbooks in English language are provided, which are published by local subject experts in collaboration with international publishers such as Longman, and are designed to promote the development of communicative aspects of the English language. There is an emphasis in pair work and small group activities to enable students to focus on communicative skills development in language classrooms. According to Jin and Cortazzi (2002: 55-56), 'these ELT methods are now at the forefront of educational change in China, teachers in other subjects are now using such interactive and communicative techniques learnt from their colleagues who teach English.'

To enter the senior middle school (that is, upper secondary) at the age of 15 or 16, the examinations including a compulsory foreign language, which is nearly always English should be taken (Jin and Cortazzi, 2002). The textbooks at this level also adopt communicative principles and put greater emphasis on oral skills and cultural content. However, in practice, grammar, reading comprehension, vocabulary and translation continue to be emphasised, typically in multiple choice examination exercises. In addition to class work, 'students may spend long hours completing English homework, reviewing vocabulary and grammar notes, going over model examination exercises and memorising texts. Some teachers require students to recite these texts in class or in their offices' (Jin and Cortazzi, 2002: 55).

English language plays an important role in the national examinations to enter university. At university, English language is the compulsory foreign language for most of the students. In order to graduate, students need to pass the English language examination.

The focus of this section is to examine the main systemic constraints in the learning and teaching of English in China, which include examination-oriented systems (Lau and Lee, 2008; Preus, 2007), traditional grammar-oriented method and materials (Arndt et al., 2000), traditional role of teachers and students (Zhou et al., 2009), learning motivation (Yin et al., 2009), and the limited number of facilities in rural areas (Hu, 2005). Ruan et al. (2015) discuss lack of motivation, lack of learners' metacognitive knowledge and inappropriate learning environment as key factors affecting the development of learner autonomy in Chinese context. These broad themes encapsulate some of the major issues discussed in literature within and outside China. Here I discuss factors identified both in China and around the world because of their resonating in many cases. These factors were identified from literature as the main areas of concern in the teaching and learning of English language. Given that learner autonomy is being developed in different countries, I felt that in some cases, the problems experienced abroad can actually be a mirror image of what happens in China. Of course there will be contextual variation but in general it is possible to extrapolate a number of issues. I will therefore approach this research work by looking at each of the aforementioned key issues, which typically affect the education systems of most institutions in the world, both internationally and from the context of the Chinese education system as well as the need for them to be addressed in China. As the field I am focusing on in this study is relatively new in countries like China, there has been little research in such contexts, hence, the need to read widely and consult with other countries exploring learner autonomy in language learning should be stressed.

2.2.1 Examination-oriented system

Many educationalists believe that examinations have great power in teaching and learning (Hughes, 1989; Davies, 1968; Vernon, 1956). Hughes (1989) claims that assessment requirements have a significant impact on the individual teaching approach, curriculum plan and syllabuses. Teachers feel that they are often compelled to implement controlling strategies[①] because of the impact of external pressures such as national examinations (Deci and Ryan, 2002). However, teachers' attempts to increase control may be counterproductive and might lead to higher levels of disaffection (Lamb, 2009). The examination-oriented system can cause many serious problems. For instance, many teachers tend to ignore subjects and activities which do not refer

---

① Controlling strategies refer to methods used by teachers to guide students which deprive students of their autonomy in their learning.

directly to passing the examination. From my prior research, since in China syllabuses are usually controlled by high school entrance examinations, many teachers are not likely to devote much time to teaching communicative skills that have no bearing on the examination requirement in Chinese secondary schools (Kong, 2009).

Furthermore, being controlled by the examination system can have negative impacts on those engaged in learning. For example, Kage (1990) carried out a research in Japan and found that when students were given tasks such as quizzes and had marks recorded in a classroom, they were less intrinsically motivated and showed a lack of competence in the final exam compared with students whose quiz grades were not recorded. Reeve (2002) also states that students are more likely to understand and utilise the newly acquired information more flexibly when they are free from the pressures of intensive exam-based learning.

However, the English learning of many Chinese students is primarily motivated by the examinations (Yong, 2015). English language is one of the three core subjects along with mathematics as well as Chinese language, and students have to pass language proficiency exams to enter junior and senior high schools. Similarly, English language is also a compulsory subject in the national university entrance examinations for all types of universities and colleges in China. Indeed, in order to obtain a bachelor's degree, in any discipline at university, one has to pass the College English Test Band 4 (CET4) (Cheng, 2008). This exam is written at the end of university studies alongside other modules on each student's course, like an exit exam. Students strive to achieve excellence in English language exams as this determines the type of school they can enroll in for further studies, for example, from junior school to senior high school level. A student has to achieve high grades in English language to be able to find a place at one of the best schools in the country which will help them to get a place at institutions on a higher rank of the educational ladder in China (Eckstein and Noah, 1993). In addition to this, because students' scores on the National College Entrance Examination have a primary effect on their career and income potential, English language teachers at each level feel a great deal of pressure to ensure that their students obtain excellent achievement in examinations, which has been stated clearly by Yong (2015: 219), saying that 'the [national] curriculum and the importance of achieving good exam results reinforce a more teacher-centred approach.' The examination system is a difficult and complex issue from a Chinese perspective, and hence there is a need to investigate this issue further in this research.

2.2.2 Teaching approach

The main approaches for the learning and teaching of English discussed in literature on China include the traditional grammar-oriented teaching approach, the CLT approach and the task-based method. The CLT approach is also referred to as task-based approach indicating that there is no difference between the two. The following section discusses the traditional grammar-oriented teaching approach and the CLT approach highlighting the problems faced in ELT in China.

2.2.3 Traditional grammar-oriented teaching approach

During a history of 5,000 years, China has boasted a long history in education which is dominated by a teacher-centred, book-centred approach, which an emphasis on replication, reviewing and memorisation. The learning and teaching of English in Chinese secondary schools has been strongly influenced by the traditional grammar-oriented method and teacher-fronted direct lecturing, which mainly includes grammar instruction, vocabulary illustration, intensive drills on language forms and text explanation (Jin and Cortazzi, 2002). Ning (2011) reiterates that teacher-centred direct teaching still plays a dominant role, where class begins with the reviewing of the material learnt the day before, followed by the new material. This is then followed by the teacher providing a discourse analysis at sentence, paragraph and passage levels. In order for teachers to run each course well, a selection of good textbooks is considered to be especially important. Rao (2002b) also notes that teachers devote almost all their effort in class focusing on the main textbook exercises, which is nice and compact, with just the right length and level, in which they can find language points they want to elaborate on, and on which hours can be spent explaining, analysing, paraphrasing, asking questions, practising patterns and reading aloud, retelling, etc. The final result of this process is that the students almost literally learn every word by heart. The author concludes that such teacher-dominated and text-focused classroom teaching results in a great emphasis on linguistic details and accuracy. There is a keen interest in the exact understanding of every word, a low tolerance of obscurity and a focus on distinct points and specific syntactic constructions. Arndt et al. (2000) note that the Chinese grammar book is the traditional and primary source of language learning material. Teaching materials deal with sentence-based grammar; different units or sections of a book are concerned with separate identifiable grammatical forms such as 'affirmative sentences' or 'present continuous' or 'comparison.' Furthermore, the grammar is based mainly on written forms and the reference material usually involves suggestions for teachers and learners to correct the usage of particular forms. Thus it can be seen that teaching approaches are restricted by the grammar-based materials. Many language teachers orient their teaching towards grammar, translation and making their subject 'academic,' 'difficult,' 'theoretical' yet with very little communication and practice. This view is echoed by Ning (2011) who claims that teaching methods in China primarily pay attention to linguistic accuracy and rote learning but with little emphasis on communicative skills and the actual use of English. In Biggs's (1996) studies, it was found that students generally adopted a surface learning approach and they spent much of the time memorising text and vocabularies.

In addition, Chinese students are usually exposed to teacher-dominated classrooms and gradually lose their learning desire and willingness in communicating in English (Ning, 2011). As a result, this traditional teaching method produces many unsatisfactory outcomes of teaching (Arndt et al., 2000), such as low speaking and writing ability. Jin and Cortazzi (2002) discover that many university graduates still find it hard to communicate in English although they have over ten years' experience in studying English.

2.2.4   The CLT approach

The CLT approach is one of the methodologies employed by language teachers with the primary aim to teach communicative competence.

In China, the movement of the CLT approach was first seen in the early 1990s. In 1992, the State Education Development Commission which is the representative of the highly centralised Chinese system of education introduced a teaching syllabus which required that secondary school teachers teach English language for communication (Liao, 2004). At the same time, the People's Education Press published a textbook series for secondary school English learners, the aim of which was to help students develop all-round ability in the four language skills (listening, speaking, reading and writing) (Liao, 2004). There are many group and pair work activities in the classroom design. This can potentially increase peer interaction as well as collaboration and foster collaborative autonomy where learners exercise a high level of control over their learning (Little, 2001). In addition, it helps teachers to realise that the purpose of teaching English is not merely to handle grammar but to achieve communication.

Preus (2007) did research regarding the tendencies in elementary and secondary education in China. He found that the Chinese government had gradually loosened its control over curriculum and assessment. China is encouraging curriculum development at the national, local and school levels, promoting a more flexible curriculum with choices for students. This reform movement seeks to de-emphasise assessment requirements and promote learner-oriented approaches which are promoted in China as a way to nurture active learners who can innovate and solve problems.

2.2.5   Traditional role of teacher and student

Towards the end of the 1970s, there was a substantial change in the roles of teachers and learners in the language classrooms in many countries including China, and learning began to gradually move away from the direct control of the teacher into the hands of the learners (Alderson and Wall, 1993). It must be noted that dramatic changes to the role of the teacher and the student were initially dominant in the west while in China teachers continued to dominate the classrooms especially before the 1980s. As early as the beginning of the 1980s, Littlewood (1981) who worked in Asia for some time made a proposition that the concept of the teacher as 'instructor' was inadequate. It is simply not enough to offer lectures or give correct answers to students. Teacher's roles should also include the overseer of learning, the classroom manager, the consultant and the communicator. A teacher has to facilitate the communication process for participants in the classroom. This view is supported by Rao (2002a) who explains that the main role of the teacher should not be the ruler, the dictator or just the speaker, but should also include the organiser, the assistant and the enlightener in a classroom. However, Rao (2002a) observes that, typically, Chinese teachers' behaviour towards students comprises of a high measure of control and restraint. Similarly, Flowerdew (1998) states that Chinese students are influenced by Confucian heritage cultures, who tend to value collectivism, cooperation, discipline and self-effacement and are willing to do what teachers tell them to do. In addition to this, Zhou et al. (2009) point out that a common and noticeable characteristic of Chinese students is that they readily accept the control and restraint of their teachers. Students often show their obedience and dependence on their teachers' authority. Chinese tradition is hierarchical, where those in lower positions of power generally obey those in high positions of power (for example, young people should obey the elders and similarly, students should obey their teachers) in society. Oxford's (1990) view holds that learners who believe teachers to be the authoritative source of knowledge would be more predisposed to avoid self-directed strategies deemed necessary to achieve proficiency in language. Ginsberg (1992) applies this to language learning, and discovers that it leads to teachers being authorities and students being passive learners. Teachers tell students what to do and students listen and obey uncritically (Ning, 2011). With teachers being considered as the 'fount of knowledge,' the final decision of what knowledge is to be taught lies with them, and the students have no option but to accept. Chinese students tend to be oriented towards pleasing their teachers in order to feel a sense of approval, which is quite consistent with the controlled way in which they are raised and instructed. Ning (2011) observes that Chinese students are usually afraid of being thought of as show-offs so they are likely to keep silent even if they have some good ideas. The role of students and teachers has to be looked at taking into account the cultural context.

2.2.6　Learning motivation in language education

Ruan et al.'s (2015) research in China acknowledges that learners' language motivation plays an important role in foreign second language learning. Success of learners is considered to be hugely dependent on their motivation. Previously, Gardner (1985: 85) indicated that 'the prime determining factor in language learning success is motivation,' because motivation, along with attitudes, determines the extent of active personal engagement in language learning. Oxford and Nyikos (1989) also find that the degree of expressed motivation is the single most powerful stimulus on the choice of language study. Students who are highly motivated use more strategies than poorly motivated students. Cook (1996: 99) observes that 'a high level of motivation is one of the key factors that lead to success in learning,' who also notes that successful learning can also result in high motivation indirectly. If a learner recognises that it is worthwhile to learn a second language, they tend to be motivated to study harder. This can result in higher proficiency, which plays a favourable role and provides greater motivation for further learning. Deci and Ryan's (1985) self-determination theory introduces two widely accepted categories of motivation: intrinsic motivation (doing an activity for the pleasure and satisfaction derived from it) and extrinsic motivation (undertaking a task because of external pressures or rewards, not out of intrinsic interest). Deci and Ryan (1985) claim that intrinsic motivation leads to more effective learning in general, but those extrinsic incentives are more necessary in the education of children. Their study takes a process-oriented view of motivation. That is, motivation can be either instigated and sustained or weakened by certain forces, such as the teaching and learning method or institutional linguistic challenges, all of which might be present throughout the learning process.

Based on self-determination theory (SDT), Deci and Ryan (2000) introduce the concept of autonomous motivation which is linked to intrinsic motivation. According to their study, this concept suggests that when students are fully engaged with their behaviour, they will perform autonomously and experience a sense of volition and willingness. Indeed, students will execute better adjustment and study well in their school settings when they are more autonomous. A similar view is held by Zhou et al. (2009) who maintain that autonomous motivation is an important factor for Chinese classroom adjustment. In line with their suggestions, autonomous motivation would tend to have higher levels of interest, perceived competence, and perceived choice whereas controlled motivation would have negative relations to the classroom adjustment indicators. In contrast, students who experience controlled motivation which involves being compelled or guided by external and internal pressures tend to be instilled with a sense of pressure, obligation and resistance. It is often the case that students learn not because they want to, but because they feel they should.

In China, many students' learning tends to be motivated by examinations (Cheng, 2008). It can even be said that getting the degree is a 'taken-for-granted' reason. However, this is often viewed as a negative influence by some researchers (e.g. Alderson and Wall, 1993). Studies have shown that examination-oriented system develops passive, unmotivated learners whose primary interest is only in passing the examinations. Ongoing research explores techniques for improving learner's motivation and learning interest. Furthermore, teachers should serve as good models for the development of learner autonomy among their students. This underscores the need for teacher autonomy which is critical for learner autonomy. Teachers should motivate students in their classrooms to develop the interest in learning the subject. In fact, 'interest' is an important issue to help students to bring about changes and to make a difference.

2.2.7　High percentage of rural areas

Hu (2005) conducts research into ELT in China based on a questionnaire involving 439 secondary school graduates from 25 provinces and municipalities of China. There are at least three practical issues in the underdeveloped regions of China. Firstly, he discovers that 70% of the secondary schools are in rural areas where there is a general shortage of qualified teachers, and teachers here typically lack competence in communication and knowledge of English-speaking cultures. Secondly, he acknowledges that rural areas do not have advanced facilities such as audio-visual or other teaching equipment for teaching and learning of English. Teaching practice is thus limited by educational resources. Thirdly, a lack of funds and teachers leads to classrooms being crowded with many students. English is usually taught in large classes (Jin and Cortazzi, 2002).

In addition to the above factors, Zhou et al. (2009) explain that most rural Chinese teachers have no choice about what they do regarding their school work. There is a deeply engrained, well-documented tendency towards uniformity in teaching approaches in Chinese rural schools (Winner, 1989). Thus, there is an urgent need to offer more professional development opportunities for teachers in rural areas in order for them to improve their skills in teaching.

In summary, this section has shed light on circumstances surrounding ELT in Chinese schools. In particular, some of the key problems and challenges bedeviling the teaching of English language have been identified. The following section focuses on learner autonomy in language learning.

2.3　Learner autonomy in language learning

My study is mainly focused on ways of enhancing the teaching and learning of English language in selected secondary schools in China. This is being done by eliciting the teachers' views on various aspects of the teaching and learning of English language, including content as well as other pedagogical and curriculum design issues. One of the key issues being explored is the role of the teacher and the extent to which teachers are autonomous. Teacher autonomy is closely linked with learner autonomy. One of the expected outcomes in the teaching and learning of English language is to guide students to become autonomous learners. This explains why learner autonomy has become an important element in language classrooms. Since my study investigates into how teachers are teaching the ELT curriculum, I decided to include the concept of learner autonomy in my literature review. It is important to understand from the outset what learner autonomy involves so that relevant questions can be raised when interviewing teachers. Therefore, although there is no research question in my study that is directly focused on learner autonomy, the concept of learner autonomy included in this section is to enable deeper understanding of the concept and to help in terms of eliciting appropriate information from teachers. Tschirhart and Rigler (2009: 71) argue that 'learner autonomy is a term that has been bandied about a great deal in the language learning literature in recent years,' who further argue that the term is a slippery notion. It is not clear whether the term is meant to refer to a behaviour or an attitude, a right or a responsibility. It seems to be most commonly understood as a psychological attribute of individual learners, implying, above all, a capacity and willingness to take responsibility for one's own learning and to actively manage it, both inside and outside the classroom (Dickinson, 1987). Like elsewhere in the world, the language classrooms in China are characterised by the effort to develop autonomous learners. The development of learner autonomy constitutes a key pedagogical goal in many English language learning classrooms across the globe. However, it must be acknowledged that the concept of learner autonomy is more developed in the western countries compared to the other parts of the world.

Fostering autonomy in language learning is mostly justified on pedagogical grounds. Nowadays in China, just like in many parts of the world, the teaching of foreign languages tends to be based on the communicative approach that focuses on the use of language in authentic, everyday situations, rather than the passive memorisation of grammar rules and vocabulary lists, and therefore presupposes more active involvement on the part of the learner (Ruan et al., 2015). According to Little (2007), effective communication depends on complex skills that develop only through using and learners who enjoy a high degree of social autonomy in their learning environment would find it easier to master the full range of discourse roles on which effective spontaneous communication depends. Nunan (2004) claims that the balance of research lends support to the view that second language learning will proceed most effectively if learners are allowed to develop and exercise their autonomy.

In addition to the reasons cited above, Ushioda (2011) cites a number of reasons why learner autonomy should be promoted in language learning classrooms. The development of learner autonomy in language classrooms has been explored in terms of understanding how teachers are fostering learner autonomy in their classrooms which remains a fundamental pedagogical goal. It is, therefore, imperative to understand why autonomy is important. Ushioda (2011) explores the nature of the relationship that exists between learner autonomy and learner motivation, citing that an autonomous learner is a motivated learner. In the same vein, Little (2007) posits that if students are involved in the management of their own learning and able to shape it according to their own personal interests, they also get their intrinsic motivation nourished and developed. Ushioda (2011) argues that developing autonomous learners also contributes to motivated students in the classrooms. There is therefore a close relationship between autonomy and motivation (Ushioda, 2011).

Autonomous learning and effective self-regulatory strategies are increasingly important in foreign language learning, without which students might not be able to exploit learning opportunities outside language classrooms. To promote learner auto-nomy, motivation, which is supported by those self-related concepts as self-efficacy and the ideal second language self, is considered to be the most crucial factor (Benson, 2001; Ushioda, 2011).

Encouraging autonomous behaviour in a language classroom is important for a number of reasons, in which perhaps the most important one is that it allows learners to take responsibility for and ownership of their own learning. The ability to learn independently empowers learners, allowing them to take learning into their own hands and enabling them to continue learning outside of the classroom or when the teacher is not present.

Experienced teachers will have a number of strategies for promoting learner independence in a classroom at their disposal, from classroom learner-centred manage-ment techniques such as pair work, group work to setting projects as homework. Helping learners to reflect on their own performance is another strategy a teacher might use to promote learner autonomy. Reflection on one's performance with a specific focus on language (e.g. grammar, pronunciation) encourages one to notice one's strengths and weaknesses.

It has been argued in literature that learner autonomy should be interpreted more broadly rather than just focusing on the ability of students to learn by themselves without teacher domination in the learning process. Learner autonomy can include other dimensions like social and political in addition to the teaching and learning aspects. It therefore becomes important to define clearly the parameters when one is dealing with learner autonomy to ensure that the audience understands the dimensions one is focusing on. In the same vein, more than two decades ago, Benson (2001) argued for the development of the different dimensions of learner autonomy, stating that individual autonomy should not be prioritised at the detriment of other aspects of autonomy including social and political autonomy. Autonomy is broadly defined as both a political right and a social responsibility.

Promoting learner autonomy may be viewed negatively by some students. For instance, there might be a feeling that teachers are no longer helping and some students can be discouraged. As a result, there are arguments that the learning of English language should be a collaborative process. Yet, when we talk about learner autonomy it should be borne in mind that this is not the same as teaching oneself or learning individually without the help of either the teacher or the other peers, but means that one can become autonomous by working collaboratively with others.

2.4　Teacher development / Professional development

My literature review also includes an exploration of teacher development in China. This is because this topic constitutes an important part in my study which seeks to find out more about how teachers think the teaching and learning of English language can be improved. The views of the teachers would be influenced by the way they are trained to become teachers, including the in-service training opportunities available to them. Teacher development constitutes an important factor in exploring ELT in Chinese schools. In a study conducted by Wang and Ma (2009), it was observed that many teachers were teaching in the same way they were taught at school. In most cases, this meant that most of the teachers were using teacher-centred approaches in teaching, despite the curriculum reform in China's basic education which began in 2001 advocating a transition from teacher-centred approaches to learner-centred approaches in teaching and learning. What it means is that teachers may not have become familiar with learner-centred pedagogies, hence, they continued to teach using the traditional teacher-centred approaches. The professional development of teachers is regarded as:

> a deliberate and continuous process involving the identification and discussion of present and anticipated needs of individual staff for furthering their job satisfaction and career prospects and of the institution for supporting its academic work and plans, and the implementation of programmers of staff activities designed for the harmonious satisfaction of needs (Billing, 1977: 22).

The work of Vrasidas and Zembylas (2008) draws attention to the importance of teacher professional development. They observe that good professional development for teachers will lead to better teaching. They also posit teacher professional development as one of the most significant elements which will impact on learner success. Vescio et al. (2008) discuss the relationship between student outcomes and efficiency of communities of learning on the improvement of teaching practice. Teacher professional development has a positive influence on students' learning and self-efficacy perceptions. This view is captured in studies carried out by many researchers who report that teachers learned to adapt teaching to individual student needs to help students improve their achievement (Lovett et al., 2008; Fishman et al., 2003).

In addition, Bullough (2008) reveals that teacher–student relationships are at the core of any quality learning experience. I think that nurturing good teacher–student relationships is closely related to the concept of teacher development. This is well articulated by Farrell (2010: 2) who indicates that different teachers hold different conceptions about such relationships and many may 'not be consciously aware of how they build, negotiate, and maintain them.' However, the nature of these relationships influences interactions between teachers and students both inside and outside the class. Teaching is a relational act because it is difficult to separate teachers and learners from teaching and learning. If teaching does not involve relationships and teachers act like well-organised machines, the class would be a very dry place. For teachers, the relational and indeed emotional investment involved in teaching includes constant monitoring of and listening to how their students are feeling, and evaluating if they need assistance with their learning. Furthermore, as Isenbarger and

Zembylas (2006: 123) have observed, 'taking the time to listen to students' problems or worries, giving advice or guidance to them, and showing warmth and love are all examples of emotional work in teaching.'

Thus, in order to enable teachers to assist their students' learning and give valuable suggestions while attending to their problems, it is necessary for them to build up trusting relationships between themselves and their students. However, building and maintaining such relationships is a hard work for teachers (Farrell, 2010). Research indicates that maintaining such caring relationships requires many emotional investment and input, such as spending extra personal time with students (Isenbarger and Zembylas, 2006; Hargreaves, 2000). In addition, teachers need to take the lead in encouraging, motivating and showing sensitivity towards their students' learning.

There are two key forms of teacher development in China, namely 'initial teacher education' or 'pre-service education' and 'in-service education.'

2.4.1　Initial teacher education

While many schools in China are trying hard to put the learner-centred principles into classroom practice, it has been observed that 'teacher education has lagged behind, with most new entrants joining the profession lacking awareness of what is going on in schools and of what learner-centred pedagogies involve' (Wang and Ma, 2009: 239). As a result, most of the new teachers tend to teach in the way they were taught in schools and are therefore in need of retraining (Wang and Ma, 2009).

Introducing learner-centred approaches during initial teacher education can help to promote awareness and to support the development of learner autonomy once they move into schools. The curriculum for initial teacher education has to be redeveloped to ensure that it is consistent with the new curriculum in schools advocating instructional strategies that embrace learner-centred approaches for the development of learner autonomy. As Little (2007: 7) points out, the demands of learner autonomy require 'an approach to teacher education that would give intending teachers the experience of being an autonomous learner and enable them to apply the same reflective processes to their teaching as autonomous learners apply to their learning.' In other words, student teachers need to be given opportunities to develop learner-centred awareness and be provided with practices by incorporating such awareness and practices in initial teacher education programmes, where teacher educators should provide opportunities for student teachers to experience, reflect on and practise learner-centred pedagogies, and furthermore, to examine their self-efficacy for teaching in a learner-centered way. This discourse shows that there is a close link between learner autonomy and teacher autonomy. Surely, teachers cannot foster the development of learner autonomy if they are not autonomous themselves. The concept of teacher autonomy is to be addressed later in 2.4.3. The following section focuses on in-service teacher education and will explore the opportunities for professional development provided to the English language teachers in schools.

2.4.2   In-service teacher education

The improvement of classroom teaching also depends on systematic staff development opportunities. A number of scholars argue that professional development produces the best results when being long-term and school-based (Raya and Lamb, 2008; Vieira, 2003). The core of professional development is about teachers learning, specifically, learning how to develop and transform their knowledge into practice for the benefit of their students' growth. Teacher professional learning is a complex process which requires cognitive and emotional involvement of teachers individually and collectively. The cognitive element addresses teachers' attempts at developing themselves professionally. Some instances may include conducting small-scale classroom research projects (action research), attending conferences and workshops related to their field of study, and reading published literature related to their profession (Richards and Farrell, 2005; Farrell, 2003). The meta-cognitive element deals with teachers and their reflections on their own concept and personality, the way they define their practice, their own emotional makeup, etc. (Zeichner and Liston, 1996; Richards and Lockhart, 1994).

Little (1995: 180) highlights that 'language teachers are more likely to succeed in promoting learner autonomy if their own education has encouraged them to be autonomous.' This view was supported by Hoekstra et al. (2009) who point out that professional development also impacts on teachers' conceptions and practice concerning student self-regulated learning. Putting teachers themselves in the position of the student enables teachers to better understand the problems and the process of learning especially from the perspective of the learner. Indeed, Ponte et al. (2004) point out that teacher technical knowledge can be improved through the process of professional development. 'Learning-by-doing' gives teachers the invaluable experience of knowing first-hand how it feels to be in the students' shoes by projects of this sort. Based on their opinions, it can be seen that teacher-continued education is a vital strategy to develop the realisation of teacher autonomy. It helps teacher's further learning and being challenged to understand the context of situation, meaning-making, participants, meaning-potential, among other language ideas, issues and conceptions. Becoming students will enable teachers to develop their autonomy as learners and provide them with the opportunity to become teachers of learning with a focus on learner autonomy. Therefore, teachers need to engage in teacher education so as to learn how to better provide teaching approaches to students. Teachers' needs will be met when they are able to make connections between their work and professional development through continued education (Vrasidas and Zembylas, 2008). It is important to create opportunities for teachers in order for them to experience autonomy as learners of teaching (Vieira, 2008).

Teacher education also plays an important role in reflective practice since teacher educators enable teachers' development to be significantly better when they 'educate' them on how to reflect instead of simply carrying out 'snapshot' observations and giving subsequent feedback (Gün, 2011). As Bailey (1997) suggests, reflection is essentially personal, teachers must reflect for themselves, which the role of the trainer should be to promote the reflection process by offering input but refraining from taking over. In China, teacher education reformation also calls for provision of more teacher professional development opportunities. This is well articulated by Preus (2007) who states that Chinese schools are instructed to promote the professional development of both novice and experienced teachers. In-service teacher education can enable teachers to reflect and hence develop their teaching approach, helping them to draw insights from their practice, and thus benefit their future teaching. Since the late 1970s, the Chinese government has viewed education as a key to economic development and has initiated several rounds of education reformation. The most recent reformation began in the 1990s and resulted in curriculum guidelines being published in 2001 and amended in 2002 (Preus, 2007). These reformations are designed to guide the Chinese educational system towards more formal professional development education.

Teachers need to hold up mirrors to their own practice, making more conscious what lies beneath the surface (Preus, 2007). Therefore, it is important for teachers to choose a colleague to observe their classes and carry the given observation tasks. Reflection is a social activity which is not just to reflect, but for the purpose of action, involving the essential element of communal dialog where there are many different voices. This view is explained by Hepple (2012), who notes that engaging with different conversational colleagues gives teachers the opportunity to discover different demonstrations of their experience. Hence, the design in the current research facilitated the reflective process through group discussions and occasions to explore classroom experiences with different voices in an attempt to maximise opportunities for dialogic learning to occur.

2.4.3　The development of teacher autonomy

One of the key questions when talking about learner autonomy is: 'to what extent can we develop learner autonomy if the teacher is not autonomous?' It appears that there is consensus on the need to focus on the development of teacher autonomy as this is vitally important for the development of learner autonomy. In other words, the two concepts are interdependent. Little (1995: 175) argues that, in fostering autonomy in language learning, the most important factor will always be 'the nature of the pedagogical dialogue.' In order to develop learners' autonomy, teachers themselves should learn to exercise autonomy in relation to their practice. Teachers, as learners, become involved in a process of autonomy, thus feeling more empowered to take charge of their own courses of action (Vieira, 1996). In addition to this, Voller (1997) claims that if students are learning how to take control, teachers may need to learn how to let go. As Smith (2001) points out, total freedom from control over professional action is not only unrealistic but also undesirable. Teachers and students are obviously assigned different roles, rights and responsibilities, and teachers' primary responsibility is the one towards their students. In this book, it will be argued as Raya et al. (2007: 49-50) say, 'when we view education as (inter-)personal empowerment and social transformation, autonomy becomes a collective interest and a democratic idea, so that teacher autonomy and learner autonomy are like two sides of the same coin.'

Having explored the definition of the concept of teacher autonomy in the preceding section, this paragraph discusses the importance of teacher autonomy according to the views proffered by teachers and other research evidence advocating for learner autonomy. The autonomous teacher knows not only what to do, but why. They have a solid network of convictions that are both practical and theoretical. The autonomous teacher can think about how children are thinking and at the same time think about how to intervene to promote the constructive process. DeVries and Kohlberg (1987: 380) note that teachers who are self-governing do not simply accept, without criticising, what curriculum specialists give them, but decide on whether to agree with what is suggested and then take responsibility for the education they are offering students.

It appears that autonomous teachers know what they should do with their students and why, and are able to justify their teaching to others. On the contrary, teachers who are not autonomous depend on others to illustrate to them what to do and cannot communicate easily with others. The statement of DeVries and Kohlberg (1987) also implies that autonomous teachers learn to make better teaching decisions by their own thinking about educational issues. In addition to this, autonomous teachers are able to set their own goals and make their own planning based on the knowledge which they have constructed (DeVries and Zan, 1994). Thavenius (1999) says that autonomous teachers reflect on their teaching roles and are able to change them. Trebbi (2008: 238) argues that the autonomous teacher may easily turn towards whatever approach he/she finds appropriate; in other words, autonomous teachers can make decisions on the appropriate approaches to teach students. It is worth highlighting that for teachers to become autonomous, the school management should be ready to give up some of its control to the teachers (Wang, 2017). It is possible for an autonomous teacher who is in control of his/her teaching to produce positive educational and developmental outcomes among students (Reeve, 2002). As a result, it is important to develop teacher autonomy in teacher education for learner autonomy.

Teachers who are autonomous can arguably contribute to learner motivation, which is connected with learner autonomy. For instance, Ushioda (2011) argues that an autonomous student is more likely to be intrinsically motivated than a teacher-dependent student. It is therefore important to consider that provision of support for the development of learner autonomy is a beneficial tool for learner motivation. The concept of autonomy support means that:

> an individual in a position of authority (e.g., an instructor) takes the others' (e.g., the students') perspectives, acknowledges the others' feelings, and provides the others

with pertinent information and opportunities for choice, while minimising the use of pressures and demands (Zhou et al., 2009: 493).

Autonomy support includes offering choices, minimising the use of pressure and encouraging independent problem solving which involves students in decision making (Reeve, 2006; Reeve et al., 1999). In addition, getting students actively involved in the actual use of English has become an important part of effective ELT classrooms. Autonomy support fosters students' inner motivation to participate in their classroom activities.

Deci and Ryan (2002) propose that a teacher's motivating style towards students can be conceptualised along a continuum that ranges from highly controlling to highly autonomy supportive. Generally speaking, autonomy-supportive teachers facilitate learning while controlling teachers' interference. There is congruence between classroom activities and students' self-determined inner motives. According to Reeve (2006), autonomy-supportive teachers increase this congruence by identifying and cultivating students' interests and preferences, and by designing classroom activities to offer more opportunities for students to have inner motivation to direct their learning. Many scholars have noted that a personal motivating style has a great influence on motivation, emotion, learning interest and performance (Reeve, 2002). Based on the summary of Reeve (2006), compared to students with controlling teachers, students with autonomy-supportive teachers display greater intrinsic motivation and conceptual understanding. There will be higher academic performance, more competence, more positive emotionality and longer persistence in school. This is because autonomy-supportive teachers are able to find ways to bring students to classroom activities and satisfy their psychological needs, such as autonomy, competence and relatedness during instruction.

However, most teachers hold a positive attitude toward controlling motivational strategies (e.g., rewards) rather than autonomy supportive strategies (Reeve, 2006). Many teachers use controlling strategies more than autonomy-supportive strategies (Newby, 2010). Indeed, many scholars (Markus et al., 1996; Ford, 1992) feel that Chinese schools do not pay much attention to the development of autonomous experiences, and that teachers themselves lack autonomy experiences. However, teacher support can only promote learner autonomy when teachers have had some experience of autonomy. As a result, my study explores ways of enhancing ELT through the development of teacher autonomy. Teachers need to be autonomous in order for them to be committed and dedicated to further the development of the learning and teaching of English in Chinese secondary schools.

It must be borne in mind that not everyone is in favour of the development of learner autonomy. For instance, there is a feeling that this is a western construct that is inappropriate in Chinese contexts. However, there are counter arguments showing that it is relevant and that it is being demanded by new curricula in China. The traditions of Chinese teaching therefore need to be addressed by finding ways of encouraging teachers to reflect critically and become more autonomous, trying things out that initially do not form part of their beliefs about learning and teaching.

In this section, an attempt will be made to define and discuss the role of teacher autonomy in ELT. A number of studies have investigated the notion of autonomy, which raises particular ideas and beliefs regarding teaching and learning. Many scholars have agreed that autonomy is a very complex concept, in terms of theory and practice, and is very difficult to 'measure' (Raya and Vieira, 2008). Indeed, most teachers claim that they are unfamiliar with the concept of autonomy (Reeve et al., 1999). In addition, research into teacher autonomy in the field of second language education is relatively recent (Lamb, 2008). The issue of teachers' own learning and teaching and their beliefs about autonomy still remains unclear. It is therefore necessary to understand the meaning of teacher autonomy in an appropriate way. In order to illustrate the term, five main dimensions of teacher autonomy in language teaching theory will be presented in this section:

- Capacity and willingness to engage with self-directed teaching such as planning lectures
- Freedom to teach what they feel is relevant
- SDPD
- Capacity to overcome constraints
- Teacher autonomy corresponding with learner autonomy

2.4.3.1 Development of teacher capacity and willingness to engage with self-directed teaching

Developing the necessary skills and positive attitudes towards teacher autonomy is regarded as crucial to the successful development of teacher autonomy (Lovett et al., 2008; Fishman et al., 2003). Vrasidas and Zembylas (2008) believe that teacher professional development will improve teachers' skill and knowledge, and this will aid teachers in their preparations toward selection of the appropriate curricula as well as making instructional decisions. Teacher professional development is not only an item of detached intellectual curiosity but also a focus of missionary purpose and passionate desire. It is important to note here that teacher professional development is being considered as one of the important catalysts for the development of teacher autonomy within the Chinese education system. The argument is that teacher professional development activities should be designed in such a way that they can provide opportunities to lead to the development of teacher autonomy.

Little (1995) defines teacher autonomy as teachers' capacity to engage in self-directed teaching, which is taking control of their teaching activities in terms of designing teaching activities based on reflection. He considers an autonomous teacher to be with a strong sense of personal responsibility for their teaching, which is exercised via continuous reflection and analysis of the teaching process and exploring the freedoms conferred to it. Autonomous teachers should be able to select their teaching materials, plan the curriculum and manage their lectures by themselves. Similarly, Aoki (2000) suggests that teacher autonomy involves the capacity, freedom and responsibility to make choices concerning their own teaching.

2.4.3.2　*Development of teaching methodology*

My literature review explores information on the experiences of teacher development in the area of teaching methodology. This is understood to be important for my study which seeks to identify what needs to be done to enhance the teaching and learning of English language. Dickinson (1987) suggests that teachers need psychological and methodological preparation in order to fully understand the impact of a new approach on learning. Gay (1987: vii) points out that teacher development programmes should be 'skill-oriented, rather than knowledge-oriented, and application-oriented rather than theory-oriented.' Innovative professional development for teachers offers a place for teachers to share their teaching experiences, expertise and offers opportunities for them to learn from others. Effective professional development encourages teachers to focus on furthering pedagogical approaches, reflective skills and teaching practice. The goal of many language teachers is to find the proper method. In addition, Raya et al. (2007) suggest that developing professional autonomy is about shortening the distance between reality (what it is) and ideal (what it should be). Professional development includes investigation of new trends and theories and practical approaches in language teaching, adaptation of academic grammar and field theory, critical assessment of the method, and systemisation of the language syllabus (Richards and Farrell, 2005).

2.4.3.3 Development of teacher knowledge

Larsen-Freeman and Freeman (2008: 147) have paid attention to various professionals' dilemmas in languages education by reviewing a relationship 'between disciplines, knowledge, and pedagogy in foreign langue instruction.' Ponte et al. (2004) claim that development in teacher knowledge can be partially perceived on three areas of teacher cognition: ideological (norms, values), empirical (connection between phenomena) and technical (methods). After teachers begin their careers, many of them start to realise that their knowledge of language teaching and learning is insufficient. Teachers' knowledge of a subject is related to their knowledge about how to design lesson plans and how to teach that subject. In addition, teachers' knowledge and beliefs about how students learn are intertwined with their knowledge of instructional strategies. Teachers' knowledge directly influences their thinking which determines their actions in the classroom. Teachers will need to think in new ways about learners, lesson plans, classroom activities, and the teaching–learning process. Such changes in thinking will require new kinds of knowledge and beliefs on the part of teachers as well as a willingness to become more 'adventurous' in their practice.

Thus, there is a need for teachers to have regular opportunities that enhance their professional knowledge. Many researchers state that teacher satisfaction amplified in professional development activities is linked to teachers' necessity and expectancy and their contribution to the enlargement of curricular understanding and self-efficacy increasing (Lovett et al., 2008). Richards and Farrell (2005) identify that teachers are generally motivated to continue their professional development once they begin their careers, who also explain that teacher development serves a longer-term goal and seeks to facilitate growth of teachers' understanding of teaching and of themselves as teachers. Professional development programmes that focus on expanding and elaborating teachers' knowledge systems are very significant in education reformation.

2.4.3.4　Development of teaching responsibility

The humanistic movement stresses the importance of qualities in teachers such as understanding, personal assumption of responsibility, and self-realisation (Stevick, 1990). The roles and responsibilities of teacher within a learner-centred approach are very important to language teaching (Tudor, 1993). In any mode of teaching, the teacher remains ultimately responsible for ensuring effective learning. According to Tudor (1993), the work of English language teachers is not only to teach language but also to develop learners as individuals. In addition, it is argued that language teachers should exploit students' affective and intellectual resources as much as possible, which will be linked into the continuing experience of students' life. Tudor identifies three main roles of teachers in their teaching. Firstly, a teacher is a 'knower,' that means they are the fountain of knowledge as well as the key in terms of determining the teaching approaches of the language in question. Secondly, the teacher is fully charged with the responsibility to identify and select the content to be covered in the classroom and how it should be taught. Thirdly, the teacher is considered to be responsible for organising all the learning activities and for providing vital feedback to the learners which is critical in terms of informing future learning.

About the first two roles, it is important to clarify that although teachers need to be knowledgeable and to gain leadership in their job, this should not compromise their commitment to the development of learner autonomy. The teachers are expected to facilitate students' learning without creating dependency syndrome on the part of the students. According to Farrell (2010) all teachers must fulfill a wide range of roles and responsibilities which include motivating students to learn and keeping the lessons interesting. In addition, Tudor (1993: 24) further points out that another role that teachers need to develop is the role of 'learning counsellor.' He continues to state that teachers need to:

1. Get to know students well enough to be able to understand both their intentions (what they need to do and would like to do) and their resources (what they are able to do);
2. Help students clarify their intentions and develop their resources;
3. Channel student participation in a pedagogically useful direction.

Furthermore, Tudor (1993: 29) highlights that teachers, in the role of learning counsellor, need at least three main sets of skills:

1. Personal skills. Evaluating students' potential and negotiating their involvement in a sensitive manner calls for an array of human and interpersonal skills. Maturity and human intuition are key qualities.

2. Educational skills. In a learner-centred mode of teaching, the teacher has to develop students' awareness and shape their ability to make the most of their knowledge and experience. Language teaching thus becomes an educational endeavour far more than a matter of skills training.

3. Course planning skills. Being open to student input and participation can make advance planning more difficult, which brings the teacher with more uncertainty than in traditional approaches. Furthermore, coordinating goal-setting and choice of methodology assumes a solid familiarity with course design and with the various methodological options available.

Helping students develop awareness in learning is a critical part of the teacher's role in a learner-centred approach, which includes the teacher making ideas and providing students with information. In addition, the teacher needs to help students to look at themselves and at language learning in an open and productive manner. This calls for skills which are designed to develop understanding and human potential (Tudor, 1993). Once the teacher has identified a potential for contribution, the next task is to assist students to frame their insights in an informatively useful form. In most cases, the teacher will need to provide some basic terminology and a few guidelines to get students thinking along useful lines (Tudor, 1993).

2.4.3.5   Development of freedom to teach what they feel is relevant
There are many factors influencing the possibility, quality and effectiveness of teacher autonomy. This section provides a broader perspective of the definition of the meaning of teacher autonomy. Identification of these factors provides a possible explanation of the problems and challenges being faced by the English language teachers in the secondary schools which is one of the main areas of interest in my study. Borko et al. (2002) investigate how educational systems and policies affect teachers' work lives and believe that policy reform environments may be supportive of teacher autonomy. The nature and operation of educational systems, policy environments and teacher working conditions determine the progress of professional development

within the school environment. In addition, school culture is an indicator of that school's ethos, tradition and beliefs. This is related to the operation of the administrative and organisational structures, and how these interact to assist or hinder teacher workplace learning. This view is supported by King (2002) who argues that professional development can either be interrupted by the school's organisational context or contribute towards obligation to learning goals and coordination in school. English departments as forms of school organisation might have positive effects on teacher professional growth and active pedagogic leadership (Knight, 2002).

Benson (2001) argues that teacher autonomy refers to a right to freedom (or an ability to exercise this right) as well as actual freedom from control. In essence, we cannot be absolutely free. Teachers should have some degree of freedom to teach what they feel is necessary in a class and to select which approach to use. It is argued that in the spirit of teacher autonomy, schools should allow teachers to have the freedom to choose the approach to teaching (although not necessarily as individuals) (Lamb, 2008). This implies that learning materials should be relevant to the learning context. In order to achieve this, schools should give teachers the freedom to select materials and ideas from outside the course as well as more freedom and authority to select their teaching objectives and classroom activities, which will help teachers to deliver the teaching/learning package successfully (Varanoglulari et al., 2008), also will encourage them to make their own decisions within the classroom setting. Bell (1999) suggests that involving teachers in the decision making processes within the classroom environment will shape classroom activities and thus encourage them to be more committed to their work. This view is also endorsed by Sahinkarakas et al. (2010) who posit that teachers are more capable of adjusting their practice if they are actively involved in identifying, evaluating and dealing with the issues involved in their practice. In addition, the content to be covered in lessons should be determined by teachers themselves. This will give more space for teachers to manage their lessons and employ appropriate strategies to develop students' motivation to learn the English language and not merely to aim to pass the examinations.

2.4.3.6   SDPD

This section is concerned with linking professional development to self-directed professional learning that is very much dependent on reflection. In line with the above statement, teacher autonomy improves along with the performance of teacher's SDPD. Many teachers hold a general belief that learning to teach can occur only through teaching experiences. Other studies demonstrate that teacher professional development is a key lever for leading education towards a better future (Vrasidas and Zembylas, 2008). The professional development of teachers is presented in the relevant literature in many different ways. For most people, teacher development is about knowledge and skill development which is in regards to teachers mastering the skills of teaching as well as the knowledge of what to teach and how to teach it. It can be packaged in courses, materials, workshops and training programs. However, it is insufficient since teachers often resist or reject knowledge and skill requirements when they experience them alone and are afraid of being criticised by colleagues or of being seen as elevating themselves on pedestals above others (Fullan and Hargreaves, 1991). There should be much more in teacher education and development than just knowledge and skill development (Wang and Ma, 2009). Therefore, in recent years, the development approaches gradually have transformed from 'outside' to 'inside.' The former usually depends on professional knowledge as well as common theories and standards that teachers apply to their own conditions; the latter is very much related to SDPD which relies on approaches that promote teachers' discovery of their own frameworks and allow them to create their own understanding and perception of what should be in their classrooms (Richards and Farrell, 2005). The reality of SDPD is in teachers taking responsibility for setting self-development goals, and managing and controlling their own learning (Richards and Farrell, 2005). However, acting in a self-directed manner does not guarantee that teachers will learn from experience. For example, some college teachers have the ability to engage in self-directed activities but they might refuse to do so because they fear taking the full responsibility of designing self-directed learning activities, which can be a time-consuming task. SDPD is very much related to reflective practice (Farrell, 2008).

McGrath (2000) asserts that autonomous teachers are those who have control over their own professional lives by engaging in SDPD. This view is further shared by Tort-Moloney (1997: 51), who says that the autonomous teacher is the one who is aware of why, when, where and how pedagogical skills can be acquired in the self-conscious awareness of the teaching practice itself. Richards and Farrell (2005) refer to self-directed learning rather than SDPD. According to their study, in self-directed learning, teachers are assumed to take responsibility for setting self-development goals, managing and controlling their own learning. However, these two concepts are very similar.

2.4.3.7   *Capacity to overcome constraints*

Vieira (2003: 219) explains teacher autonomy as the willingness and ability to manage constraints within a vision of education as liberation and empowerment. In addition, Lamb (2000) finds it important for the teachers themselves to go through this process, reflecting critically on their setting and the forces which come into play, to articulate ideas, and to find ways of moving ever closer to those ideas:

> As with pupils, teachers need to understand the constraints on their practice but, rather than feeling disempowered, they need to empower themselves by finding the spaces and opportunities for manoeuver. (…) Critique (resistance) needs to be linked to transformation rather than resignation (Lamb, 2000: 127).

2.4.3.8   *Teacher autonomy corresponding with learner autonomy*

The concept of teacher autonomy in English learning has been widely discussed in the literature and it is generally accepted that teacher autonomy is an important ingredient in the development of learner autonomy (Feryok, 2013; Raya et al., 2007; Tschirhart and Rigler, 2009; Chan, 2003). Teacher autonomy is defined as a teacher's ability and willingness to help learners take responsibility for their own learning by Thavenius (1999: 160). As the two concepts are interrelated, it is important to interpret the dynamic relationship between teacher autonomy and learner autonomy. Learner autonomy involves learners taking responsibility for their own learning. Little (1999) describes how the development of learner autonomy depends on the development of teacher autonomy. On the one hand, teachers' own learning and teaching experiences and their beliefs about autonomy play an important role in the development of learner autonomy (Lamb, 2008). On the other hand, 'an autonomous teacher is thus a teacher who reflects on her teacher role and who can change it, who can help their learners become autonomous, and who is independent enough to let their learners become independent' (Thavenius, 1996: 160). Learner autonomy does not mean learning without a teacher but it removes the need for a teacher's lecturing or domineering position in teaching and learning context (Little, 1999). Learner autonomy concerns a capacity which can be cultivated and explored in the classroom with the help of teacher autonomy. As argued by Raya et al. (2007), there is a close link between teacher autonomy and learner autonomy, the two concepts being considered as two sides of the same coin. Any discourse involving the development of learner autonomy would be void if no mention of teacher autonomy is made. It is against this background that my study focuses on teacher development and teacher autonomy in addition to learner autonomy.

The focus throughout this book is not to make a judgement about which answer is right or wrong, neither is it the purpose of this research work to analyse these five issues noted. What it seeks is to deepen the understanding of the complexity, principles and values of teacher autonomy as it pertains to SDPD in China. China is encouraging curriculum development and promoting a more flexible curriculum with choices for students (Preus, 2007). The aim of new textbooks was to help students develop the ability to use English for communication (Liao, 2004). Based on the textbooks, teachers are expected to support learners by helping them integrate knowledge, skills and attitudes into personal competences. However, 70% of the secondary schools are in rural areas which are short of qualified teachers, and teachers here are typically lack communication competence in teaching (Hu, 2005). In addition to this, many schools still pay too much attention to examinations and apply traditional grammar teaching approaches. It is difficult for teachers to apply the CLT approach in teaching. Therefore, teacher professional development becomes an important key to improve teachers' disposition and capability to solve ELT problems in Chinese secondary schools.

2.4.3.9 *Reflective practice*

One of the key elements in teacher development is the ability to reflect on one's practice, both on teaching or research activities. Reflective practice is being considered here as it constitutes an important aspect of teacher professional development linked with learner autonomy. For instance, one of the key issues to be discussed in my study is whether English language teachers are reflective practitioners or not. Interest in finding out will determine the extent to which reflectivity impacts on ELT in Chinese schools under study. There are many articles explaining the importance of promoting reflective practice and more practically the opportunity offered by reflective school portfolios as triggers for change (Ross and Bruce, 2007). The roots of the term 'reflection' are traced back to Dewey (1933: 9) who defined it as action based on 'the active, persistent and careful consideration of any belief or supposed form of knowledge in the light of the grounds that support it.' Fendler (2003), in addition to Dewey (1933) and Schon (1983), refers to reflection as having a Cartesian basis, which views knowing about the self or self-knowledge as a valid means of knowledge generation. In the realms of teaching and education, 'when teachers are asked to reflect on their practices, the Cartesian assumption is that self-awareness will provide knowledge and understanding about the self' (Fendler, 2003: 17). Most of the techniques resorted to in training reflective teachers indirectly draw upon this Cartesian view of reflection.

In another classification, Jay and Johnson (2002) identify three steps that are important for effective reflective practice. The steps one has to undertake are description, comparison and criticism. Each step plays a pivotal role, for instance, during the descriptive stage the teacher has to define which elements of his/her class should be the focus of attention during reflection. The second stage, that is, comparison, is the phase during which the teacher starts 'thinking about the matter for reflection from a number of different frameworks' (Jay and Johnson, 2002: 78). Schon (1983) contends that the comparison stage consists of the teacher's attempt to develop a new perspective guided by lessons drawn from other practitioners. In a way, one compares his/her thinking with others' about a given phenomenon. By doing so, one can identify good practice or more effective ideas for improving their own practice. This ability to detach oneself from the limits of one's experience will enable us to 'discover meaning we might otherwise miss' (Jay and Johnson, 2002: 78). This process enables one to develop a better idea or a full picture of the teaching and learning milieu. Last but not least, the critical stage consists of the reflective practitioner's active evaluation of the different ideas or perspectives leading to the uptake of new methods or ideas to enrich their practice. In other words, during the critical stage, important decisions are made regarding new ways of thinking about organising teaching and learning activities in future.

Reflection is not an easy process since it requires critical thinking skills, self-direction, and problem solving ability coupled with personal knowledge and self-awareness (Lee, 2007). Larsen-Freeman (cited in Bailey, 1997: 4) has noted, 'awareness is the first step towards being able to change our teaching practice.' Many studies support the idea that teachers learn from experience through reflection on the nature and meaning of teaching experiences (Richards and Lockhart, 1994; Schon, 1983). These studies rely primarily on reflection as an instrument for teacher's professional development. Several methods can be used to encourage teachers to engage in reflective practice, including using reflective journals and compiling their own biographical notes (Braun and Crumpler, 2004).

Richards and Farrell (2005) identify teacher's learning as reflective practice. Reflection is the process of critical examination of experiences and leads teachers to have a better understanding of others' teaching practice. It's not merely reflective but rather critically reflective, which reflects the work, context and consequences of one's teaching, as well as teachers' skill, efficiency or kindliness in performing it (Carr and Kemmis, 1986). The significant importance of engaging in reflective practice emerges when teachers interpret the data they gather during their own teaching to make changes in their future teaching activities (Gün, 2011). Additionally, the reflective approach has a favourable impact on individual reorganisation and knowledge restructure. It is essential to give teachers opportunities to consider their teaching process so that they can become more aware of their own beliefs and how they are influenced by those beliefs to foster learners' second language acquisition (Raya, 2006). The best outcomes for teacher development can be obtained when teachers are provided with focused input sessions related to reflecting on different aspects of their classroom teaching (Gün, 2011). As early as the first half of the 20th century, Dewey (1933) has defined a reflective teacher as one who critiques their own practices, comes up with some ideas on improving their performance to enhance students' learning and then employs those ideas in class. Therefore, a reflective teacher is a very important component in teaching and learning.

According to Zeichner and Liston (1996: 6), reflective teachers:

1. Examine, frame and attempt to solve dilemmas of classroom practice;
2. Are aware of and question the assumptions and values they bring to teaching;
3. Are attentive to the institutional and cultural contexts in which they teach;
4. Take part in curriculum development and are involved in school change efforts;
5. Take responsibility for their own professional development.

The crucial question is how reflection can be carried out more effectively by teachers, which explains why I included this aspect in my literature review. It is important in my study to establish whether the ELT practitioners are reflective and how they use reflexivity to promote the development of learner autonomy. It is insufficient for teachers to reflect on their teaching by simply asking them to answer some questions on questionnaires by which they are merely 'reacting' rather than 'reflecting.' It is not significant for teacher development to simply ask teachers to complete a 'reflection sheet' after a classroom and expect them to think 'critically' about their teaching (Gün, 2011). Brandt (2008: 37) also believes that feedback alone is insufficient and that feedback and reflection should be:

> integrated in the form of reflective conversations with a number of features including the assigning of greater prominence to reflection, and to the presence of a facilitator and language learners.

Given the importance of reflective practice in the development of learner autonomy, establishing appropriate methods of developing teachers' capacity to reflect on their teaching is significantly important (Posteguillo and Palmer, 2000). Posteguillo and Palmer (2000) reiterate that the process of reflection should instead focuses on the 'what' and 'why' rather than the 'how' of questions, since they are directly associated with the procedural concerns of teaching. Focusing on the 'why' of questions is important for critical reflection and this is how a deeper understanding of one's own teaching can be generated. In order for teachers to bring themselves to the level of awareness of what they do and the related reasons, critical reflection is required with regards to how teachers reflect on their practice (Bailey, 1997). The reflective teaching and learning training helps teachers to reflect critically on teaching in order to increase their ability to identify strengths and weaknesses and to take action towards becoming more effective teachers, with the ultimate aim of identifying teacher educators' strategies to help teachers to engage more successfully in reflective behaviour (Bailey, 1997). It also helps teachers in the profession and assists them with their teaching difficulties.

2.5 Summary

This chapter presented the reviewed literature on various topics related to my study. The topics covered in the literature review include: ELT in China, which focused on the development of ELT in China, highlighting the problems and challenges being faced, including teachers' perspectives on ELT. A number of previous studies have identified problems and challenges bedeviling the teaching and learning of English language in Chinese schools. However, few studies have explored the recent developments in ELT in China, making my study more relevant. My study explores aspects of ELT at secondary school level with a view not only to identify problems but also to consider ways of addressing the problems and challenges to improve the teaching and learning of English language. One of the major changes in the teaching and learning of English language has been the transition from teacher-centred approaches to learner-centred approaches. Literature shows that while the new curriculum emphasises the shift in approach towards teaching in order to promote learner autonomy, few teachers are actually translating this into practice in their classrooms. Many new teachers are reportedly unaware of the new approach and, hence, they teach in the same way they were taught in schools, that is, they still make use of teacher-centred approaches. My literature review has also focused on teacher development or professional staff development and it is evidenced that the teacher education curriculum is not consistent with recent changes in the ELT curriculum. As a result, my study is to explore teachers' perspectives on learner autonomy and teacher autonomy. It has been argued in literature that for teachers to be able to promote learner autonomy, they must be autonomous themselves. In other words, there is a clear connection between learner autonomy and teacher autonomy. My study explores teachers' perspectives also on:

- The content of the ELT curriculum
- How teachers design and carry out the ELT curriculum
- The problems being faced in the teaching and learning of English language in schools
- What can be done to ensure effective teaching of English language in schools
- What opportunities exist for teachers to develop professionally in schools

- What role does SDPD play in the teaching of the English language

One of the key goals of the study is to help teachers to critically reflect on their teaching in order to bring about an instructional improvement in their classes. Given the limited research on teachers' perspectives on the learning and teaching of English language in Chinese secondary schools, my study will focus on this area and aim to bring to light what teachers think as important change agents in ELT. The next chapter presents the research methodology and methods used in generating answers to the main research questions highlighted in Chapter 1.

CHAPTER 3

Research Methodology and Ethical Considerations

3.1   Introduction

In Chapter 1, I have outlined the research questions of my study. In this chapter an attempt will be made to make explicit the process used in generating the responses to the research questions, that is, the research methodology. This includes defining the theoretical framework, research design, research approach, research methods and the ethical considerations that guided the conduct of my research. In this introduction section, I will define and make explicit my conceptual understanding of methodology and how the concept is being interpreted and applied in my study.

Research methodology has been defined differently by various authorities. For instance, Denzin and Lincoln (2000) define methodology as how we gain knowledge about the world while Hennink et al. (2011) posit that methodology is how we collect research data. The ideas are made clearer by Sikes (2004: 16) when she refers to methodology as:

> The theory of getting knowledge, to the consideration of the best ways, methods or procedures, by which data that will provide the evidence basis for the construction of knowledge about whatever it is that is being researched, is obtained. Methodology is concerned with the description and analysis of research methods rather than with the actual, practical use of those methods.

Sikes brings up an important idea of justifying the methods to be used in a study and this view is supported by Wellington (2000: 22) who interprets that methodology 'is the activity or business of choosing, reflecting upon, evaluating and justifying the methods you use.' Wellington et al. (2005: 97) also view that 'methodology refers to the theory of [generating] knowledge and the activity of considering, reflecting upon and justifying the best methods.' This view is supported by Clough and Nutbrown (2006: 27), who indicate that 'one of the tasks for a methodology is to explain and justify the particular methods used in a given study.' Researchers have to be able to justify methodological cases to indicate why they choose a particular approach and specific procedures for their research (Sikes, 2004). This is because different methodologies and procedures can produce different kinds of evidence and have different philosophical underpinnings, which can also influence the outcomes or the nature of the data generated from a particular study. It is important to notice that all the authorities cited above make a clear distinction between method and methodology. Sikes provides a simple way of differentiating between method and methodology, explaining that method is about doing whereas methodology is about understanding what you are doing (Sikes, 2004). The aim of my methodology section is in agreement with the declaration in Cohen et al. (2000: 45) which states that methodology should seek:

> to describe and analyse these methods, throwing light on their limitations and resources, clarifying their presuppositions and consequences, relating their potentialities to the twilight zone at the frontiers of knowledge. It is to venture generalisations from the success of particular techniques, suggesting new applications, and to unfold the specific bearings of logical and metaphysical principles on concrete problems, suggesting new formulations.

He further explains that the aim of methodology is to help the researcher to understand the research process itself but not the research outcomes. Research is best regarded as 'the process of arriving at dependable solutions to problems through the planned and systematic collection, analysis, and interpretation of data' (Cohen et al., 2000: 45).

In line with the views proffered by Sikes (2004) and Wellington et al. (2005), this section will involve discussion of theoretical framework, research design, research approach, research methods for data collection and analysis, including the ethical aspects of the study. Firstly, the theoretical framework underpinning the study is to be discussed.

3.2 Theoretical framework

The conduct of my study has been guided by the interpretivist knowledge framework. There exist different research paradigms including positivism, interpretivism and pragmatism. A paradigm, providing specific methodological frameworks for researchers, has been defined as a 'model or framework for observation and understanding which shapes both what we see and how we understand it' (Babbie, 2007: 32). A similar view is held by Denzin and Lincoln (2008: 31), who define a paradigm as a 'net that contains the researcher's epistemological, ontological and methodological premises.' Researchers are guided by these different research paradigms as argued by Prasad (2005: 8) who says 'researchers are often trained in one particular scientific paradigm, with specific guidelines on how to conduct research.'

My study is mainly a qualitative inquiry, which hence falls within the interpretivist paradigm. Interpretivism, also referred to as constructivism (Bryman, 2004), is a research perspective which emerged as a reaction to positivism. Here I must highlight the tenets of both positivist and interpretivist paradigms to clarify the existing differences between the two approaches to research in terms of differences in the ontology, epistemology and methodological orientation. The methodology that is adopted in research is embedded in the ontological and epistemological assumptions of the researcher. Researchers are bound within the ontological and epistemological premises which are the basic set of beliefs that guide them to interpret and understand the world (Guba, 1990). Ontology refers to the nature of reality and how we view the world, for example, the question of 'what kind of being the human being is' (Denzin and Lincoln, 2008: 31) or to reflect on 'the nature of phenomena, or entities, or social reality.' Some ontological perspectives require qualitative research; Hennink et al. (2011) give an example that where reality is assumed to consist of meanings, perceptions, beliefs and underlying motivations, they can be examined through qualitative research.

Epistemology is a theory of how we can come to know things while ontology a theory of what exists and how it exists. In other words, epistemology refers to the nature of knowledge and what is possible to know and understand, that is, 'the relationship between the inquirer and the known' (Denzin and Lincoln, 2008: 31).

Chikwa (2012) claims that epistemological assumptions guide the researcher's judgement of the appropriateness of different methodological choices in an inquiry. Thus one of the fundamental considerations of any research inquiry is an understanding of what counts as knowledge in that inquiry.

Below I am going to describe in more detail the differences in the epistemology of the positivist and interpretivist paradigms. Different research paradigms are underpinned by different philosophical positions. For instance, positivism, which is traditionally known to be the scientific approach to research, emphasises:

> the objective measurement of social issues, where it is assumed that reality consists of fact and that researchers can observe and measure reality in an objective way with no influence of the researcher on the process of data collection. (Hennink et al., 2011: 14)

The objective measurement separates the researcher from the researched data and denies the interaction and co-construction of data collection with human beings. Research is thus assumed to be value-free. In addition to this, positivism involves an epistemological approach, whereby researchers formulate a hypothesis before conducting the study and then test the hypothesis by collecting empirical data. One of the major criticisms levelled against positivism is its assumption about objective measurements which according to Lincoln and Guba (1985) has potentially 'produced research with human respondents that ignores their humanness' (cited in McKenzie et al., 1997: 178).

The interpretive paradigm emerged and provided a new way of thinking which was different from the positivist perspective by acknowledging that the positionality of researchers has influence on the collection and outcomes of research data. 'Although researchers may use instruments for collecting data such as interview, observation, document analysis, the "researcher" is the key instrument in the qualitative research, who actually gathers the information in the process of data collection' (Creswell, 2009: 175). In addition, interpretivism highlights the significance of 'interpretation and observation in understanding the social world' (Snape and Spencer, 2003: 7). Contrary to positivism, the interpretive paradigm acknowledges that research is value-laden, and is an integral component of qualitative research. From viewpoint of interpretivism, human action is meaningful (Denzin and Lincoln, 2000). It has a meaning for human life and people 'act on the basis of the meanings that they attribute to their acts and to the acts of others' (Bryman, 2004: 14). The interpretive paradigm recognises that 'reality is socially constructed as people's experiences occur within social, cultural, personal and historical contexts' (Hennink et al., 2011: 15). Furthermore, the inter- pretive paradigm acknowledges that people's understanding and experiences of reality are subjective; hence, there can be various perspectives on reality rather than a single truth as proposed in positivism. Also, interpretivism supports that it is possible to understand the subjective meaning of action in what positivists would consider to be an objective way (Denzin and Lincoln, 2000). Interpretivism encourages the researcher to interpret the participants' actions and the social world from their point of view. I consider that it is impossible to be objective in any research endeavor no matter how hard we are trying to.

Interpretive data are generally qualitative. Denzin and Lincoln (2000: 3) point out that 'qualitative researchers study things in their natural settings, attempting to make sense of, or interpret, phenomena in terms of the meanings people bring to them.' In addition to this, qualitative research offers opportunities of face-to-face interaction between participants and researchers over time in the natural setting. The researcher collects the data by direct communication with participants, observing their behaviour and action within their context (Creswell, 2009). However, it is worth noting that in some cases, it is possible to generate qualitative data using questionnaires where the researcher does not have to meet with the participants in person. Generally, qualitative research methods are applied to get to know behaviours, perceptions, beliefs or experiences of people. My study adopts a qualitative research design which is to be discussed in the following section.

3.3　Research design

My study involves working with teachers, eliciting their views regarding the learning and teaching of English in China. Data collection involves some face-to-face inter- views with teachers to recognise their perspectives and experiences towards ELT and attending their classes to observe the interaction between teachers and students. After observing the classes I had discussions with the teachers to understand why they behaved and interacted with students as I had observed. This helped me to gain access to the teachers' perspectives around teaching and learning approaches. As a result the study lends itself to the interpretive research paradigm.

In this paragraph, I will define qualitative research and make explicit my rationale for using the qualitative research design. Qualitative research is an umbrella term that covers a wide range of techniques and philosophies. It is an approach that allows the researcher to examine people's experiences in detail, by using a specific set of research methods such as in-depth interview, focus group discussion, and observation. This approach also allows the researcher to identify issues from the perspective of study participants, and to understand the meanings and interpretations that they give to behaviours, events or objects. It is important to note that one of the reasons why qualitative researchers study participants in their own environments is that this gives them the opportunity to explore the impact of the contextual factors of the participants. Denzin and Lincoln (2008: 4) state that qualitative research 'involves an interpretive, naturalistic approach to the world. This means that qualitative researchers study things in their natural settings, attempting to make sense of, or interpret, phenomena in terms of the meanings people bring to them.' Qualitative data analysis is interpretive, whereby researchers seek to interpret the meanings that participants themselves give to their views and experiences. Due to the in-depth nature of qualitative research, few study participants are needed, as the purpose is to achieve depth of information rather than breadth by 'mining' each participant deeply for their experiences on the research topic (Hennink et al., 2011).

Qualitative research is critiqued in literature as being subjective, difficult to replicate, lacking of generalisation and transparency. However, in the following section I will discuss the criticisms levelled against qualitative research and provide my responses to them with a view to clarify my adoption of the approach.

3.3.1   Critique of qualitative research

Lincoln and Guba (1985) suggest that the criteria for judging a qualitative study are different from that used to judge a quantitative study. The following sections will discuss the criticisms levelled against qualitative research, where I would also discuss the criteria considered useful for judging the quality of my study, which is mainly qualitative.

3.3.1.1   Qualitative research is subjective

Qualitative research is easy to be criticised as being too impressionistic and subjective. Quantitative researchers point out that qualitative findings depend too much on the researcher's unsystematic perceptions about what is important, and also depend too much on the close personal relationships that the researcher normally strikes up with the people studied (Bryman, 2004). Furthermore, in qualitative studies, the researcher is said to frequently begin the study in a relatively open-ended way and requires a gradual narrowing down of research questions or problems. In addition, it is said that the consumer of the writings developing from the research is given few hints as to why one area was chosen for study instead of the other (Hennink et al., 2011). However, I feel that these criticisms are being framed from a quantitative research perspective. A qualitative study such as mine is systematic and follows a well thought-out structured process (as shown in this chapter) that is honest and acknowledges the important roles of both the researcher and the participants of the study. The integrity of the data is in the findings and the writing is comprehensive. In my study I would maintain my role as a researcher and avoid my own views overshadowing the views of the participants as far as possible.

3.3.1.2   Qualitative research is difficult to replicate

The difficulty of replicating the study is another critique levelled against qualitative studies. The argument goes that the main instrument of data collection during qualitative research is the researcher, therefore, what is observed and heard depends very much on the predilections of the researcher (Bryman, 2004). But in the case of quantitative research, since the instruments used by the researcher are designed by the researcher and therefore, the views and theoretical perspectives of the researcher are bound to influence the research process as well. Although the qualitative study may be difficult, even impossible, to replicate, given the nature of the conditions under which it is conducted, the main objective for conducting this study mainly cannot be replicated. Anyway, if the findings are interesting, another study can always be designed that can then be conducted in another setting. It is impossible to replicate social settings but the insights from the study can always be used to guide the design of a similar study.

3.3.1.3　Qualitative research is difficult to generalise

It is often suggested that the scope of the findings of qualitative research is restricted particularly in participant observation and structured interviews. It is hard to know how the findings can be generalised to other settings due to the limited number of individuals in certain organisations or locality. In this way, quantitative researchers question on how it can be possible for one or two cases to represent the whole. It is impossible to achieve the whole picture as suggested by positivists. But my case study makes use of different data collection tools to generate thick descriptions of the teaching and learning of English language in the participating schools, which helps to bring out a comprehensive analysis of the situation obtaining in the participating schools from the perspective of the participating teachers. It is true that the findings cannot be applied to other contexts but what is significant for me is the idea of generating some important insights that can be utilised by other researchers as a starting point for further research at scale.

3.3.1.4　Qualitative research lacks transparency

Bryman (2004) describes how other researchers criticise qualitative research as being devoid of transparency. There are opinions that some qualitative research reports are unclear and do not clarify how participants are chosen including details regarding the research procedures. But qualitative research reports do generally provide details of the research process including the focus of the study, the methods used and the limitations of the study. As shown in my current study, all the methods and procedures followed in the conduct of my study are described fully. It is therefore not justified to say that qualitative research lacks transparency. A study should be conducted ethically and one of the ethical requirements is transparency.

It is true that qualitative research is conducted differently from quantitative research. So, the same lenses used in judging a quantitative research should not be simply applied. In conducting my study, I looked at all the different criticisms in qualitative case against qualitative studies for my study being carried out systematically, ensuring that findings would be credible and that the report would be an honest reflection of the situation regarding the teaching and learning of English language in selected Chinese schools. The following section focuses on the criteria for judging a quantitative study.

3.3.2 Criteria for judging the quality of a quantitative study

In this section, I intend to discuss the criteria used to judge the quality of a quantitative study to provide a basis for comparison with the parallel criteria adopted in my study. It is clearly shown in research literature, for example, Lincoln and Guba (1985) and Bryman (2004), that there exist different criteria for judging the quality of an inquiry within the chosen research paradigm. It is significant to adopt a suitable one for judging the quality of an inquiry.

The criteria used to judge the quality of a quantitative research are explained by Bryman (2004) as consisting of three most prominent elements, namely reliability, replication and validity. Firstly, reliability is fundamentally concerned with issues of consistency of measures because an unreliable study cannot give a valid account. Guba and Lincoln (1989: 235) define that:

> Reliability refers to a given study's consistency, predictability, dependability, stability and accuracy, and the establishment of reliability for a given study typically rests on replication, assuming that very application of the same, or equivalent, instruments to the same phenomena will yield similar measurements.

According to Bryman (2004), researchers need to be sure that all the design indicators are related to each other. Otherwise, some of the items may not be related to design.

The second criterion is validity which has four aspects: measurement validity, internal validity, external validity and ecological validity (Bryman, 2004). Measurement validity is mainly applied to quantitative research and to the search for measures of social scientific concepts. Primarily, it involves the 'question of whether a measure that is devised of a concept really does reflect the concept that it is supposed to be denoting' (Bryman, 2004). The internal validity also relates to the issues of causality. Lincoln and Guba (1985: 290) define internal validity as 'the extent to which variations in an outcome or dependent variable can be attributed to controlled variation in an independent variable.' They assess the internal validity as the essential means for determining the 'true value' of a given inquiry, that is, 'the extent to which it establishes how things really are and how they work.' In addition, the issue of external validity referred to 'the question of whether the results of the study can be generalised beyond the specific research context' (Bryman, 2004). Finally, ecological validity is concerned with the question of whether social scientific findings are applicable to peoples' every-day, natural social settings. It seems that the more the social scientist intervenes in natural settings or creates unnatural ones, the more likely for findings to be ecologically invalid. As can be gleaned, the concepts here refer primarily to positivist or quantitative research. Surely, this cannot be applied to qualitative research.

3.3.3   Alternative criteria for qualitative research

Lincoln and Guba (1985) propose that it is necessary to have specific terms and ways to judge and assess the quality of qualitative research that provide alternative terms to reliability and validity used by quantitative researchers. They propose two main criteria for evaluating a qualitative research: 'trustworthiness' and 'authenticity.' Trustworthiness is made up of four criteria, namely:

- Credibility, which parallels internal validity
- Transferability, which parallels external validity
- Dependability, which parallels reliability
- Confirmability, which parallels objectivity

In my study, I adopt a new way of conceptualising quality of research and this involves using new language different from that applicable to quantitative research. Following is a brief description of each of the four concepts outlined above.

3.3.3.1   Credibility

The significance of this emphasises the multiple accounts of social reality. If there can be several possible accounts of an aspect of social reality, there are the feasibility or credibility of the account that researchers arrive at that defines its acceptability (Bryman, 2004).

3.3.3.2   Transferability

Qualitative research typically entails the intensive study of a small group, or of individuals sharing certain characteristic, so qualitative findings tend to be oriented to the contextual uniqueness and significance of the aspect of the social world being studied. As Lincoln and Guba (1985: 316) state, whether findings 'hold in some other context, or even in the same context at some other time, is an empirical issue.'

Therefore, transferability is an important criterion of qualitative study. It is important in a qualitative study to focus on context, so a similar study can be conducted elsewhere but without necessarily anticipating similar results as differences in contextual factors affect the conduct of the study. Generalisations are not possible as qualitative researchers pay attention to context and acknowledge the impact of different contextual factors on the conduct of a study.

3.3.3.3 Dependability

Guba and Lincoln (1989) suggest the idea of dependability as a parallel to reliability and argue that, to establish the advantage of research in terms of this criterion of trustworthiness, researchers should adopt an 'auditing' approach. This involves ensuring that complete records are kept at all stages of the research process, for example, establishing research questions, as well as selecting research participants, fieldwork notes, interview transcripts, data analysis and so on.

3.3.3.4 Confirmability

This concept is parallel to the conventional criterion of objectivity. Like objectivity, confirmability is concerned with assuring that data interpretations and outcomes of inquiries are rooted in contexts and persons apart from the researcher and are not simply figments of the researcher's imagination (Guba and Lincoln, 1989). Confirmability ensures that while complete objectivity is impossible in social research, the researcher can be shown to have generated data that are credible. Unlike the conventional paradigm which roots its assurances of objectivity in method—that is, follow the process correctly and have findings that are divorced from the values, motives, biases or political persuasions of the researcher—the constructivist paradigm's assurances of integrity of the findings are rooted in the data themselves. This means that data (constructions, assertions, facts and so on) can be tracked to their sources, and that the logic used to assemble the interpretations into a structurally coherent and corroborating whole is both explicit and implicit in the narrative of a case study. It should be apparent that researchers have not overtly allowed personal values or theoretical inclinations manifestly to control the conduct of the research and findings (Guba and Lincoln, 1989).

3.3.4　Authenticity

In addition to the four trustworthiness criteria outlined in the preceding section, Lincoln and Guba (1985: 232-237) suggest criteria for authenticity, which raise a wider set of issues regarding a wider political impact of research.

- Fairness. Does the research fairly represent different viewpoints among members of the social setting?
- Ontological authenticity. Does the research help members to arrive at a better understanding of their social milieu?
- Educative authenticity. Does the research help members to appreciate better the perspectives of other members of their social setting?
- Catalytic authenticity. Does the research act as an impetus to members to engage in action to change their circumstances?
- Tactical authenticity. Does the research empower members to take the steps necessary for engaging in action?

The central point of the discussion of Guba and Lincoln's (1989) ideas is that they differ from other writers in seeking criteria for evaluating and assessing qualitative research that are different from quantitative research. Given that my research is a qualitative one, I applied the ideas proffered by Guba and Lincoln (1989) in the ways of evaluating the quality of my study. For instance, to ensure the credibility of the interview data, after transcribing the interviews I sent the transcripts to the interviewees for them to authenticate the transcriptions, for the data to be a true representation of the views shared by the participants. By being given them the opportunity to go through the transcripts, the participants were able to endorse and in some cases to add more information they may have overlooked during the interview session, which helped to generate credible data. Also a 'researcher-qua-researcher' stance could be confirmed, making sure that my personal values and other existing theoretical positions did not colour the data. In addition, I also provide contextual details of each school involved in the study to help the reader to interpret the results of my study correctly with rich contextual background information, including the type of school, the class sizes, the teacher qualifications and experience, among other things, which help to give a clear picture of the data. The use of interviews and observation as data collection methods also helps to generate data that is credible in line with the parallel criteria discussed by Guba and Lincoln (1989).

3.4　Research strategy

There are many terms that have been used to classify research approaches. Sikes (2004: 16) states that the term 'methodology' itself can be used 'to denote the overall approach to a particular research project, to the overarching strategy that is adopted.' Thus case study, life history and action research become examples of methodological approaches. Denzin and Lincoln (2000) use the term 'strategy' to refer to the kind of research approach adopted. I use the term 'research strategy' here to denote the type of research adopted which is in this case a case study. Since the concept 'research approach' might cause unnecessary confusion as this might mean more than a strategy adopted, I must stress that in some cases the two concepts are used interchangeably in my thesis especially when I make reference to quotations by other authorities. This section is to describe my choice of a case study and make explicit the rationale for choosing this particular research strategy.

3.4.1　The advantage of case study

Clough and Nutbrown (2006) define that a research approach should be seen as being constructed (for particular purposes) rather than selected (for any general usefulness). As indicated earlier, my study involves working in partnership with three secondary schools and each school constitutes a unit of analysis involving participating English language teachers and students. In this case, my study can be considered as a multiple-case study. The notion of 'case study' has been widely examined. A case study focuses on the characteristics of an individual unit, which may be a school or even one person. In each of the participating schools in my study, the participants include English language teachers and students from their classes. The adopted approach helps me to understand the interaction of factors involved in the phenomenon under study, that is, the teaching and learning of English language.

The reasons why I adopted case study as my research strategy are based on the following aspects.

Firstly, Bell (1999: 10) states that a case study is a particularly appropriate strategy for the individual researcher because it 'provides an opportunity for one aspect of a problem to be studied in some depth within a limited timescale.' The practical advantage of a case study is that it is a small-scale research, which requires few resources and leads the researchers straight into the action.

Contrary to a quantitative study where the researcher manipulates variables with a view to understanding cause-effect relationships, in a case study scenario, the researcher is not interested in dealing with large samples; instead, they focus on a single unit to come up with thick descriptions of the phenomenon under study. The unit of study can be a single school, a child, a hospital, a class or a community. 'The purpose of such observation is to probe deeply and to analyse intensively the multifarious phenomena that constitute the life cycle of the unit with a view to establishing useful insights about the wider population to which that unit belongs' (Cohen and Manion, 1994).

My study involves working with three Chinese secondary schools as discussed before. The choice of the three schools is made for their representativeness enabling me to establish common trends and patterns. For example, I included both private and public schools as this would help me to identify how the teaching of English language is being managed in different contexts. Here case study is a useful research strategy, which helps to explore in depth teachers' perspectives on the learning and teaching of English. Denscombe (1998: 38) posits that one of the most important values of a case study approach is that 'it allows the researcher to deal with the subtleties and intricacies of complex social situations' within the focus of one or few instances. Case study is concentration upon a particular instance in order to reveal the ways in which events come together to create particular kinds of outcomes. The case study seeks holistic explanation and justification. It tends to be 'holistic' rather than deal with 'isolated factors' (Denscombe, 1998: 31). In one case, many elements work together providing an in-depth insight into how different factors affect each another. An effort is made to explore in detail how teachers think the teaching and learning of English language can be improved in the schools in China. My study looks at a holistic picture including the curriculum design issues, the text-books being used and the appropriateness of the content and methods being used to teach the language. In addition, teachers' own views regarding the effectiveness and ways of improving the teaching and learning of English language are elicited. This is achieved by the use of different data collection methods, which is one of the celebrated advantages of using a case study.

Secondly, Yin (2009: 143) explains that a case study is 'an empirical inquiry that investigates a contemporary phenomenon in depth and with its real-life context, especially when the boundaries between phenomenon and context are not clearly evident.' Applying case study as a research approach because it encourages the researcher to interpret situations, use judgement and arrive at a promising course of action. In light of Yin's assertions, the essence of the case study is that it is an enquiry in a real life context. The case study approach helps the researcher to understand a real-life phenomenon within the contextual situations and identify factors from the conditions in which they arise, which are very relevant to the phenomenon of research. In this research, data collection will take place in China and the main target is the learning and teaching of English language in Chinese secondary schools. There are many influential factors involved in this research such as cultural issues, educational system, examination format and objective facilities. Adopting a case study helps to develop a comprehensive understanding of the teaching and learning of English language in the participating schools.

3.4.2 The justifications of case study

Case study is criticised by some authorities in terms of its nature and the difficulty of generalisation. As Stenhouse (1985: 266) points out:

> In case study the relationship between a case, and a collection of cases that may superficially resemble a sample, and any population in which similar meanings or relationships may apply, is essentially a matter of judgement.

However, some authors disagree with 'generalisation.' Denscombe (1998: 36-37) makes the following statement:

> The extent to which findings from the case study can be generalised to other examples in the class depends on how far the case study example is similar to others of its type.

Indeed, Stenhouse (1985: 266) goes on to argue that the 'nature of generalisation' is the merit of case study:

> Case study reaches after the restoration of prudence, and also of perceptiveness,

the capacity to interpret situations rapidly and at depth and to revise interpretations in the light of experience.

Therefore, the value of case study needs to be re-estimated.

3.4.3   Participants of the study

My study involves working with three secondary schools in Hangzhou, China, the city I live in, which makes easier for me to access the schools and the teachers. I arranged meeting with the school heads by email and phone calls. Once appointments were made, I visited each of them in person and talked about my study. I provided information sheet for my study including the ethical approval letter from the University of Sheffield, as well as promised to share the findings of my study with them at the end of the study. This helped to get the school heads on board, making it easier to talk to the teachers thereafter.

Nine ELT teachers, three from each school, participated in the study. In addition, students who belonged to the teachers in the study also participated, especially during lesson observations. A total of 18 classroom observations, two per each participating teacher, were conducted and these facilitated discussions in interviews with teachers and provided useful data on classroom activities and the overall interaction between teachers and students.

3.4.4   Research sampling

During the study, I had to identify schools that were convenient and helpful in terms of generating data to respond to the main research questions out of many schools in China. And since it was impossible for me to have the time and resources to conduct a survey of all secondary schools, teachers and students in China, or even in Hangzhou, I had to adopt a small sample by purposive sampling. As Creswell (2007: 125) defines, 'purposive sampling, used in qualitative research, means that the inquirer selects individuals and sites for study because they can purposefully inform an understanding of the research problem and central phenomenon in the study… researchers can sample at the site level, at the event or process level, and at the participant level.' I could only work with English teachers in secondary schools in teaching and learning of English because this was the main focus of my study. I was interested in finding out the teachers' perspectives on the current learning and teaching situation in China and how they were trying to bring in positive change to the situation through their SDPD. In addition, within the schools, I was interested to see what kind of opportunities and support was provided by schools to foster teacher professional development. Given that my study is a qualitative one, I could not make use of random sampling techniques as this was inappropriate. Different qualitative sampling techniques exist, including quota sampling, snowballing and convenience sampling. Quota sampling is appropriate when one is interested in working with a sample that represents all the minority groups in the population. However, in my study, this was not important. Snowballing is useful when working with a sample of participants who are hard to come by. In my case, schools are not difficult to identify. What I did was to look at the schools that were close to my address to avoid travelling long distances. In a way, the schools and teachers were selected considering convenience and academic purpose.

3.4.5 Ethical considerations

My study was conducted in line with the University of Sheffield's code of practice on research ethics. This section is to discuss the ethical principles and how they were applied in the context of my study.

Hennink et al. (2011) claim that ethical challenges in qualitative research may be more pronounced than in other types of research due to the nature of qualitative research and the complexity of the research processes, which involve dealing with different institutions and people. In qualitative research, researchers usually want to hear the voices of participants. Therefore, qualitative methods are applied to get to know perceptions, beliefs and feelings of participants. The intimate relationship between researcher and participant requires that we consider carefully the ethical principle of 'doing no harm,' by keeping the acquired information secure and by making the data anonymous. Otherwise, the privacy and security of the participants could be compromised. Furthermore, Creswell (2009) posits that many ethical issues arise during the stage of data collection. Therefore, I carefully considered access to research settings, informed consent, voluntary participation, privacy and confidentiality in the process of data collection and how to deal with the potential harm of the research process to the participants.

3.4.5.1   *Permission to conduct research and gaining access to schools*

Permission to conduct the study was sought and granted by the University of Sheffield through the Department of Educational Studies Ethical Review Committee. I contacted the head of each school in writing asking for permission to do my study and this was granted. I did not have to go through any other authorities before contacting the schools. The school heads then helped me to get in touch with the English department staff via department heads.

3.4.5.2   *Informed consent*

Flynn and Goldsmith (2013: 10) define informed consent as follows:

> The term informed consent implies that subjects know and understand the risks and benefits of participation in the research. They must also understand their participation is completely voluntary.

According to Hennink et al. (2011: 63), 'individuals should be provided with sufficient information about the research, in a format that is comprehensible to them, and make a voluntary decision to participate in a research study.' This view is supported by Newby (2010: 357) who argues that 'consent is more than a signature on a form. We must be sure that people understand in what (and on what basis) they are participating.' Researchers must ensure that participants are provided with adequate information about the study and the procedures during the interview or discussion (Hennink et al., 2011). In conformity with these principles, I provided information on the nature of my study and what involvement in the study would mean to every participant. I emailed each participant a detailed information sheet and a participant consent form before engaging them in the study. Everyone had the chance to read and raise any questions before making a decision whether to participate in the study. Furthermore, I always asked my potential participants (the English language teachers) to go through the participant information sheet and to confirm their willingness to participate in the study. Before embarking on the interview, I asked whether the participant was still comfortable to participate in the study. In addition, I clarified any questions to them to make sure that they fully understood the nature of their involvement in this research. It is important to keep participants informed about the nature and the purpose of the research throughout the research process.

3.4.5.3 *Voluntary participation*

Seeking permission is an essential part of any research project. In this research, participation in the study was voluntary. It is important to respect the participants and their willingness to participate. I was lucky to have the support of the school heads in each school, with whose support it was easy for me to talk to the teachers and get their consent. To me the teachers expressed willingness to participate but it is possible that they all agreed because they did not want to disappoint their school heads. Participants had the right to refuse getting involved in the research without facing any consequences. Before I conducted interviews, I also asked the participants if they wanted to be recorded or not. Thankfully, all my participants accepted to be recorded. I also explained to them that I would delete all the recordings when the research was complete. Additionally, all participants were informed and reassured that it was within their right to withdraw from the research arbitrarily.

3.4.5.4 *Maintaining anonymity and confidentiality*

It is important to keep the acquired information secure and make the data anonymous (Hennink et al., 2011). To ensure anonymity, I made use of pseudonyms for the names of participants and school in my study. In my interviews, I avoided mentioning concrete information about the interviewees or other persons mentioned that could lead to their identification. I also informed the participants that the interview and observation data were to be analysed and reported anonymously. It was my responsibility to protect the identity of my research participants and to ensure that all data records were kept confidential at all times. In addition, authorisation was given by participants for me to use the data in conferences and any other scholarly activities in the consent form they signed at the beginning of the study before presenting any data related to them in the research. In addition, no third party had access to the recorded data without the participants' permission, except of course, the supervisor and the examiners if they feel the need to access the records.

3.4.5.5 Minimisation of harm

Sieber (1993: 14) states that 'ethics has to do with the application of moral principles to prevent harming or wronging others, to promote the good, to be respectful and to be fair.' Israel and Hay (2006: 96) argue that '...in social sciences, research harm is generally more likely to involve psychological distress, discomfort, social disadvantage, invasion of privacy or infringement of rights than physical injury.' It is important to consider carefully the ethical principle of 'doing no harm' (Hennink et al., 2011). The influence of bioethics means that harm is not only thought of in physical terms, but also includes psychological, social and economic damage (ESRC, 2005). From the Ethical Conduct statement, there is an important responsibility for the researcher to carefully assess the possibility of hurting research participants and thus should minimise the possibility of harm (Bryman, 2004). In my study I ensured that there was a friendly atmosphere between myself and the participants and that the participants never felt under pressure to provide me with information. For instance, during the interview, the participant was all free to choose the questions to answer and could easily communicate that to me. I deliberately adopted this approach to relieve the participants of any potential stress during the study.

In the following section I will focus on the research methods used in the study for the purpose of generating data.

3.5 Research methods

This section describes the data collection methods used in the conduct of my study. Clough and Nutbrown (2006) discuss the distinction between methodology and method stating that methodology provides the reason for using a particular research recipe whilst methods are some of the ingredients of research. They argue that one of the tasks for a methodology is to explain and justify the particular methods.

Clough and Nutbrown (2006) describe that a method turns out not to be a spanner—or even a micrometer—but rather something which has to be painstakingly custom-built from other drafters' cast-offs which, whilst providing a general guidance, were not made for this particular job. Sikes (2004) uses the term procedures to refer to methods, which are the specific research techniques that are used to collect and analyse data. Wellington (2000: 17) asserts that 'methods can and should be mixed.' In order to have an in-depth understanding of the phenomenon under study, which means here the teaching and learning of English language in Chinese schools, I attempted the use of triangulation of data collection methods. Cohen and Manion (1994: 254) define triangulation as 'the use of two or more methods of data collection in the study of some aspect of human behaviour.' This view is echoed by Flick (2007: 4) who provides the definition of triangulation in a more comprehensive way in qualitative research:

> Triangulation means that researchers take different perspectives on an issue under study or more generally speaking, in answering research questions. These perspectives can be substantiated by using several methods and/or in several theoretical approaches. They are, or should be, linked. Furthermore, triangulation refers to combining different sorts of data on the background of the theoretical perspectives, which are applied to the data. As far as possible, these perspectives should be treated and applied on an equal footing and in an equally consequent way. At the same time, triangulation (of different methods or data sorts) should allow a principal surplus of knowledge. For example, triangulation should produce knowledge on different level, which means insights that go beyond the knowledge made possible by one approach and thus contribute to promoting quality in research.

I made an effort to triangulate data collection methods in my study, using lesson observations as well as individual interviews with the participating English language teachers. The aim was to achieve the generation of credible data from different sources. Wellington (2000: 50) advises researchers to consider a 'horses for course' matrix (a question-methods matrix) during the early stages of research planning. Denscombe (1998) states that:

> Good social research is a matter of 'horses for courses,' when approaches are selected because they are appropriate for specific aspects of investigation and specific kinds of problems. They are chosen as 'fit for purpose.' (cited in Wellington, 2000: 50)

In Table 1 I indicate the research questions in one column and the corresponding research methods in the other column, as a description of how each data collection method was developed and used in the study.

Table 1   Research questions—methods matrix

Research questions	Research methods
1. What are the teachers' perspectives on the content of the ELT curriculum?	Interview
2. What are the teachers' perspectives regarding how they design and teach the ELT curriculum?	Interview and observation
3. What are the teachers' perspectives on the key problems being faced in the teaching and learning of English language in schools?	Interview and observation
4. From the teachers' perspectives, what can be done to ensure effective teaching of the English language in schools?	Interview and observation
5. What opportunities exist for teachers to develop professionally in schools?	Document analysis and interview
6. From teachers' perspectives, what role does SDPD play in the teaching of the English language?	Interview

The following section will describe the methods used for data collection in my study. In each case, I will describe the method, making explicit why I chose the method, and subsequently explain how the method was implemented.

3.5.1   Semi-structured interview

The interview is probably the most widely applied method in qualitative research. Bryman (2004) claims the flexibility of the interview is what makes it so attractive, though pointing out that there exist different types of interviews and not all of them are flexible. Many authors define interview in various ways. Wellington (2000) posits that the purpose of a research interview is to look into a respondent's perspectives or life history, from whose view an interview is indeed a conversation with a purpose. The function of a research interview is to give voice or platform to a person or a group of people to make their perspectives known. An inter- view enables a researcher to follow up their ideas to investigate participants' motives, feelings, values, perspectives, experiences and so on. It is important, however, to notice that the interviewers should not play a leading role and not treat the interview as their platform rather than the interviewee's (Wellington, 2000). In addition, researchers should avoid bias towards different respondents (Wellington, 2000).

I made use of qualitative interviews as I was mainly interested in eliciting the views of the interviewees. In qualitative interviewing, rambling or going off at tangents is often encouraged—it gives insight into what the interviewee sees as relevant and important. In particular, I adopted semi-structured interviews for my research, where the researcher has a list of questions or particular topics to be covered, but the interviewee has a great deal of flexibility in how to reply. Questions may not follow on exactly in the way outlined on the schedule and some questions may not be included in the guide but can be asked as the interviewer picks up on ideas presented by interviewees. However, all the key questions will be covered in each interview to ensure consistency and to generate responses to the main research questions (Bryman, 2004).

In a semi-structured interview, it is possible to obtain 'open-ended' answers from respondents while keeping a clear list of issues and questions (Denscombe, 1998). This method allows me to develop my ideas and speak widely on the issues or problems. One important point to bear in mind is that researchers need to be generally flexible in their approach to interviewing in qualitative research. Bryman (2004) warns that in a semi-structured interview, researchers should not turn the interview into a kind of structured interview but with open questions. This emphasises the need for flexibility and not being mechanical. Flexibility is important in these areas as changing the order of questions, following up leads, and explaining contradictions in answers. In line with my epistemological assumptions, I believe that knowledge can be generated through discovery and investigation of people's subjective explanations. In this case, when conducting interviews I focused on eliciting views of the participants rather than guiding them to give me some predetermined information.

I did not consider using structured interviews and unstructured interviews for my research. In structured interviews, the researcher has a clearly specified set of research questions that are to be investigated (Bryman, 2004). This interview involves a high control over the order of questions and the range of answers, as well as a predetermined list of questions and pre-coded answers. Hence, the respondents can hardly offer broad answers and the response tends to have a level of standardisation (Denscombe, 1998). Compared to structured interviews, it appears that semi-structured interviews have more potential to generate innovative and unexpected points from open-ended answers. My research emphasises greater flexibility in the formulation of initial research ideas and a focus on the interviewees' own perspectives. The aim of the interview in my study is to discover and not to reconfirm assumptions. As a result of this, restricted and closed questions are unsuitable for the type of data I attempt to generate for research. Unstructured interviews can focus on the interviewee's thoughts. The interviewee chooses the topic and follows their ideas to pursue their thoughts (Denscombe, 1998). In this context, a single question might be asked to kick start the conversation and this can be followed up by several prompting questions on issues of importance to the interviewer (Bryman, 2004). As can be gleaned from the description, this type of an interview is closely related to a conversation (Burgess, 1994). Thus, the unstructured interview is not suitable for my study since I here had an idea of the key issues that I wish to be covered during the interviews. Of course this is not to say I did not entertain any new themes which came up during the conversations. Participants were free to share their views including new themes, but in a guided way.

3.5.1.1　Interviews with teachers

Interviews were conducted with English language teachers from three different secondary schools, all located in Hangzhou, China, which was determined by proximity to where I lived. The interviews took place some time after the observations had been carried out, to provide a picture of the teaching and learning of English language in the participating schools and to provide a concrete basis for discussion. Each interview was arranged in advance and conducted in a quiet environment where there were no disruptions from other teachers or students. I contacted each of the participating teachers by mail to agree on a suitable time for the interview. In addition, I would always give the teacher a call a day before the interview to confirm their availability for the interview The interviews took an average of 30 minutes and were conducted based on a guide designed to elicit responses (See Appendix). The questions on the interview guide were formulated in line with the main research questions to ensure that interviews generated responses to all the main research questions.

　　Prior to the interview, each participant was provided with an information sheet where the purpose of the research was clarified. It was also made clear that participation was to be voluntary and participants were free to withdraw from the study at any point if they felt the need to do so. I made it explicitly clear to them that their information was to be treated in confidentiality and all recordings would be deleted at the end of the study. All the interviews were recorded and later transcribed for final content analysis. The purpose of this qualitative content analysis was to explore the existing practice with a view to identifying how it might be enhanced. Ultimately, I was keen to find out whether any alternative professional skills could be developed.

I interviewed a total of nine teachers who were teaching English as the second language in three schools. The interview questions refer to the key problems of learning and teaching ELT in China and how to improve ELT through teacher professional development. The design of the teachers' interview was based on two major considerations: firstly, the teachers' perspectives on the current situation of English teaching in schools, which includes the content of ELT curriculum, the teaching approach and the key problems of ELT in china; and secondly, on teachers' perspectives on their role as agents of change in the ELT regarding SDPD in the learning and teaching of English. The interview allowed me to ask the teachers to report on their perceptions of their own roles and responsibilities, their perceptions of their students' learning motivation, and how they engaged with self-professional development.

3.5.1.2 *Checking the quality of the interview data*

In this section I am going to explain how I checked the quality of the data obtained through interviews. Lincoln and Guba (1985) consider member checking as the most critical technique for establishing credibility. When I finished my drafts of the interview transcription, I asked participants to view the credibility of findings and interpretations. According to the statement made by Stake (1995: 115), participants should play a primary role 'directing as well as acting in case study research. They should be asked to examine rough drafts of the researcher's work and to provide alternative language, critical observations or interpretations.' Based on this validation strategy, I emailed all teachers whom I interviewed and asked them for feedback. Most of them were very cooperative and agreed to look at the interview accounts and provided some feedback to me. The approach involves sending data, analyses, interpretations and conclusions back to the participants so that they can judge the accuracy and credibility of the accounts.

3.5.2 Observation

Observation is an important method in research that enables researchers to systemati-cally observe and record people's behaviours, actions and interactions. It also allows researchers to obtain a comprehensive depiction of social settings or events in order to situate people's behaviours within their own socio-cultural context (Hennink et al., 2011). In addition, observation is especially beneficial for providing an introduction to the study context, particularly when starting a new research project or when working in a new social context (Hennink et al., 2011). Observation includes watching what participants do, listening to what they, observing and how they say it and how people interact. Thus, rather than asking participants about their perspectives and behaviours, as researchers do in interviews, observation provides direct details and behaviours of participants. Therefore, Mays and Pope (1995: 182) contend that the observational method used in 'social science involves the systematic, detailed observation of behaviour and talk: watching and recording what people do and say.' Similarly, observation is 'used to understand and interpret cultural behaviour' (Mulhall, 2003: 306). My study included 18 visits to schools and lesson observations across the three schools. Lesson observations were conducted to help me identify issues to follow up in the interviews with the teachers. I was able to ask teachers why they had done certain things during the lessons, how they felt about their teaching including how they could improve their practice in future.

Clough and Nutbrown (2006) define observation as simply 'looking'—'looking critically, looking openly, looking with the knowledge of what we are looking for, looking for evidence, looking to be persuaded, looking for information.' The purpose of the observation is to enable researchers to perceive ideas, which might be missed and to determine concepts that participants might not bring to mind in interview situations (Cohen et al., 2000). It involves conducting multiple tasks. During an observation, researchers are systematically watching, listening, questioning and recording people's behaviours, expressions and interactions. Researchers need to make decisions on what, when, whom and how to observe and record observations (Hennink et al., 2011). The methods of observation fall under the interpretive paradigm and are often used within an ethnographic fieldwork approach. Observation is used in combination with in-depth interviews, in order to provide complementary data to understand issues from different perspectives (Hennink et al., 2011). As highlighted earlier, in my study I observed teachers in order to facilitate discussions in interviews. However, it is not sufficient to collect the data through interviews, which can only provide general perceptions rather than what actually happens. However, direct observation can be particularly useful to discover whether teacher and student behave in the way they claim to behave. The idea is to generate data that portray a comprehensive picture. Observation allows us to study people's behaviour in 'strange' situations such as classrooms (Wellington, 2000).

In addition to this, Creswell (2009: 181) claims that in qualitative observations, the 'researcher takes field notes on the behaviour and activities of individuals at the research site.' This can also help researchers to better understand why teachers and students act in the way they do. Observation is a highly skilled activity for which an extensive background knowledge and understanding is required. Interviews are insufficient to reflect teachers' perspectives towards learning and teaching of English language in China. There is a need to have classroom observation which is attempting to find out the actual language learning and teaching activities that teachers asked their students to participate in the class. It can be seen as manifestation of language teaching behaviour. A total of nine classroom observations were made with nine teachers in three different schools.

3.5.2.1 The types of observation

Observation can be structured or unstructured, participant or non-participant. Each approach has both strengths and limitations. Different kinds of observation can be conducted depending on what the researcher seeks to achieve. In this study, participant observation is employed as my research method. Lessons in three different schools were observed within three months. Denscombe (1998: 200) defines participant observation as:

> the method in which the observer participates in the daily life of the people under study, either openly in the role of researcher or covertly in some disguised role, observing things that happen, listening to what is said, and questioning people, over some length of time.

Participant observation can often provide valuable and insightful data. The essential advantage of participant observation is that it preserves the naturalness of the setting (Denscombe, 1998). Participant observation uses the researcher's 'self' as the main instrument of research, therefore offers opportunities for researchers to see things as they normally occur. It is:

a systematic and disciplined study which, if performed well, greatly assists in understanding human actions and brings with it new ways of viewing the social world. (May, 2001: 174)

Denscombe (1998: 203) identifies three types of participant observation:
- Total participation, where the researcher's role is kept secret
- Participation in the normal setting, where the researcher's role may be known to certain 'gatekeepers,' but may be hidden from most of those in the setting
- Participation as observer, where the researcher's identity as a researcher is openly recognised

Therefore, I adopted the role of participation as observer in my research. For its primary advantage which is to gain informed consent from the participants and avoid ethical problems such as failure to acknowledge the rights of participants. I participated in classroom activities, taking notes of the process of lessons and obtaining teaching materials under the permission of teachers.

3.5.2.2   *Strengths and limitations of observation*

There are several strengths and limitations for observation data collection method. On the one hand, Flick (2014) suggests three contributions along with three limitations of the method of observation. As for contributions, firstly, compared to interview, observation involves a longer period in the field and in contact with the persons and contexts to be studied; secondly, theoretical sampling can be applied in observation more easily than in interview studies; finally, the interaction with the field and the object of research may be realised most consistently. As for limitations, firstly, observation attempts to focus on events as they naturally occur while the act of observation impacts the observed in any case, therefore, the result of observation can be doubtful; secondly, the attempt by the observer to avoid being identified poses problems in analysing the data and in assessing the interpretations which did not constitute any problem to me as my study did not involve hiding my identity to the participants, where participants knew that I was a researcher and I was observing them for a particular purpose; thirdly, the number of the members cannot be restricted due to the public field. In addition, not all phenomena can be observed in situation.

Furthermore, Hennink et al. (2011) provide a list of strengths and limitations of observation as shown in Table 2.

In my study, observations were made to enable an insight into the teaching and learning of English language. I wanted to appreciate the classroom dynamics and ensure that I raised appropriate questions during my interviews with teachers. Teachers knew that I was not drawing any conclusions from the lesson observations only; instead, I was using this approach to ground myself into the issues around the teaching and learning of English. I knew exactly what to look at as I had defined my research questions so I did not need massive experience as an observer. I took notes and ensured that as far as possible, the notes were not coloured with my own views and values. The method helped me to understand the interactions between teachers and students during teaching and learning in English classrooms.

Table 2   The strengths and limitations of observation

Strengths	Limitations
Provides familiarity with cultural milieu	Time consuming (continued and repeated immersion in setting)
Provides context to behaviour	Recording field notes is cumbersome
Explains behaviour	Simultaneous observing and recording can be difficult
Documents unspoken rules of behaviour	Field notes may be subjective
Less intrusive than interview methods	Researchers need to refrain from interpretation
Provides insight into people's interactions	Needs skilled observers
Helps avoid participants, post-hoc rationalisation of behaviour	Limited as a stand-alone method
Complementary to other methods	

3.5.2.3   Field notes of observation

Hennink et al. (2011: 194) state that 'conducting an observation requires skills not only in observing social situations but also in recording observations.' Taking clear and detailed field notes is important, which become useful data for research analysis. It is challenging to write field notes with observation. Hennink et al. (2011:195-196) suggest some strategies for taking field notes as shown below:

- Writing notes continuously while observing;
- Taking short breaks from observing to write field notes, and then elaborating on these later;
- Becoming familiar with the social setting to find a place where you can observe and take notes;

- Using sketches or drawings to improve the detail of field notes;
- Labelling each filed notes with a data, time and place;
- Developing your own shorthand technique to note brief points that you can expand later;
- Including notes on people, activities and the physical environment itself.

In addition, Hennink et al. (2011) mention that when observing a social setting such as a classroom, it is useful to include the interactions happening in the class in field notes. For example, who talks to whom, whose opinions are sought, who are the listeners, and what is the body language of the speakers and listeners. Observing body language in such social setting can indicate the power dynamics in the social setting. For example, if the person is always standing and speaking while others sit and listen, this may identify that the person is in a leadership role. In the classroom observation, it is one of the ways to indicate whether the class setting is teacher-centred or not.

A field diary is another way to record researchers' thoughts and interpretations about what they observe. It includes ideas, feelings, opinions, disgust and shock (Hennink et al., 2011). One of the advantages of writing a field diary is that 'it keeps field notes free of interpretations' (Hennink et al., 2011: 197). It is also helpful to be reflective and critical of the iterative process in observation. A field diary enables researchers to note down their thoughts on emerging ideas.

In my study, I decided to take down notes in my small notebook that I used as a field diary. While I sat in the classroom, I took notes on anything related to the focus of my study, for example, the methods the teachers were using, how the textbook was being used, the role of students including the interaction between teachers and students. This was helpful as a reminder of issues to discuss with the teacher during the interviews. Interviews provided opportunities to explore further issues that I would have observed in the classroom. To ensure that the observations were complementary to the interviews I made sure that each of the nine teachers were observed before the interview.

3.5.3　Documentary research

The term 'documents' covers a very wide range of different kinds of sources (Bryman, 2004). The documents for educational research might be of paper sources, electronic sources, visual sources or aural sources (Wellington, 2000). Furthermore, Bell divides documentary data into primary and secondary sources, where primary sources 'are those which came into existence in the period under research' such as conferences and school meetings, while secondary sources are 'interpretations of events of that period based on primary sources' such as books, journals, diaries, government publications and official statistics (Bell, 2005: 125). In my study, I included documents like annual reports, minutes of meetings, prospectuses (of a school or college), lesson plans, examination papers, schemes of work, curriculum documents, web pages, photographs, government papers and policy documents.

Furthermore, Wellington (2010: 113-114) suggests that documents can be applied in three critical stages in research:

1. The exploratory stage

Documents can be used to open up an area of inquiry and sensitise researchers to the key issues and problems in that field. This can be especially useful in an area in which the problems have not been clearly conceptualised or formulated. Through studying documents, research questions can be articulated or hypotheses can be created.

2. The complementary stage

As well as being of value at the outset of research, documents can enrich a study throughout the research process, i.e. as a complement to other methods and approaches, for example, case study.

3. The concluding stage

The main advantage of using documentary sources is their accessibility. To gain the material the researcher simply needs to visit the library or use the World Wide Web. A large amount of information is available without much cost, and without the need for authorisation or ethical problems (Denscombe, 1998). In other words, compared with people as a source of data, document analysis poses fewer problems and issues. However, the materials associated with the document analysis may be written with particular aims, which are different from the researcher's purpose. Therefore, researchers should show a critical analysis of the various sources and carefully evaluate their credibility. Scott (1990: 6-8) summarised four basic criteria to evaluate documents as addressed below:

- Authenticity: Is it the genuine article? Is it the real thing?

- Credibility: Is it accurate? Is it free from bias and errors?
- Representativeness: Is the document typical of its type? Does it represent a typical instance of the thing it portrays?
- Meaning: Is the meaning of the words clear and unambiguous? Are there hidden meanings? Does the document contain argot and subtle codes?

The four criteria have some applicability to educational research, so Wellington (2010) considers them in detail. Firstly, 'authenticity' refers to the source and the authorship of a document (Wellington, 2010). This criterion could be used to measure the identity or origin of a document. Secondly, 'credibility' refers to the extent to which a document is genuine and truthful (Wellington, 2010). For example, in an interview transcript it is whether the participants provide genuine information, that is, being honest in the responses to the interview questions, whether they tell 'the truth' , or in some cases, whether it is accurate. Both credibility and authenticity are akin to the idea of validity. Thirdly, 'representativeness' refers to the 'general problem of assessing the typicality or otherwise of evidence' (Scott, 1990: 7). It relates to the idea of 'generalisability' (Wellington, 2010). However, Scott (1990) declares that research does not always want or seek 'typical evidence.' The significant skill is to evaluate how typical or atypical it is before any inferences are drawn. Finally, 'meaning' regards the assessment of the document themselves. As Scott (1990: 8) says, 'what is it and what does it tell us?' This is probably the most important and most contentious aspect of documentary research. In my research, I will use documentary analysis in order to evaluate the ELT curriculum, teaching materials, background information of participating school, and professional development opportunities for teachers in China. Documentary analysis was also useful in terms of informing my interview discussions with teachers. I was able to identify issues that needed clarification and focus during interviews with teachers in each school.

This section looked at the different data collection methods, including semi-structured interviews, lesson observation and document analysis. A brief description of what each method involves is provided and in addition, the rationale for the adopted method in my study is discussed. As argued earlier, the study triangulated data collection method in an attempt to generate credible data to respond to the main research questions. The following section will look into data presentation.

3.6　Data Presentation

As discussed in the preceding section, this study involved the use of different data collection tools, including interviews, observation and document analysis. This section will look at how the interview data were generated and processed for subsequent analysis.

3.6.1　Recorded and transcription

In qualitative research, 'the interview is usually audio-recorded and transcribed whenever possible' (Bryman, 2004: 330). May (2001: 138) claims that although transcription is a very long process, 'recording can assist interpretation as it allows the interviewer to concentrate on the conversation and record the non-verbal gestures of the interviewee during the interview.' This view is echoed by Bryman (2004) who posits that qualitative researchers are frequently interested not only in what interviewees say but also in the way they say. It is better for researchers to use audio-records instead of making notes, because the interviewer is supposed to be highly sensitive to what is being asked, following up interesting points, drawing attention to inter-viewee's answers; thus, it is better if the researcher is not bothered by having to focus on getting down notes on each interviewee's saying. Most people agree to the request for the interview to be recorded; however, there will be people who are self-conscious or alarmed at the prospect of their words being preserved and might refuse recordings. When faced with refusal, researchers should not stop but still go ahead with their interview (but not recording), as it is highly likely that useful information will still be provided. However, it is also important to have flexibility in coping with audio-recording equipment breakdown and refusals by interviewees to allow a recording to take place. In addition, it is a common experience that the interviewee may continue to talk and in most cases bring up some interesting issues after the interviewer has turned off the recording device. Although it is not possible to start recording again, it is important to take down some notes after the interview as the conversation may actually contribute to the research story.

Flick (2014: 389) also states that if 'data have been recorded using technical media, their transcription is a necessary step on the way to their interpretation.' In line with this apt observation, all the recorded interviews need to be transcribed. Transcription is a necessary and basic step in qualitative research. Hennink et al. (2011) contend that transcription is an act of representation in qualitative research, and the purpose of the research influences the type of transcription conducted. For example, linguistic and conversational analysts focus on the nature and structure of dialogues, therefore the transcription may include the diction, accents, length of pauses, lengthened words, word emphasis or sounds. Some people might think that transcription is simply a translation of verbally materials into a written format. However, this is too simplistic given that during a conversation a number of other features, for example, body language or intonation, need to be captured as they define meanings. Transcribers need to be 'trained in much the same way that interviewers do' (Bryman, 2004: 332).

I had to transcribe all the interviews by myself in order to keep with the ethical commitment to the participants' confidentiality and anonymity. The problem with transcribing interviews is that its being very time-consuming. On average, transcribing a thirty-minute interview took me half a day, for I had to translate Chinese into English first and then conducted the thematic analysis of the translated transcripts. However, despite being a time-consuming process, it practically assisted me to become more familiar with the data and this was beneficial for the purposes of data analysis. Moreover, transcription has the advantage of keeping intact the interviewee's words by building up the amount of text to be analysed (Bryman, 2004). Qualitative data are not untreated until all the interviews have been completed and transcribed. There are good grounds for making analysis an ongoing activity, because it allows the researcher to be more aware of emerging themes that they may want to ask about in a more direct way in later interview. In light of this, after each interview I listened several times to the audio record and tried to identify the main themes emerging from them. This was very helpful as I kept adding questions on emerging themes during interview sessions.

There are different transcription systems; however, a standard has not yet been established (Flick, 2014). According to the statement of Strauss (1987), it seems very reasonable to transcribe only as much and as exactly as required by the research questions. It is reasonable to think that a transcription system should be easy to write, easy to read, easy to learn and easy to search. Occasionally, I added contextual information by writing a brief note about the interaction, particularly in the way of saying. This was done immediately after the interview to ensure that I captured every important detail. These little notes assisted me to look at the transcriptions later. I also kept more detailed field notes that I did not include with transcriptions. Some interviews or at least large portions of them are sometimes not very useful, perhaps because interviewees are reticent or not as relevant to the research topic as they are supposed to be. Actually, it is a common phenomenon among qualitative interviews, since some qualitative interviews may be regarded as uninspiring and uninteresting by interviewees. If I found some interviews not terribly illuminating, I may not include them in the transcription. Therefore, it would be better to listen to these interviews first, at least once or twice and then transcribe only those portions that the interviewer thinks are useful. However, the researcher may miss certain things or need to go back to the tapes at a later stage in research analysis to try and find something that only emerges as significant later on.

3.6.2　Translation of data

In my case studies, interviews were conducted in a different language from that of the study, therefore, the transcripts needed to be translated from Chinese to English for data analysis. I conducted interviews in Chinese because I did not want to limit the participants' capacity to express their thoughts due to language barrier. Hennink et al. (2011) consider two approaches to translating a record interview. The first approach is producing a verbatim transcript in the original language of the interview and then translating this into a second transcript in the language of study. The second approach is to conduct translation and transcription simultaneously leading to a single transcript in the language of the study. This includes a translator listening to segments of the recorded interview, considering an appropriate translation and then writing down the translation into a transcript. However, simultaneous translation and transcription may lose some of the detail in the translated transcript and it may easily cause translation errors. Therefore, I chose the first translation approach, which has the verbatim transcript in Chinese and then translated this into a second transcript in English. Although this is a time-consuming approach, it helps to check for accuracy and appropriateness, while bringing about a transcript in the original language for reference during data analysis. In order to maintain anonymity and confidentiality, I decided to carry out translation and transcription by myself. I have explained how I took field notes during lesson observations earlier. I also translated the notes from Chinese to English in order to make use of them in my final data analysis. The limitations of translation are that although an effort is made to convey the message as it is from the participants' perspective, there is no use of direct words from the participants, which might affect the meanings from them.

3.7　Data analysis

Given that my study generated qualitative data mainly, data analysis has involved the use of qualitative data analysis techniques, which is to be explained in more detail in the following paragraphs.

3.7.1　The nature of qualitative data analysis

Qualitative data obtained from the interviews and observations including document analysis were analysed using the thematic analysis approach. In the first place, the data were transcribed and coded. Creswell (2009: 184) states that 'qualitative data analysis is conducted concurrently with gathering data, making interpretations and writing a report.' Qualitative data analysis is sought to interpret the meaning of participants' views, feeling and experiences.

However, dealing with qualitative data is not easy. Qualitative research generates vast amounts of data in non-standard format. There is an inevitable tendency within qualitative data that is 'over-collected' and 'under-analysed' (Wellington, 2000). This poses a challenge for the researcher to interpret and analyse the data. Eventually, many researchers find out that they are limited by 'time, words or energy when it comes to analysing, interpreting, discussing or "locating" the data' (Wellington, 2000: 135). Hence, during my research process, I had to carefully evaluate the collective data and make a record, which helped me to avoid 'over-collecting' data while 'under-analysing.' The data analysis process is not a linear sequence but a circular process (Day, 1993). Being aware of the nature of the process of data analysis, I have developed a good understanding of the data, which facilitated a deeper analysis of emerging themes. The following section discusses the thematic analysis approach that I used in the analysis of my study findings.

3.7.2 Thematic analysis

Thematic analysis is a type of qualitative analysis, which Braun and Clarke (2006: 79) defined as:

> a method for identifying, analysing and reporting patterns (themes) within data. It minimally organises and describes your data set in (rich) detail. However, frequently it goes further than this, and interprets various aspects of the research topic.

Thematic analysis is considered the most appropriate method for any study that seeks to discover themes or patterns using interpretations such as mine, providing the opportunity to code and categorise data into themes. The processed data can be displayed and classified according to its similarities and differences. In order to achieve this, the process should include coding, categorisation and noting patterns, that is, different level of themes could be provided (Braun and Clarke, 2006). By gathering data using different instruments (for example, observation and interviews in this study) with participants in different environments, thematic analysis will produce and present the data more effectively and reflect the reality of the data collection. Braun and Clarke (2006: 86) identify six steps that can be followed in search of patterns across the data, including:

1. Familiarising with the data

The familiarisation process involves transcribing of the data from audio recordings to a word document. Here after transcribing, each transcript was translated from Chinese to English language. A hard copy of each transcript was read through several times, with extracts of interest highlighted and initial thoughts written and revisited.

2. Generating initial codes

Once all the nine interviews were transcribed and translated into English, the transcripts were read through systematically looking for features in the text that were of interest with regards to the research questions.

3. Searching for themes

After the data set had been read, re-read, coded and re-coded all of the codes created were collated into possible themes. Consideration was given to how different codes could be combined to create overarching themes, which was an iterative process.

4. Reviewing themes

This phase is about reviewing and refining the themes (Braun and Clarke, 2006). Each created theme was read through with the coded text extracts to check that the themes were grounded in the codes.

5. Defining and naming themes

The themes were revisited and re-read for several times, creating an opportunity to revise, ensuring that the story told was clear and credible. This also aided in developing the names for each theme.

6. Producing the report

The final stage of thematic analysis involves the final analysis and the write-up of the findings.

In my study, I made use of the steps outlined above in the analysis of the data. Other forms of qualitative data analysis exist, for example, grounded theory. However, although grounded theory is very similar to thematic analysis in terms of their procedures for coding themes or coding from data (Braun and Clarke, 2006), it is not appropriate for my study. For grounded theory, data collection and data analysis processes run parallel (Strauss and Corbin, 1998), where analysis data is undetermined before starting a study; and if sample used was determined and defined like in the case of my study, thematic analysis is more appropriate (Creswell, 2009). Grounded theory was not appropriate for me because I had in mind some themes drawn from the main research questions and themes derived from literature that influenced my data analysis.

3.8   Summary

This chapter has presented and discussed the methodology, methods and procedures followed in conducting the study, has made explicit that the study at hand was a small-scale qualitative study which involved working with three secondary schools in a selected region in China. A multiple-case study strategy was adopted. The methods used for data collection included semi-structured interviews, observation and document analysis. Qualitative data were generated and the chapter discussed the approach to qualitative data analysis using thematic analysis. In addition, the chapter looked at the ethical considerations in the conduct of the study, including principles of gaining access, informed consent, voluntary participation along with maintaining confidentiality and anonymity of participants. I have provided details on all the processes and procedures involved, ensuring that the rationale for choices made has been provided. The following chapter will focus on the presentation of the primary data generated in the study.

CHAPTER 4

Data Presentation and Analysis

4.1 Introduction

This chapter contains data generated from my study, through different methods including interviews, classroom observations and document analysis. This is based on data collected in China from nine individual teachers from three secondary schools involved in the study. The study investigates the teachers' perspectives on ELT as well as their role as agents of change in ELT, and also sought to investigate what the teachers think needs to be done in order to improve the teaching and learning of English language in Chinese secondary schools. A number of issues were explored, including teachers' perspectives on the content of the ELT curriculum, the design and teaching of the ELT curriculum as well as the key problems being faced in the teaching and learning of English language in schools. The main research questions addressed in the present study are listed below:

A. Teachers' perspectives on ELT

- What are the teachers' perspectives on the content of the ELT curriculum?
- What are the teachers' perspectives regarding how they design and teach the ELT curriculum?
- What are the teachers' perspectives on the key problems being faced in the teaching and learning of English language in schools?

B. Teachers' perspectives about their role as agents of change in ELT

- From the teachers' perspective, what can be done to ensure effective teaching of the English language in schools?
- What opportunities exist for teachers to develop professionally in schools?

- From the teachers' perspective, what role does SDPD play in the teaching of the English language?

As stated earlier, data included in this chapter are derived from different sources, including semi-structured interviews and lesson observations. In the first part of this chapter, data from the lesson observations and from each school are to be presented separately, while the second part of the chapter focuses on the presentation of interview data. During interviews, in most cases I raised slightly different questions with each teacher, and I analysed each interview transcript separately as Smith (1995: 9) says, 'a single respondent's transcript may be written up as a case study in its own right.' I divided the data into three groups according to the schools and the teachers. For each school, I provided background information to enable the readers to gain insight into some of the contextual factors influencing the teaching and learning of English language, including information on the school policy statements, course contents and related materials. The following section is to present the observation data. Although analyses will focus primarily on observations first and then interviews, appropriate, cross references of the two will be made.

4.2   Data from lesson observations

By involving lesson observations on each of the nine teachers in the study, I wanted to develop a deep understanding of the context in which the teaching and learning of English language took place. The lesson observations were meant to complement the interview data. Each teacher was observed before the interview session to facilitate the interview conversation. This is why I stated that although each interview used the same interview guide questions there were some slight differences in the conversations held with each teacher, whether will be further explained later in the interview data section. Lesson observations were conducted during the period between 6th February and 10th March 2012. I observed nine teachers from three secondary schools who were teaching English language courses. Each teacher was observed on two occasions. The three schools were in the same province located in the southern region of China. The schools will not be identified by their exact name here, but to be referred to as School A, School B and School C. The average class size in each school was between 40 to 50 students. The students were all taught together on the

English course for six hours/week. The students were of mixed levels of attainment and of normal gender distribution. Allocation to classes was done on 'first come first served' basis. As for details about lesson observations from each of them, for each school, there is a section on information about the school, which is then followed by the presentation of the lesson observation data. Below is a list of themes used:

- Background information about the school
- Lesson observation data
  - ➢ Teaching methods
  - ➢ Teaching and learning materials used
  - ➢ The role of the teacher

4.2.1   School A

School A is a private school, which was established in 1995. It consists of primary, secondary and high school parts, covering the whole curriculum like any other school in China; however, the school places a particular emphasis on the teaching and learning of English language. The secondary school which I worked with enrolls students aged between 13 and 15. It has a total of 900 students divided into 18 classes of 50 students each. There are many teachers in the school but only nine of them are English language teachers. English language is taught at three levels[①] in the school namely level 1, level 2 and level 3. I selected two English language teachers from level 3 for my study, because they were the only ones available and willing to participate in the study. Though ideally there shall be a representation of teachers working with students at all the three levels. From the information provided on the school website, it can be known that the school had made an excellent reputation for itself in the teaching of English language since 1995. I hoped to understand what made the school successful in the teaching and learning of English language. As I interacted with the school staff and students, also from the policy documents, for example, the school's strategic plan, I noticed that the school encourages the deve-lopment of each student's particular interests and talents, whether academic, artistic and athletic or any other interests the students may have. They encourage students to develop their ability to study on their own and offer them many opportunities to

---

① Level refers to year of study, so level 1 is year 1, level 2 is year 2 and level 3 is year 3.

improve their initiative and creativeness, which can also be seen during the interviews with teachers as will be discussed later. On the other hand, School A expects their teachers to foster healthy and socially responsible behaviours among students on their way to adulthood. Accordingly, there are many expectations from the curriculum. Although schooling in general has many purposes, the curriculum is the school's main instrument for promoting the learning of specified knowledge, skills and attitudes. In an effort to promote the learning of English language, the school encourages the teachers to use different teaching methods in English classes. Furthermore, the school holds many English activities, such as English Saloons, English Speech Contests and Cambridge English lessons.

As has indicated in the preceding section, three teachers were selected to participate in my study. All of the three teachers had more than ten years' working experience in teaching English, with Mr Chen[1] having 22 years, Mrs Lu 16 years and Mrs Cao 12 years. Data from lesson observations are to be presented below. Of the three teachers, it was noted that Mr Chen had an opportunity to go to Australia as part of his professional development to develop his communication skills in a native English speaking environment.

4.2.1.1   Lesson observation data

Each of the three teachers was observed teaching on two occasions. This was meant to help me develop a deep sense of the methods the teachers were taking, the teaching and learning materials they were using in the classrooms as well the role played by the teacher during the class time. These different elements identified during lesson observations are to be discussed below. Some evidence from document analysis and discussions held with teachers immediately after the lesson observations will be used to substantiate the issues and observations made during the lesson observations.

4.2.1.2   Teaching methods

I am aware that the teaching of English language can be achieved by the use of different methods and teachers are in most cases free to select the methods they want. When I went to observe lessons, I wanted to develop an understanding of which specific methods or approaches the teachers were using in their classrooms. I observed that two

---

① Note all teachers' names used are pseudonyms.

of the three teachers (namely Mr Chen and Mrs Cao) I was working with in my study in School A were applying the CLT approach in their classes and the other teacher was using the traditional grammar teaching approach (Mrs Lu). There is a general consensus amongst the two teachers, Mr Chen and Mrs Cao, who stated that communication is the goal of teaching and learning English language. Mr Chen believed that comparative studies will stimulate students' learning motivation and excite their creative thinking and as a result, he sets group work activities for his students. Given that Mr Chen and Mrs Cao were both using the same approach to teach the English language, I decided to use one example to show how the approach was being used, which would be enough to demonstrate what the two teachers were doing and the choice of Mr Chen's example was based on his teaching experience, which was 10 more years longer compared to Mrs Cao's so it was helpful to take the example of a more senior teacher.

I observed Mr Chen on two different days: 6th February 2012 and 13th February 2012. His class consisted of 42 students who were seated in seven rows and six columns. There were 22 boys and 20 girls mixed up in the class, no separation between girls and boys. Generally, I observed that the teacher enjoyed a very good relationship with the students and similarly, the students appeared to get along very well with each other. This set a good atmosphere for learning in the classroom. In the first class, he had four objectives listed on his lesson plan, which he shared with me before the lesson started:

1. To understand description words, that is, adjectives: exciting, busy, dangerous, boring, difficult and so on

2. To utilise description words to describe one's own favourite jobs

3. To use descriptive words to characterise some jobs

4. To develop good listening practice, and help develop reflection

The lesson was based on content drawn from the course book entitled *Go for It* (Nunan, 2007), in particular sections B 1a—3a of Unit 4: I want to be an actor. According to the teacher, students were supposed to master the following key points by the end of the session:

1. Use 'because it is...' to describe personal favourite jobs

2. Use proper and accurate adjectives to express the view of some jobs

3. Understand and make use of the language points in the three advertisements

I observed that during the session the teacher asked students to recall vocabulary and grammar learnt in the previous lesson. There is much repetition in the teaching of vocabulary and grammar. At the beginning of the lesson, Mr Chen asked students to read and recite vocabulary, by which, it means students practised the pronunciation the new words and phrases learnt in the lesson. The words were placed in groups as shown below and students had to read all them.

Step 1: Pronounce new words and phrases

Group 1: money/give/get	Group 2: wear/uniform
Group 3: dangerous/thieves	Group 4: work late/go out/dinners
Group 5: talk/meet/ask	

The teacher also provided students with the opportunity to practise correct grammatical constructions. He read them first, asking students to repeat after him. I found that the teacher was setting grammar patterns for students to use in conversations. When I asked the teacher after the lesson, he told me that the purpose of the task was to help students to learn vocabulary and grammar patterns by heart. This was also clearly articulated in the lesson plan. For example, in order for students to understand descriptive words, such as exciting, busy, dangerous, boring and difficult and then to use these words to describe their own favourite jobs, Mr Chen set several learning and teaching steps as shown here. All the activities were being done in English ensuring that students had opportunities to develop the much needed communication skills.

Step 2: Introduce a series of similar dialogues

In the following section, a number of dialogue activities were conducted. Each dialogue was introduced by the teacher using PowerPoint slide and then reading all the parts first with students repeating after him. He also gave students examples of questions that they were to be asked based on the dialogue content to give them an opportunity to practise speaking skills. The same pattern was used in all the dialogues. For instance, the following dialogue would be put up on a PowerPoint slide, where 'T' stands for teacher, 'S' stands for student with S1 and S2 indicating student 1 and student 2 respectively.

> **Dialogue 1**
>
> T:　　Do you want to be a doctor?
>
> S 1:　No, I don't.
>
> T:　　Why?
>
> S1:　Because it is difficult.
>
> And then Mr Chen turned to another student.
>
> T:　　What does Jack think of the doctor?
>
> S2:　He thinks the doctor is difficult.
>
> T:　　What do you want to be in the future?
>
> S2:　I want to be a thief.
>
> T:　　Why?
>
> S2:　Because it is exciting.
>
> T:　　Well, maybe you want to be a policeman in the future.

The teacher motivated students by praising them when they got things right and providing support and hints when it was necessary. For example, when student 2 (S2) in the above dialogue mentioned that he wanted to be a thief, the teacher did not criticise him but suggested a more seasonable answer like being a policeman instead of being a thief. Students were able to make mistakes and learn from their mistakes in the classroom. The lesson was very lively as students participated actively. Students took turns to talk during the session with the teacher providing feedback to each student as they worked on different activities.

> **Dialogue 2**
>
> More students involved in the dialogue encouraging the development of listening and speaking skills.
>
> T:　　Do you want to be a bank clerk in the future?
>
> S3:　No, it's boring.
>
> T:　　What do you want to be?
>
> S3:　I want to be a teacher, it is interesting.
>
> Mr Chen asked another student.
>
> T:　　What does S3 want to be?
>
> S4:　She wants to be a teacher.
>
> T:　　Why?
>
> S4:　Because she thinks it is interesting.

Through these dialogues, students were able to understand and use grammar correctly.

Step 3: Choose the correct description words and complete the sentences below

---

interesting, busy, exciting, boring, difficult

My work is _____, but kind of dangerous, thieves don't like me.

I want late, I'm very _____ when people go out to dinners.

I like talking to people, I meet _____ people every day and ask them question.

This activity was for writing where each student had to complete the task in their notebooks. The teacher used a PowerPoint slide to show the sentences to the students. I copied the exercises as they were and I noticed that in some cases the teacher also made grammatical mistakes. For example, the second sentence in this example does not make sense at all, yet students tried to answer all the questions. It can be said that there were some problems when teachers tried to model English language.

Step 4: Express ideas: use the description words to describe one's own favourite jobs

---

Dialogue 1

T: What do you want to be?

S5:   I want to be a writer. It is an interesting job.

T: OK, good idea, very good. Thank you!

Mr Chen asked another student.

T: What does S5 want to be?

S6:   S5 wants to be a writer.

This activity appeared to be similar to the one in Step 2. The teacher explained that in some cases he repeated activities to ensure students had a good opportunity to practise. In this case, emphasis was placed on students' ability to read, pronounce and to apply the descriptive words more widely.

Dialogue 2

T: What do you want to be?

S7:   I want to be a farmer.

T: Why do you want to be a farmer?

S8:   It is busy but has lots of fun.

In this activity, students were doing something similar to the previous activity (in Step 2). As highlighted earlier, the teacher used many repetitions to enable students to understand and be able to use vocabulary and correct grammatical constructions. In my view this was in line with the CLT approach which places more emphasis on developing students' communication skills.

4.2.1.3   Group work and pair work

From classroom observation, I found that teachers set various group work activities as well as pair work. One teacher explained to me in our conversation after the lesson that he used group work tasks to give learners more opportunities to use the language for themselves. Group processes involved students reflecting on their learning experience and discussing what actions should be maintained or changed in order to improve the effectiveness of the whole group. Working in small groups ranging from two to five students each, students would be asked to revise the activities done in class including new similar activities to get the chance to practise language use. The aim of group work according to the teacher was to offer learners more opportunities for language production and thus enhancing their fluency and effectiveness in communication, basically involving three steps: students thought individually on a given topic, then took turns to exchange ideas with their peers, and finally they were selected to share their peer's ideas with the class. Normally, the task was based on textbook learning materials.

During lesson observations, I observed that all the three teachers in my study were employing group work. To illustrate what was happening in School A, an example from one of the teachers will be used. On the 8th March, I attended Mrs Lu's class, who was interested in developing students' English speaking skills through the use of group work and pair work activities. For instance, she showed a picture to students and asked them to make conversation in pairs about the picture. The students were given three minutes to have a dialogue with their peers and later five pairs were asked to present their work to the whole class. Some of the questions she gave them are: What is the family doing? What is the girl doing? What is the man doing?

The presentations by students were guided by what is shown in the picture. For example, what the first pair presented is like the following:

> S1: Hi, what is the grandfather in the picture doing?
> S2: He is reading a newspaper.
> S1: What are the other three people doing?
> S2: They are watching TV.

On 10th February, I had the opportunity to attend Mrs Cao's class, where I found the atmosphere very relaxed. She was teaching a grammar lesson where students worked in groups as well as individually. In that session, they were practicing the use of the following structures:

for + a period of time
since + time point

Mrs Cao showed four different pictures using a PowerPoint illustrating people engaging in different activities (guitar, piano, swimming and reading) and gave a conversation example for students to practise with their peers. After that, she asked four pairs of students to present their conversation to the whole class.

> **Activity:**
> T: How long have you been playing guitar?
> S1: I have been playing guitar for 1 hour.
> S2: I have been playing guitar since 1 hour ago.

The students were meant to practise using the constructions shown above. S2 came up with an incorrect construction in class. When I asked the teacher for clarification, the teacher acknowledged that sometimes students failed to come up with the desired structures; however, she tried to encourage them to keep trying.

As can be seen above, the activities being used by the teachers are repetitive in nature and as explained earlier on this is an approach used by the teachers to help students to understand new vocabulary and correct grammatical constructions. The teacher, Mrs Cao, explained to me that use of pictures also helps students to visualise and easily understand the new words. As highlighted earlier, two of the teachers, Mr Chen and Mrs Cao, were using the CLT approach while Mrs Lu using the grammatical approach more. However, the above example of Mrs Lu shows she focuses on the development of the students' communication skills too, which needed to be addressed in her classes.

4.2.1.4   Teaching and learning materials

I observed that the course book (*Go for It*) contains many pictures and different topics to enhance student understanding. In addition, there are many activities that provide students with opportunities to develop listening skills in the course book.

The lesson by Mr Chen was very dynamic with the teacher giving students different activities to practise listening and speaking skills. For instance, after completing the above table, students were asked to listen to the tape and repeat the sentences loudly with the teacher emphasising the key points such as descriptive words used in the conversation. I noticed that the teacher was responding to the students' needs, giving them more opportunities to repeat the activity until they understood. Furthermore, the teacher moved around the class identifying those students who were having difficulties in completing the tasks and helping them. She used a question and answer approach to establish student understanding.

I also observed Mrs Cao teaching a lesson on grammar on 10th February, in particular the present perfect progressive/simple past tense/present progressive tense. In this particular case, the teacher was not using the course book but carefully chosen teacher-created materials, which were based on what students had learnt from the course book in the previous lesson. During the first part of the lesson Mrs Cao conducted a revision of the previous lesson, which had focused on the simple past tense. After that, she introduced an activity where students were to practise the use of different grammar structures. The teacher wanted students to understand how the words 'for' and 'since' are used in different sentence structures. Using a PowerPoint she explained how the two words are used in sentences as illustrated below:

> for + a period of time
> since + time point

The teacher selected learning resources that appealed to students to keep the lesson interesting and easy to understand. For example, to enable students to practise the use of the above grammatical structures, the teacher showed a picture of Jackie Chan a famous actor among students and asked them to give different answers to the question 'how long has Jackie Chan been acting?'

Students showed great enthusiasm to participate in this activity. They took turns to give different answers as shown below:

---

1. Jackie Chan has been acting for 51 years.

2. Jackie Chan has been acting since 51 years ago.

3. Jackie Chan has been acting since 1961.

4. Jackie Chan has been acting since he was 7 years old.

There was a buzz in the classroom with students eagerly talking and giving their answers, which I interpreted as students found this activity very interesting and they engaged very well throughout the lesson. The teacher gave them more activities similar to the one above to ensure that the students understood the use of the two different grammatical structures.

Mr Chen and Mrs Cao were using the communicative approach. This was discernible in their lesson plans as well as in the types of activities they developed with students in the class. Students were given more opportunities to practise reading and pronouncing the words and phrases in English. While the two teachers focused on teaching grammar in a communicative way, Mrs Lu adopted a different approach. Students in her class spent most of the lesson time practising grammar. The teacher, Mrs Lu, clarified to me that they did not have much opportunity to practise speaking and listening compared to students in the other two classes. The final English exam does not have a speaking test, hence, this teacher chose to focus on grammatical aspects that were examinable rather than spending time on speaking practice. In the lesson I observed, Mrs Lu used different activities to give her students opportunities to practise grammar. The lesson was 40 minutes long, but Mrs Lu gave students many activities including the three examples shown below, which indicate the emphasis placed on the development of grammatical skills of students. The activities were mostly written ones with no opportunities for students to practise speaking and pronouncing the words and phrases in English.

In Activity 1, Mrs Lu gave some words to students and asked them to make sentences as shown below.

Activity 1: Make sentences

are, Lisa, talking, to, who, Tim, and

S1: Who are talking to Lisa and Tim?

S2: Who are Lisa and Tim talking to?

Activity 2 involved the teacher asking students to practise raising questions with each other.

Activity 2: Ask a question on anything about the highlighted part of the sentence

She comes <u>from America</u>.

Question: Where does she come from?

In Activity 3, the teacher asked students to identify the appropriate verb to complete sentences. This was an exercise focused on the development of students' grammatical skills.

Activity 3: Fill the blank with a proper verb

1. It's time to _____ (play) football.
2. _____ (put) on your shoes, please!
3. My father is over there. He is _____ (clean) his car.
4. Don't _____ (do) it like that. Does it like this?
5. Jim is good at _____ (swim).
6. Would you like to _____ (play) football?

By looking at the students working on grammatical activities I observed that students lacked enthusiasm as they worked through many grammatical activities over a short time with limited opportunities to converse with their peers. Apart from the grammatical activities in the main course book, the students were also expected to do homework activities from another textbook. I felt that there were too many written activities for the students.

4.2.1.5   The role of the teacher

From my observations, I found that teachers play different roles including organising, guiding and supervising students in the class. All the three teachers in my study organised creative activities and imaginative situations for students to practise speaking skills in English. For example, teachers would show students a picture and ask them to create and narrate a story about it. However, as explained earlier, there was variation in the amount of practice that students got. For instance, Mrs Lu indicated that her students did not get as much of that as students in Mr Chen's and

Mrs Cao's classes.

In addition, teachers provided guidance on students' learning of new words. For instance, at the beginning of a lesson, Mrs Cao showed a PowerPoint with 10 words and asked students to read each word three times. After that, she asked students to stand up one by one and read out them loudly in the class. It seems students were used to doing this; they spontaneously stood up and took turns to read out the words. The words that the teacher used here were: collect, collector, marathon, skate, raise, stamp, shell, kite, globe, coin.

I noticed that Mrs Cao did not translate the words to Chinese; instead, she asked students to give the meaning of the words in Chinese. This strategy of asking students to translate the meaning of words in Chinese inspired students to participate actively, stimulating their enthusiasm and interest in giving answers. This was done before students read the words and it appears to have helped students to learn the words quickly. It was evident that students were engaging with the assigned work and expanding their vocabulary.

As highlighted earlier on, teachers demonstrated that they were facilitators in their students' learning during and after the lessons. For example, Mrs Lu required every student to memorise the dialogues in the course book and she used her free time to supervise the students practising the dialogues in her office. She indicated that the purpose of doing this was to improve students' grammatical skills through sentence construction during the dialogues. She also told me that she had to work extra hours to supervise students effectively. Furthermore, teachers provided learners with opportunities in the classroom to use the language for communication. The school English language teaching policy revealed that it was important for teachers to appreciate that students' willingness to engage in communication and to have the freedom to use the language as a key role in their learning. The dialogues that students participate in enable teachers to provide useful formative feedback to students, which I was able to see during the lesson observations.

4.2.2　School B

School B is a public secondary school, which was founded in 1954. From the school website, it is shown that the school has a student population of 800 and 80 staff members. The students enrolled are between 13 and 15 years old. There are a total number of 23 classes across levels one to three. The English department has 12 teachers, all possessing a bachelor's degree in ELT. Unlike in School A, in this school I selected a single teacher from each level of study, that is, level 1 to level 3. From the school's strategic plan document, I read that the school's vision is to achieve a people-oriented and harmonious development of students. The school records also show that it has been identified as a Conduct-standard School by the Municipal Board of Education, that is, a school with an excellent reputation for student behaviour, and has been voted into the province's Satisfaction Schools category over the last six years. Looking at their school curriculum, it can be seen that the school encourages the development of the students' all-round abilities but puts moral education in the first place. The main purpose of the school is to develop quality education with basic moral standards. The school aims at producing students who fit well in the society with a high level of responsibility and a sense of caring, hardworking and respectful of the human relationships. It pays more attention to the students' mental health education and its counsel position is rated as an 'excellent counsellor centre' by the city's department of mental health education. Furthermore, the school emphasises the need for efficiency of classroom teaching, adherence to teaching reformation, teaching and research work and pursues 'light burden, high quality' teaching mode. The school is geared to embracing new methods of teaching and learning and teachers enjoy being facilitators in the students' learning process. The school places emphasis on the dignity of individual values rather than just focusing on the provision of subject knowledge.

With regards to teaching and class management, the school holds a 'learner-oriented' educational philosophy (as enshrined in the school's strategic plan document). According to the teachers in my study, in order to improve the quality of teaching and learning of English language, the school encourages teachers to develop innovative ideas in their teaching and to make use of staff development opportunities, for example, workshops and seminars arranged either by other schools or the Ministry of Education agencies. In addition, teachers are also encouraged to give open lectures to other colleagues. They ask teachers to read advanced teaching materials and also to explore new teaching methods. Finally, the school requires teachers to think about how to apply their knowledge to practical teaching and learning in classrooms, as well as how to meet the needs of different levels of students.

As indicated in the preceding section, three teachers were selected to participate in my study. The teachers' working experience ranges from 15 to 20 years, with Mrs Zhou having 20 years of teaching experience as an English teacher, Mrs Yang 17 years and Mrs Zhu 15 years. Data from lesson observations are analysed below.

4.2.2.1   Lesson observation data

Data from lesson observations analysed here are using the same themes as in School A. Again, some supporting evidence drawn from document analysis will be used to substantiate the issues and observations made during lesson observations.

4.2.2.2   Teaching methods

Unlike teachers in School A, I observed that teachers in School B were applying the Task-based Language Teaching (TBLT) approach in their classes. As explained in Chapter 2, task-based language learning and teaching approach consists of teachers giving students multiple tasks during the lesson. Teachers in this school were using the TBLT approach throughout different levels.

Another teacher from this school employed body mime in the teaching and learning of English. For example, when she asked about a particular sport, she would ask another student to demonstrate the action. When I asked the teacher about why she was using the approach, she commented that the approach was helpful for some of the students, in particular, students with low attainment levels.

On 20th February 2012, I observed the class of Mrs Zhou who was teaching level 1. She was teaching Unit 4 which had been taught in School A two weeks before. It appears the private School A started two weeks earlier than the public School B. Similarly to Mr Chen in School A, I observed that Mrs Zhou had four objectives to achieve in her lesson and these were drawn from the four main components of the course book. These objectives are:

1. Function: talk about jobs

2. Grammatical structure: 'what' questions, 'where' questions, present tense, to want, to work

3. Target language: What does he do? What do you want to be?

4. Vocabulary: doctor, reporter, policeman, bank clerk, shop assistant, dangerous, exciting, boring

The lesson was based on content drawn from the course book entitled *Go for It*, in particular Section A 1a—3a of Unit 4 (Lesson 3): I want to be an actor. The same book was being used in School A. With thirty-five students were in attendance, the class size was smaller than in School A and this might have impacted on teacher and student interactions and the overall effectiveness of language learning.

I observed that in the beginning of the session the teacher asked students to have conversations based on the previous lesson. It provided many opportunities for students to interact with the teacher and among themselves. These kinds of tasks helped students to develop listening and speaking skills among others skills. From classroom observation, I found that teachers set many group work and pair work tasks. In my conversation with the teachers after the observation, I was told that the aim of group work was to offer learners more opportunities for language learning and thus enhancing their fluency and effectiveness in communication. The following is an example of one of the group work tasks used by Mrs Zhou. After explaining the example below, Mrs Zhou gave students two minutes to find out their peer's parent's job and write down the information in their note books. (Please note that 'T'=teacher and 'S'=student).

Task 1: Group work

T:　What does your father do?

S:　He is a doctor.

T:　Does he like his job?

S:　No, he doesn't.

T:　Why?

S:　It is a difficult job.

After working in pairs, the teacher allocated students into six groups. Students would continue to discuss and get to know each other and the jobs of their parents in the same way they did in pairs. More opportunities to practise speaking were provided by the teacher who asked students from one group to ask questions to students in another group concerning their parents' jobs.

The lesson plan showed a number of different activities to be done by students and it was clearly articulated that these activities were meant to encourage students to develop speaking skills. For example, after the above activity which involved discussions about jobs between pairs and groups of students, the teacher went on to give students another task where they were to talk about their dream job making use of new target words (descriptive words, including interesting, dangerous, exciting and busy).

Mrs Zhou wanted students to talk about their dream jobs with their peers. She started this topic by asking students the following question: 'Do you want to know what my dream job is?' In this case, she was using her own examples and prompted students to talk. When asked by students for the answer, she would say: 'I don't want to tell you, you need to guess.' The teacher then presented a PowerPoint with a riddle:

Task 2: Dream job

my dream job

It is interesting.

But sometimes it is kind of dangerous.

I'm busy and meet many people every day.

Using the information provided in the PowerPoint, students were meant to guess Mrs Zhou's dream job. She provided some hints and ultimately students found out that the answer was 'reporter.' This activity generated a lot of interest among students and they all participated enthusiastically. Following this, the teacher asked students to engage in similar conversations.

Students were then asked to listen to a tape-recorded conversation where people were talking about jobs. After listening to the conversation, the teacher asked students to write a report based on the conversation.

Task 3: Write a report

Betty's father is a _____, and Betty wants to be a _____, because _____.

In our group, my father is a _____. And/but I _____, because _____.

A few students were then asked to present their report to the whole class. At the end of the lesson, the teacher gave students a task to do at home as shown below:

Task 4: Home work

Make a survey: What do your friends want to be? Why?

Write a report: My Friend is... He/She wants to be..., because it's...

4.2.2.3   Teaching and learning materials

As with School A, the main textbook in School B is *Go for It*. In addition to this, teachers in this school make use of other materials such as English newspapers and other resources. Articles in such materials, which contain well-known characters like Harry Potter, encourage students, in particular the high performers or students with high levels of attainment, to do more independent reading in order to widen their horizon and to enhance their reading skills. The teachers provided opportunities for students with high levels of attainment to go beyond the expected standard in order to keep them motivated and engaged. In other words, the teachers differentiated the tasks taking into account the students' levels of attainment.

One particular feature of School B, unlike School A, that I noticed was that teachers encouraged students to learn English songs. It was interesting to see one student come to the teacher and sing a complicated English song very well. Additionally, students were also asked to share reading materials or movies that they found particular interesting in class. However, these tasks were being done by students in level 1 and level 2. According to the teacher of level 3, her students focused on preparing for examinations as this constituted the primary goal for final year students.

4.2.2.4   The role of the teacher

No major differences were observed between teachers in School A and School B. This means that teachers in School B engaged in similar roles to teachers in School A, which included organising, guiding and supervising students. Although they used TBLT, in principle they maintained the same role as teachers in School A, planning and facilitating student learning. This emerged clearly in the interviews that were held after the lesson observations as will be discussed later. The level of student engagement is the one feature in School B that appears to be different from School A as teachers here tend to give more tasks to students during the class. Furthermore, the use of authentic learning materials stands out for teachers in School B compared to teachers in School A. Noticeably, the teachers were making use of newspaper articles and asked students to bring to class learning materials of their choice, including videos and songs.

4.2.3　School C

School C is a relatively new school, having been established at the beginning of 2000. As with School B, this school is a public school with over 1,200 students divided into 38 groups (classes) across level 1 to level 3, and a total of 90 staff members. The staff profile records show that the school has got a well-qualified English language teaching team, which consists of 24 members. Four of the teachers were awarded the title of national 'Fine' teachers, which is the highest professional recognition title in China, while eight teachers recognised as 'Fine' teachers in their city or in the province. In addition, 60% of the teachers graduated with first class in their first degree. I selected three English teachers for my study. The teachers had teaching experience which ranged from less than 1 to 5 years. It was notable that English teachers in this school were relatively young compared to teachers in the other two schools. Two of the three teachers, namely Miss Zou and Miss Li, had 5 years of ELT experience whereas Miss Fang had less than one year of ELT experience. All the three teachers had graduated with a first class in their bachelor's degree course which was BA English Language. In addition, they all had a teaching quali-fication but as can be seen from their work experience, they were pretty much at the beginning of their careers, particularly Miss Fang. As I interacted with the teachers, I noticed that they were very enthusiastic and positive about their work as English language teachers.

The school has got well-designed learning environments. Each classroom consists of both digital and non-digital technologies. For instance, the digital technologies include computers, good audio systems, projectors and microphones in each classroom. Microphones are used by teachers who have large class sizes; the audio systems are for listening practice and the computers are mainly used for PowerPoint presentations.

The school has excellent achievements in English, and their students demonstrate higher speaking skills compared to students from the other two schools. These data were available from the ranking tables of English language results in the region and the school head also commented on this during our conversations. For example, one of the students was awarded first place in the city's award, and another student came second in English language competition held at provincial level. Although these results only highlight performance of two students, it is worth mentioning that in the other two schools, no student has received awards at either city level or provincial level, which to some extend shows the difference in academic achievements between School C and its counterpart schools in this study. Talking to the teachers in the school, I learned that at that moment, the school was looking for a way to foster students' comprehensive development, that is, rounded students who were good academically and demonstrating mastery of other soft skills needed in society and in the world of work. The school was working towards providing high quality education which is not only examination-oriented. There are many different English competition events among teachers and students. For example, in the first semester of 2012, the school held an English 'free young' drama play for the second year students. There were eight scripts: *Wu Song Fought the Tiger*, *Catch the Rabbit*, *Snow White*, *Do Re Mi*, *Aladdin*, *The Red Queen Tries Hats*, *The Tiger and the Fox*, *The Gift of the Magi*. In order to encourage students and teachers, the school set four individual awards (best male lead award, best female lead award, best male supporting actor award and best female supporting actor award) and seven cooperative awards to different classes (best creativity award, best drama award, best performance award, best co-operation award, best co-ordination award, most popular award, best scenario award). This was a strong incentive to encourage students to learn English.

Another positive aspect of the school is their commitment to continuous professional development. The teachers in my study expressed that every Wednesday teachers got together for up to three hours to discuss pedagogical issues, including defining teaching purposes for each lesson, selection of content to be covered in lessons and teaching approaches. The school requests teachers to complete a lesson plan for every class, which should include the aims of the lesson and the activities to be done during the lesson (they include tasks like dialogues, new words, grammar and homework). In addition, the plan should include the teaching approach and the teacher's reflection on the lesson.

4.2.3.1　*Teaching methods*
School C requires the teachers to integrate 'guidance case study' teaching techniques into second language learning classrooms. The goal of guidance case study is to stimulate students' self-awareness and group cooperation abilities. The principle of guidance case study is to let students engage with the learning material and prepare

for class time activities before they come to class to present it. Basically, using this approach, students are assigned work to do in small groups outside the classrooms. The teacher assigns students to the groups, forming groups of mixed levels of attainment. This approach to teaching and learning of English language places emphasis on collaborative learning. According to the English teachers in my study, the advantage of this approach is that it allows advanced students to help the less advanced students with their studies. Moreover, it was considered that guidance case study approach is likely to facilitate the learners' capacity to communicate in the target language because it provides more opportunities for comprehensible input, real-life experience of language use and positive group interaction. The ultimate goal of the guidance case study approach is to generate more interaction and meaningful negotiations in the process of completing designated tasks. Students are encouraged to get meaning across instead of simply focusing on the accuracy of the language forms. Despite the perceived benefits of the approach, I noticed that teachers found it challenging, and therefore were unwilling to implement. They shared their fears during the interviews, which were conducted after the lesson observations.

On 6th March 2012, I observed a teacher from this school, Miss Zou, who had 5 years of teaching experience. The lesson was based on content drawn from the course book entitled *Go for It* and there were fifty-two students in attendance. From the lesson plan, the lesson focused on grammar, that is, the use of direct and reported speech. At the beginning of the lesson, the teacher explained to her class that the language goal was to enable students to report what someone said.

As with other teachers in the study, I found Miss Zou was quite adept at encouraging students to answer questions. She motivated students to take risks, and her students were not afraid to give wrong answers, which helped them to learn a lot. If a student had no idea, she would provide a hint to help them find out the answer. Using PowerPoint, Miss Zou illustrated many examples of conversations to students, like the ones shown below:

Activity 1: Focus on grammar

A. You should do your own work.

B. What did he tell his brother?

C. He told his brother that he should do his own work.

A. I am not mad at my brother anymore.

B. What did he tell us?

C. He told us that he was not mad at his brother anymore.

The teacher encouraged students to find out the similarities and differences in these two conversations. Moreover, she highlighted the words with past tense, passive voice and third person singular (as shown above) to help students to understand the grammatical structures. Although the main target for this lesson was to help students understand how to transform direct speech to reported speech, Miss Zou also wanted to help students to become familiar with the use of past tense, passive voice and third person singular. She further presented twelve different direct and reported speech examples with simple present tense, simple past tense, simple future tense and past future tense during the same lesson. I noticed that the use of multiple examples helped students in their learning as more students getting involved in the discussions each time the teacher used another example.

The teacher used many activities, some of which are shown below, and explained that this was meant to help the students learn more grammatical constructions. For example, the students were asked to talk about good and bad habits to practise using different sentence patterns. Please note that in the following dialogues, 'T' stands for teacher and 'S' stands for student and where a number is used, for example, 'S1' means student 1.

Activity 2: Good and bad habits

T: We are supposed to... / We are supposed not to...

S1:   We are supposed not to watch football at night.

S2:   We are supposed not to get up later.

S3:   We are supposed not to read too much novels.

T: But I think you can read as much as you can.

Miss Zou asked students to play a game called 'guessing and reading for the truth.' The game consisted of two parts, in the first part students had to guess the answer to a question posed by the teacher. Below is an example:

> **Activity 3: Guess**
>
> Why didn't Xiao Li talk to me?
>
> A. I did something sorry to her.
>
> B. She copied my homework and we have a big fight.

In the above example, the teacher put the question and two answers on the PowerPoint slide and students would try to work out (guess) the correct answer. In the second part, the teacher would present the correct answer to the class highlighting the grammatical aspects that students should focus on as shown in answer B.

In my conversation with the teacher, I learned that the topic was not only related to grammar but also helped students to receive good moral education. Furthermore, it encouraged students to develop interest in guessing an answer to a question during a conversation. To further develop students' communication skills, after the guessing and reading for truth activity, the teacher gave students a 'reading for communication' activity, which was based on the content covered in the previous task. In this case, students were asked to work in pairs and the teacher provided them with some guidelines to come up with a dialogue. Using the narrative in the previous example, students were asked to act as the writer of the dialogue and were supposed to report the whole story to the teacher (one student acted like the writer while the other student acted like the teacher in the dialogue). So the student acting like the teacher would ask questions whilst the other student would answer all the questions during the dialogue. In order to encourage students to participate effectively, the teacher would award additional marks for each of the following points (two marks each):

1. Speaking without looking into the book

2. Narrating the complete story

3. Fluent and logically connected ideas

4. Correct use of body language

5. Being imaginative and creative

After working in pairs, students were given the chance to present their work to the whole class.

The teacher praised the students whose job was well done and gave them high marks. It was evident that these students had grasped the content of the previous activities. From one lesson, the teacher managed to develop students' reading, listening and speaking skills.

Towards the end of the lesson, students were given homework to write a story in their own words based on the ideas developed in the various activities done in the classroom. This was intended to enable students to reinforce what they had learnt during the lesson and to prepare themselves for the next lesson.

4.2.3.2   Teaching and learning materials

In addition to this, teachers created other learning materials that students used for preparatory work, that is, work to be alone before coming to class. For each lesson, teachers had to get together to discuss the key activities including the aims of the session, the intended learning outcomes, the methods of delivery, content and tasks for students. After the meeting, one of the teachers would put together all the ideas for a single unit and distribute to all the teachers. They take turns to produce materials for each unit. Examples of the materials made by the teachers are the ones discussed in the above activities, with similar materials prepared for each lesson.

4.2.4   Summary of lesson observation data

The preceding sections presented data obtained from observations and document analysis. Data from each school has been presented separately but where possible comparisons have also been made. The three schools presented similarities and differences in the way they teach English language.

Among some of the similarities, I observed that the three schools were using the same basic textbook *Go for It* for different levels starting from level 1 to level 3. Generally, all the schools had very large classes of students. In a way, the class size impacts on the methods and activities that teachers plan and organise for their students. In the different approaches being used from one school to the others, there is still an emphasis on engaging students in their own learning. It is quite noticeable that teachers are in the main facilitators in the students' learning process.

Each school has its own teaching philosophy and it was interesting to observe some variations in terms of teaching methods used by teachers in the same school, for example, two of the teachers in School A were using the communicative approach while the other teacher was using the traditional grammatical approach. The approaches used in each of the three schools are summarised below (see Table 3).

Table 3 A summary of the approaches used in teaching English language
in the three schools

School	A	B	C
Teaching approach	• CLT • Traditional grammatical approach	• Task-based learning	• Guided case study

The observations made are important and the main themes emerging from the data will be discussed in more detail in the following chapter. The following section presents primary data generated from interviews with the teachers. It is likely that some of the themes will be similar to those discussed in the preceding section as the interviews were also informed by the experiences from lesson observations.

4.3 Interviews with English language teachers

In addition to lesson observations and document analysis, my study involved conducting semi-structured interviews with English language teachers. As indicated in Chapter 3, the interviews followed the observations in order to give me a picture of the teaching and learning of English language in the participating schools and to provide a concrete basis for discussion. A total of nine teachers from three schools were interviewed, which were conducted at the teachers' school premises. In each case, the teacher would find a quiet room in the school where the interview would be conducted without interruptions from other staff members or students, to ensure that the atmosphere was conducive for a good conversation. I used a digital voice recorder to record all the interviews. In the first place, I made sure that there was a good rapport between myself and the interviewees. Before each interview, I introduced myself, highlighting the purpose of my study and clarifying any questions that the teachers had to make them feel comfortable. I chose to ask simple questions at the beginning of each interview, for example, those like 'how long have you been teaching the English language?' and 'what does your job involve?' before I moved my discussion to focus on the details of learning and teaching of English language. This was a deliberate effort to make them feel comfortable and to create an atmosphere which would facilitate discussion of issues of interest in relation to English language teaching and professional development. Each interviewee took time to explain to me their perspectives on the key problems being faced in the learning and teaching of

English language in schools and they further talked about possible solutions to these problems. I was very happy to have an opportunity to talk to them in a relaxed atmosphere and appreciated the data they provided.

After each interview, I translated and transcribed the audio files. I did not include annotations about voice stress, accent, paralinguistic features, precise duration of pauses, or signalling of instances of conversation overlap, with the only focus on the key issues that would help answer my research questions. I will make use of some of the extracts from the interviews as I write my findings. I have eliminated the features of the response, for they could interfere with readability. For example, where there is unnecessary repetition or unfinished sentences, I would delete these provided the meaning of what remained was unaltered. It is to reduce and display the data, which illustrate the perspective of each individual respondent within each of the categories specific to the research questions so that the reader is able to track the meaning of my analysis. The interviews of all three teachers from one school and their perspectives on various aspects of the teaching and learning of English language are reported together. Teachers' perspectives are elicited on the following sub-themes:

- Content of the ELT curriculum
- Design and teaching of the ELT curriculum
- Current situation of ELT in the school
- Role of teachers agents of change in ELT
- Opportunities to develop professionally in the school
- Role of SDPD in the teaching and learning of English language

As before, names of schools and teachers will remain anonymous for confidentiality purposes. Schools will be referred to as A, B, C while pseudonyms will be used for teachers' names.

4.3.1　Interview data from teachers in School A

Between 13th February and 17th February 2012 I held three interviews, with Mr Chen, Mrs Cao, Mrs Lu in School A.

4.3.1.1　Teachers' perspectives regarding the content of the ELT curriculum

According to the teachers in School A, in secondary schools in China, English is a compulsory subject and is based on a rigorous curriculum typically with one set of textbooks which contain practice activities in listening, speaking, reading and writing. Similar to observations made earlier during lesson observations, the teachers indicated that the main course book was *Go for It*. The purpose of the course book is to improve the students' overall competence in each of the four skills categories mentioned. The book contains more practice in listening; indeed, some of the listening activities are not linked to the listening test but aim to develop the students' practical ability in communicative skills. Teachers are also able to pick up useful information from the local context, for example, newspapers and videos, to help students to improve their listening ability. The views of the teachers in this school were captured by one teacher with the following statement:

> The course book *Go for It* has four sections: reading, speaking, listening and writing. It is hard to say whether the curriculum has any particular trends. Compared to the previous books, it added more listening and speaking practice. The materials are connected to students' daily lives, so it is easy for them to relate to the topics. (Mrs Cao)

Teachers were happy that the course book provided enough opportunities for students to learn grammar. There was consensus that a focus on grammar is important in helping students to understand and grasp the meaning of vocabulary and make sense of sentences. For instance, in an interview with Mrs Lu, she highlighted that 'I think grammar is very helpful to understand the meaning of the words. Grammar can help students to make sense of the sentences.' My conversations with teachers in School A show that for them, the curriculum content is exclusively the course book *Go for It*.

4.3.1.2   *Teachers' perspectives regarding how they design and teach the ELT curriculum*

This section focuses firstly on curriculum design and later on teachers' perspectives on how they teach the English language curriculum. Regarding the designing of the ELT curriculum, teachers in School A indicated that although they got a standard lesson structure, each teacher had the flexibility to choose activities to focus on in each lesson. There were differences in the number of activities in each of the skills categories that each teacher used. For example, one teacher placed more emphasis on grammar while another teacher would place more emphasis on speaking and listening skills.

When asked to reflect on the factors that influenced the design of the lesson plan, all the three teachers highlighted the impact of examinations. This showed that examinations were the most important factor to them. To emphasise the importance of examinations, one teacher said:

> To be honest, for me, no matter what kind of lesson plan, the ultimate aim is to make sure students pass their examination. As Deng said, 'a black plum is as sweet as a white.' How to design lesson plan is not so important, the key is to ensure that it works well for the examination. (Mrs Lu)

What Mrs Lu said resonates with the perspectives of the other two teachers in the school. It was noticeable that each teacher placed emphasis on what they considered important for students' success in examinations. Mrs Lu indicated that sometimes she did not feel the need to adhere to the original lesson plan, but chose to focus on the needs of students which in some cases meant digressing from the plan.

Mrs Cao and Mr Chen felt it important to have a well-structured lesson plan. Mrs Cao claimed that she considered the purpose of each lesson and ensured that students were prompted to contribute during and after lessons. The teachers highlighted three important aspects of lesson design as indicated below:

- The design of an effective lesson plan takes time, diligence and an under-standing of the students' abilities. Therefore, it is important to consider the purpose of the lesson, for example, why the students need to learn it and what they are supposed to learn.
- Lessons need short activities or trigger activities at the start in order to attract the students' attention and stir up their interest before the actual lesson begins.
- It is necessary to consider all the activities that students can engage in and think about how to guide them to do in-class activities. The purpose of teaching is to motivate students to take in what the teacher is teaching.

Mr Chen emphasised that lesson planning involves careful thinking and strategising. For example, regarding spoken language, he considered the proper form to teach the spoken language and the way to give students meaningful practice in producing spoken English language. In addition, Mr Chen said that he used to think about how to set the target and deal with the possible difficulties he might meet in the class when

115

designing a lesson plan.

> Thinking and strategy are very important in making a lesson plan... I design the
> lesson plan by myself. My class [sessions] are different from [what is in the book].
> Like this class, I am always thinking about how to set the target and how to deal
> with the possible difficulties which students may meet. (Mr Chen)

The other aspect of English language discussed by the teachers is the need for
teaching and learning centred on how students learn the language. As Mr Chen's
belief, students' learning strategy is developed by the teacher. Therefore, it is important
to guide them in a proper way, for example, to develop students as good listeners:

> Students' learning strategy is developed by the teacher. Only 10% of the teachers
> might notice that training students to be good listeners is very important. I always
> teach students that listening is respect to others. (Mr Chen)

Where there is a dialogue task, studengts need to communicate and present.
According to the teachers, students tend to be self-centred and may not be interested
in listening to other students speaking. It is important to train students to listen to their
peers speaking. To clarify his point, Mr Chen made reference to how he encouraged
students to listen to each other during a lesson by asking them to comment on answers
provided by their peers.

Another important sub-theme that emerged from the interview data with the
teachers in School A is listening to feedback from students. The teachers made use
of feedback from students in their designing of the lesson plans. They indicated that
they were flexible enough to change the lesson plan during the session to ensure that
they reflected on students' learning needs. 'There is a need to change something in
the class according to students' reflection and understanding... As a teacher, I can tell
how much they understand according to their reflection' (Mr Chen). If students get
confused, teachers will spend more time to clarify issues to them. In the same vein,
Mrs Cao argued that to use students' feedback was an important skill for a teacher.
Students' countenance and body language can tell what they are feeling in the class.
If the teacher, therefore, takes care of their feelings and teaches according to their
level and standard, it will be very helpful. Additionally, Mr Chen pointed out that
'lesson plans are dead, but students and teachers are living.' There should be mutual

communication between students and teachers.

Each lesson plan should include a variety of activities, according to the teachers. In this regard each teacher pointed out that they included collaborative activities including pair work, role plays and brainstorming in class. To illustrate their usage of different activities, Mrs Cao found out that level 1 students liked to do role plays as they found this interesting. For level 2 students, Mrs Cao reported that she encouraged them to read children's literature such as Harry Potter and then asked them to give a three-minute speech in the class. Many students were enthused with this since they would have read the books or watched the movies.

> I set pair work, role plays and brainstorming in my class room; I give them different topics and ask them to discuss with their peers or in a group and then show their findings to other students. Many students are positive and show great enthusiasm in doing these activities. They would like to enhance their memory and I encourage them to present their work to the class. If they do well in the presentations, I will add a credit to their semester [grade]. (Mrs Cao)

All the three teachers stated the possibility that students found themselves engaged with the learning of English through the teachers' use of different activities. For instance, Mr Chen trained students to imitate his pronunciation and accent and encouraged them to attend the reading competitions. He asked students to read loudly and to imitate the pronunciations and accents. For example, in the morning reading session, students might present the paragraph which they think they can read best. It seemed many students liked to participate and most of them were motivated by their presentations. The school has reading competitions, English songs and other activities, which are beneficial towards the improvement in students' learning interest and speaking ability of the English language.

4.3.1.3   Teachers' perspectives regarding the current situation of ELT in the school
During the interviews, teachers were asked to reflect on the current situation regarding ELT in the school. A number of issues were raised in the conversations including the effectiveness of the current course book and the role of examinations in the learning and teaching of English language. These two appear to be the most important issues around ELT in the school and will be discussed in the following paragraphs.

ELT appears to be impacted on significantly by examinations. Mrs Lu mentioned that currently, 'they added the listening testing to the examination... however it still lacks the speaking part. The examination system needs to be changed, but, there are too many students in China, it is hard to change the situation immediately.' All the three teachers from School A said that in general English teachers placed emphasis on the teaching of grammar rather than the speaking skills because the examination won't focus on it. Furthermore, syllabuses are controlled by the high school entrance examination which is set at local authority level, that is, beyond the school. Therefore, English teachers in China are not likely to spend much time on speaking practice, which has no bearing on the examination requirement. It appears that here the teachers in the study were speaking about the general approach used by English teachers in Chinese schools because in my lesson observation, it was quite evident that the participating teachers focused on speaking skills too.

Teachers felt that the examination was being changed and was becoming more challenging for the students. For example, Mrs Cao indicated that the difficulty of the examination was being increased: 'Firstly, there are few direct answers we can find in listening test. On the contrary, there are many calculations.' The listening part requires good listening skills and in addition to that, students need to be able to do some mathematical calculation, like the question: 'The time now is 8 pm, the plane is leaving in 15 minutes, at what time is the plane leaving?' As highlighted above, this type of question is complex for students as they need to do some calculation and then structure the answer using correct grammar. The teacher added that 'it is a good tendency to add culture and daily communication to examinations. However, Chinese students lack such backgrounds' (Mrs Cao). The teacher strongly felt that students never get to experience these kinds of things, that is, the use of phrases that are typically English.

Some of the changes to the examination such as the inclusion of listening tests were identified as positive. For example, Mr Chen highlighted:

There are many differences. In the past, examination tends to test grammar and vocabulary but currently it pays more attention to application competence [not speaking skills though]. For the listening, there are two examinations for the high school entrance. The system will pick the higher scores as students' final mark.

Personally, I think it more reliable and applicable. (Mr Chen)

Teachers agreed that examination was the main factor motivating students to learn. The feelings of the teachers were well articulated by Mr Chen, who said, 'Examination is the main motivation. I would like to say 80% of the students are motivated to learn because they want to pass examinations and access a place at a good high school. The other 20% are motivated by their interest to learn another language.'

There were mixed feelings among the teachers regarding the impact of exam-oriented teaching on students' learning. Mrs Lu and Mr Chen said that the examination has both a negative and a positive impact on the learning and teaching of English language. On the one hand, for students who are willing to study, the examination is good for them, helping them to be guided in their study and to aim to achieve high marks, which enables them to learn the language very well. On the other hand, for those who are not good at studying, examinations can be a daunting experience. Contrary to the views of the other two teachers, Mrs Cao believed that for most of the students, the examination played a positive role in their learning of English language. Examinations might stir up students' learning interests.

Despite feeling that examinations could encourage language learning, Mrs Cao also believed that teachers should not rely on this, stating that:

> Students' learning motivation is very crucial. During the learning and teaching process, give more encouragement to students. Encourage them to speak more. I would like to prepare an excellent lesson plan and arrange interesting activities to attract student's attention. Moreover, building up good relationships with students is another effective way to encourage them to study.

As indicated by Mrs Cao, it is the case that a number of factors including how the teacher motivates students play an important role in facilitating students' learning.

4.3.1.4　*Teachers' perspectives on their role as agents of change in ELT*

I was also interested to establish what teachers think about their role as change agents in ELT. One of the key issues that emerged from the interviews in this school was that being a reflective practitioner is an important ingredient in terms of introducing meaningful changes to the learning and teaching of English language. Teachers in

School A held a positive attitude towards classroom reflection. Mrs Cao stated that a reflective approach helped her to consider how to re-organise classroom materials and tasks and how to restructure individual knowledge. Mr Chen mentioned that schools required teachers to complete the teaching reflection form and he believed that reflection was a way to perfect a teacher's role.

> Yes, we have requirements in school; we need to fill the teaching reflection paper. Personally, I think it is a good way to perfect a teacher's role... because students help teacher to improve. So, if I found students have a problem with understanding content, I will change my class activities and plan for the next time. (Mr Chen)

Mrs Lu reflected on every lesson and she stated that, '... If the lesson is effective, I will be very happy. If students find it hard to follow their lesson, I will think about what I missed and how should I improve my practice.'

4.3.1.5 Regarding opportunities that exist for teachers to develop professionally in the school

A number of opportunities for continuous professional development were cited by teachers during interviews, including lesson observations in the school, seminars and specific training programmes like public lessons organised by the school. School A provided a conducive environment for teachers to improve their practice, offering a place for teachers to share their teaching experiences and expertise so they could learn from each other. These kinds of in-service professional development activities help with teaching and stimulate teachers to alter or strengthen teaching and educational practices. The following observations were made by Mrs Lu:

> The school arranged some lecture observations and research activities. Generally speaking, lesson observation is encouraged for new teachers. They present their lesson and get feedback from other teachers at the end of the lesson. (Mrs Lu)

The school also provides teachers with opportunities to develop themselves outside the school. This was highlighted by Mr Chen who indicated that:

> As an English teacher, there are many opportunities to develop professionally, such as further studies, theory learning and practical training. The main way for us is to attend seminars, public classes and specific training programs. (Mr Chen)

These approaches used in and outside the school are beneficial to teachers and can help students to experience high quality teaching. However, teachers also indicated that due to pressure from excessive workloads and other administrative responsibilities they did not always have the time to engage meaningfully with professional development activities. One of the issues they cited was the large class sizes which made it difficult to provide individual support to students.

4.3.1.6   *Regarding the role that SDPD plays in the learning and teaching of English language*

I asked the teachers how they engaged with the in-service professional development opportunities. This is because without engagement, without genuine interest, there can be no focus on meaning or outcome. Teachers typically want to achieve an outcome, as a result want to engage in training. This question deals in general with how teachers learn and improve by engaging in workshops, attending public lessons, observing others or applying discussions of lesson plans to the classroom. Mrs Lu highlighted that staff development opportunities helped them to reflect on their practice including the selection of appropriate teaching methods. She stated that, 'there exist different teaching methods; however, it is not advisable to apply everything in the class without thinking.' She added that every class had different student levels and it was important for teachers to understand how to respond to the needs of each student.

> After attending continuous teacher training programmes, it is easy to stir up enthusiasm and one would try to apply everything learnt. However, I find that it is improper to apply everything to my class. Actually, what I do in the class is pretty much dependent on the students' level and reflection. (Mrs Lu)

Referring to how she made use of 'public lessons,' that is, lessons open to other teachers to come in and observe providing constructive criticism. Mrs Cao stated that she would prepare for opportunities to be observed by her peers believing that the feedback from other teachers would be very useful:

> If I have a public class, I will prepare it very carefully and at least try to teach twice before I give a public lesson. I feel that I learn much by giving public classes and receive a lot of useful feedback from the teachers. (Mrs Cao)

Mr Chen stated that he never stopped learning from his colleagues and books.

> Since I started teaching, I gradually realised that I lacked experience and was limited in my English speaking capacity. Therefore, I decided to continue to improve my English speaking skills. Now I am learning from my colleagues and from books. (Mr Chen)

Teachers in School A mentioned that they had on-going discussions with other teachers regarding teaching approaches. They would exchange different views, agreeing and disagreeing, explaining, and organising their arguments. The importance of understanding how teachers work together and share practice with their colleagues was reflected in the interview data. Mr Chen shared his experience of the discussions held with other teachers. He stated that he liked 'to discuss with other teachers how to present a class, how to attract students' attention and stir up their interest.' Sometimes he felt his colleagues were like mirrors for him to view his own practice in the discussions.

> We have discussions concerning how to design lesson plans, how to arrange classroom activities, how to present classes effectively, how to improve students' learning interest and so on. (Mr Chen)

I asked the teachers for their perspective regarding setting personal goals towards improving English teaching. Mr Chen pointed out that setting a goal was important for a teacher to develop professionally. It is hard for a teacher to develop speaking and listening capacity without setting goals regarding these skills. In particular, there are many teachers who have many years of teaching experience, whose goal is the examination and whose experience proves that the traditional teaching approach is good for examinations. Therefore, it is hard for them to develop speaking and listening skills without setting a goal regarding these capacities. Moreover, Mrs Lu emphasised the importance of setting goals highlighting that:

> Setting a goal has an important impact on our teaching. However, how to carry out and reach the goal is another separate challenge. I used to set goals before the new semester; however, carrying this out is very hard. (Mrs Lu)

In the same vein, Mrs Cao emphasised the need for teachers to set goals for their professional development stressing that teachers need to be encouraged to do this:

Not only do students need motivation to study, but teachers also need encouragement to undergo further study. Setting personal goals is a good idea to help me to improve my teaching. For every class, I have set the goals for students and for myself. I hope I can present interesting and useful lessons to the students. (Mrs Cao)

Finally, I asked teachers what they think about responsibility. All of them agreed that responsibility was very important to a teacher. Mrs Lu said that, 'a responsible teacher is a self-motivated, self-developed and self-managed person.' Furthermore, she added that if a teacher had responsibility, they would respect students and encourage them to improve their learning approaches and not just criticise them.

Mrs Cao pointed out that 'teaching is not an easy job, thus it takes time to set one's mind on teaching. A teacher needs to think about the best way to present knowledge and to prepare students for life.' A responsible teacher does not simply accept, without critically reviewing the curriculum given by specialists, and think about whether to agree or disagree with what is suggested. She explained the importance of being a responsible teacher:

> As a teacher, I believe that responsibility is very important. Without it, no teacher can do a good job... We need to be aware that we are models to students not only in academic achievement but also in character and virtue. Therefore, we need to be careful about what we teach the students. (Mrs Cao)

Similarly, Mr Chen has highlighted that teachers should take responsibility for the education which they offer to students. Teaching is a lifelong job, where a teacher is like a 'farmer' and a student is like a 'plant.' Mr Chen was emphasising the amount of time that students spend in school. A teacher probably stays with students three years, five years or even eight years. Teachers need to help students to build up good learning habits.

> Responsibility is an important factor in our teaching life. A responsible teacher pays attention to students' lifelong development. Why do I set so many conversations in pair work and group work? This is because if I focus on examinations only I will not help students to develop fully in their learning of the English language. Teachers are like farmers and students are our plants. (Mr Chen)

According to Mr Chen, teachers ought to consider students' lifelong development more than their academic achievement.

4.3.1.7   Summary of interviews with teachers from School A

The preceding section presented interview data from the three teachers in School A. Regarding the teachers' perspectives on the ELT curriculum content, the interview data showed that the content for the ELT curriculum was exclusive to the use of the course book *Go for It*. The interviews looked at the teachers' perspectives on the design of ELT. It emerged that the teachers felt that although they had to use a standard lesson structure there was flexibility to choose activities they wanted individually. The lesson plan was, however, affected by factors like examinations. There was consensus on the impact of examinations on the way teachers designed the lesson plan. When teachers reflected on the current situation regarding ELT, it was shown that the effectiveness of the current ELT relied more on the role of examinations and the effectiveness of the current course book. Teachers also pointed out the lack of time to engage in meaningful professional development due to heavy workloads and large class size. Reflection was highlighted as being the key in the role of teachers as change agents. Teachers also felt that there existed opportunities for professional development with the school providing opportunities for the teachers to engage in SDPD. It was evident from talking to teachers that they were passionate about their job and they sought not only to help students pass examinations but to prepare them for life. For instance, despite the emphasis on grammar in the examinations, teachers continued to develop their students' speaking skills too. The teachers demonstrated a great sense of responsibility and willingness to engage in their professional development by participating in school-based professional development as well as out-of-school activities. The teachers were quite resourceful, identifying materials from the local context to provide scaffolding for their students' learning. These issues will be discussed in more detail in Chapter 5. The following section focuses on interview data from School B.

4.3.2   Interview data from teachers in School B

Between 27th February and 2nd March 2012 I held three interviews with Mrs Zhu, Mrs Zhou and Mrs Yang, three secondary English teachers teaching in School B I have observed. Details about the school and the levels they were teaching have been discussed earlier.

4.3.2.1   Teachers' perspectives regarding the content of the ELT curriculum

One of the main questions I asked English language teachers was about their views regarding the content of the ELT curriculum. This included teachers' views about the content covered in the course book. All the teachers interviewed claimed that the new course book *Go for It* not only emphasised the students' reading abilities but paid attention to their comprehensive competence in the four skills (reading, writing, listening and speaking). It was highlighted that emphasis was placed on the development of listening and speaking skills. The current curriculum system is different from the previous one, and currently, there are more activities aimed at developing each one of the four skills. This view was supported by Mrs Zhu who believed that the current curriculum helps students to develop comprehensively.

> Generally speaking, the curriculum helps students to make progress in reading, writing, listening and speaking. My colleague also agreed that the students' English learning skills have improved after using the new course book *Go for It*. (Mrs Zhu)

There was consensus that the new course book was effective in promoting students' learning. Again, it can be seen that to those teachers similar to School A, the content of the ELT curriculum is exclusive to the course book.

4.3.2.2   Teachers' perspectives regarding how they design and teach the ELT curriculum

Regarding the designing and teaching of the ELT curriculum, teachers in School B talked about how they plan lessons together. Each one of the three teachers interviewed was responsible for teaching two classes. First, they design lesson plans in a co-operative way and then develop individual lesson plans. Mrs Zhu regarded lesson plans as a systematic way of going about planning instructions. She claimed that before she started to design a lesson plan, she asked herself the following questions: 'Why do we want an effective curriculum? How can we help students learn more than they do now? How can students learn different things? How do we increase their interest?'

In addition, Mrs Yang pointed out that the design of the lesson plan was purposeful and deliberate. It is not just to have a lesson of teaching but a course with a purpose to improve students' learning. Knowing the different tasks and problems at each step is significant in making the lesson plan. Furthermore, Mrs Yang indicated that towards the final goals, the lesson plan served as the means and procedure, which could be very creative. Therefore, it requires invention, novel concepts and innovative thinking at every stage of the lesson plan.

> If I am not sure what my goals are in a lesson, I may not know whether I will be able to accomplish the tasks or not. So, when I design the lesson plan, I need to be as clear as possible about what the main purpose and the real targets are, so that students can respond accordingly. (Mrs Yang)

Teachers in School B are able to design the lesson plan and arrange classroom activities by themselves; they make use of guidelines provided in the national syllabuses. There is centralisation of national syllabuses, exam standards and common practice among teachers.

> We can design the classroom activities and the way to present knowledge to students by ourselves. However, one thing is certain: all the activities should contribute to the achievement of goals set out in the national syllabuses. (Mrs Zhou)

It can be seen that teaching and learning is very much influenced by examinations because the examination will be set around the goals in the national syllabuses. Mrs Zhu indicated that there was differentiation in what students were taught at different levels.

> For the first and second year students, I pay attention to students' all-around competence development... I would like to train students in pronunciation and encourage them to imitate the intonation. However, in year 3, if they can pass the examination, that's fine. (Mrs Zhu)

The teachers stated that during teaching they were concerned about the students' feedback in the class. They prepare the lesson plan before class and consider students' reflection according to students' level and then think about how to respond to them. After each class, the teachers collect feedback from students and use this when preparing subsequent teaching. They expressed their willingness to change lesson plans to suit their students' needs. The key factor in lesson plans is to provide room for continuous correction and improvement. For instance, Mrs Zhu claimed that she amended or changed some details in class according to students' reflection. She teaches two classes and after delivering the first lesson she makes changes to the lesson for the next group in light of the lessons drawn from the first group. She explained:

> According to students' feedback, I will amend or change some details of my teaching. I have two classes. If I realise that students in Class 1 found it hard to follow or understand something, I will consider improving the teaching framework or reducing the difficulty in Class 2. So, generally speaking, the second class experiences a richer learning experience compared to the first class. (Mrs Zhu)

Similarly, Mrs Yang also considered students' feedback to see whether they can follow each stage of teaching in the class or not. If she found that students were having difficulties, she would try to respond to the needs of the students as explained below:

> When I teach in the class, I care for the students' reflection to see whether they can follow me or not. If I find they are stuck, I might change the content or slow down the teaching speed to give them more instructions concerning the areas of need. (Mrs Yang)

Teachers' flexibility and willingness to respond to the students' needs during lesson delivery plays an important role in facilitating students' learning.

4.3.2.3 *Teachers' perspectives regarding the current situation of ELT in school*

I asked teachers to reflect on the most difficult aspects of learning and teaching English in Chinese secondary schools according to their experiences. Mrs Zhu stated that it was hard to say because the situation in China was very complicated, with many differences in language teaching between different places. She added that there were huge differences between schools in rural areas and urban areas. However, Mrs Zhou and Mrs Yang viewed that improving students' interest was the most challenging aspect in the learning and teaching of English language, adding that 'a good learning habit requires learning interest' and quoted Einstein's saying, 'Interest is the best teacher.' The teacher viewed student interest as a direct motivation to push students to study.

We also had some discussions regarding the current situation on examinations, materials, teaching approach and learning motivation. It was easy to see the problems of the learning and teaching of English language from the interview data. Furthermore, some changes and developments taking place in the learning and teaching of English language were discernible.

With regard to examinations, Mrs Zhou claimed that the current testing pays more attention to students' communication competence compared to the past. She added that the listening scores have been changed. However, it must be noted that examinations are still dominated by grammatical aspects and vocabulary.

> The assessment now pays more attention to listening. In 1992, there was no listening in English testing. For the past two years, they increased listening scores from 20 to 25 in the examination. Basically, the current testing is more focused on communication. (Mrs Zhou)

Mrs Zhou pointed out that the current examinations reduced the grammar points but added more vocabulary. There is no oral testing, but there is communicative English. For example, in multiple-choice questions, it may say 'would you like to...,' which is a spoken language format but appears in the written examination. In addition, Mrs Yang mentioned that the difficulty of writing and reading was increased, while adding more language traps in the context of the word. For example, the following is a multiple-choice question in the high school entry examination.

Look, there is a stick, under the _____.			
A. table	B. stone	C. glass	D. chair

It is easy for us to choose under the 'stone' or under the 'table'; however, the answer is under the 'glass.' Because 'look' implies visibility, and only glass allows visibility, which can be seen through. It does not test grammar ability but is a grammar trap. The teacher felt this kind of testing is meaningless.

> The difficulty of writing and reading has been increased. Moreover, the difficulty of multiple-choice testing has been increased. Apparently, it reduced the grammar element in the multiple-choice. There is an extra trap in the context of the word. (Mrs Yang)

With regards to teaching and learning materials, since 2003, School B started to use the course book *Go for It*. According to all the participating teachers in the school the aim is to improve learning motivation and build students' confidence through step-by-step progression. There are many listening practice and group work activities to improve students' listening and speaking ability. As highlighted before, the course book focuses on communicative skills and the content tends to relate to the students' real life.

> The book contains many interesting pictures and includes many topics for students. As a result, it helps students to open their thoughts. *Go for It* contains many group work activities which are good for speaking practice. The content is more meaningful and caters for communicative competence. (Mrs Zhou)

However, there is a contradiction between the focus of the course book and the examination. The course book *Go for It* aims to improve the learner's speaking and listening ability while the examination focuses on grammar and vocabulary. Earlier Mrs Zhou expressed that there was an increase in listening in the examination, but this does not mean to say listening is now dominating all other skills. She was just commenting on the increase in the time allocated to listening, which was increased slightly. Teachers expressed concern about how to find a good balance between teaching students to pass the exam with a good score while at the same time, maintaining high level of motivation during class activities. For example, students find it boring to concentrate on the grammar and yet, teachers are afraid of spending more time on speaking practice which is not examinable. This makes it difficult for teachers to manage the class.

Mrs Zhou and Mrs Yang also mentioned that the listening practice activities were not organised in a logical sequence. In the same vein, the teachers observed some irregularities regarding the speed of listening activities and the level of difficulty of vocabulary. This was well articulated by Mrs Zhou.

> The listening practice does not follow a coherent pattern. The speed was supposed to progress from slow to fast, and the word difficulty should be increased from year 1 to year 3. However, sometimes, the year 1 listening speech is faster than year 2. There is also too much new vocabulary that is hard for students to follow in the beginning. (Mrs Zhou)

Secondly, the way in which the content in the course book is structured is a little bit messy. For example, there is the present continuous tense in Unit 1, but after a few units, the present continuous tense comes up again. Mrs Zhou suggested that it should cover consolidation first and then incorporate new knowledge.

> *Go for It* keeps presenting new knowledge and then after a while asks students to review it. To be honest, it does not work very well. Actually, I feel it will be better if we cover consolidation first and then learn other new knowledge. (Mrs Zhou)

A. Teaching approach

All the teachers interviewed emphasised that students play an active role in the class. They highlighted the need to ensure that students were engaged during the lessons, and the teachers' role should be that of facilitating students' learning. For example, in the first interview, Mrs Zhou expressed her desire to help students build up a good habit of active learning. She said that every student needed to participate in speaking, listening, writing and reading activities in each class.

> I would like to adopt the learner-centred teaching approach. The student is the main part in the learning and teaching of English language. Even the best teacher cannot take the place of their students in learning things. I try to help students build a habit of participating actively in the learning process rather than being passive learners. (Mrs Zhou)

This view was supported by Mrs Zhu who also believed that students should be active participants in class. In this regard, teachers should focus on what the students are learning and try to provide opportunities to encourage them to learn. The role of the teacher is to support the learners rather than 'spoon-feeding' them.

> Students should play an active role in the learning and teaching of English language. As teachers, what we have to focus on is not what we are doing but what the students are doing to learn. Students' actions are the drivers of learning... What I do, is providing support to the learners rather than giving them all the information. (Mrs Zhu)

Mrs Yang cautioned that the learner-centred teaching approach is a good way of learning and teaching English language. However, it should not be misinterpreted to mean students are able to take over the class. Teachers still needed to help them by setting up clear learning objectives and activities.

> Students are not mature enough to suggest the teacher what to do. A good teacher will design appropriate learning objectives and select relevant materials and strategies that can support students to learn effectively. (Mrs Yang)

B. Learning motivation

The teachers unanimously agreed that the examination was the main factor that motivates students to learn English language at the current stage. Students tend to focus more on examinable materials in class.

> Most of the students aim to pass examinations and then go to a good high school which can assist them to enter a celebrated university... although many students wish to speak and write excellent English, they seem to care more about examinations. (Mrs Zhu)

On the other hand, Mrs Zhu believed that students' interest in the subject played a pivotal role in their learning. The teacher indicated that there was a need to ensure that students were supported to develop interest in the subject because without interest it could be hard for students to learn. In this case, although being an important factor, examinations alone cannot help students to learn. Although teachers agreed that examinations formed the main factor for the motivation of students, they also expressed mixed feelings about the effectiveness of examination-oriented motivation. For example, Mrs Yang suggested that the influence of such motivation was very negative to students' learning of the language. In particular, although examinations focus on grammar, many students do not think they need to learn the complicated grammar, stating that 'if they become a taxi driver, what they need is the simple communicative language' (Mrs Yang). Not everything they learn to pass examinations is necessarily important for real life communication.

However, Mrs Zhu and Mrs Zhou hold different perspectives from Mrs Yang, who believed that the impact of examination depends on students. Students study hard because of examinations, which is the positive drive to learning. However, if students only learn for examinations, it will have a negative impact on their long-term development.

There are many testing systems in school and society; and I feel it is a very positive matter. However, regarding the learning emotion, if students have to learn English because of examinations, then it is very negative. (Mrs Zhu)

Discussions with the teachers demonstrated that there were a number of factors that influence students' learning of English language.

4.3.2.4 Teachers' perspectives on their role as agents of change in ELT

Teachers were asked for their perspectives on what they could do to bring about changes in the learning and teaching of English language. A number of ideas were suggested by the teachers. First of all, teachers claimed that they carried out class-room reflections every day. They believed that building a good relationship between teachers and students would help in the learning and teaching of the English language since the learning atmosphere was very important. In addition, it was suggested that it was necessary to divide students into classes of different levels in order to meet their needs. Finally, it was also mentioned that curriculum and assessment reformation played a significant role in the learning and teaching of English language. Below is a list of the ideas suggested by teachers regarding what they could do to bring about changes in the learning and teaching of English language.

A. Classroom reflection

Teachers in School B claimed that teaching reflection was very important to their practice. Reflection helps teachers to identify areas in need of improvement as well as to reinforce good practice. Through reflection, teachers are able to identify problems in teaching materials, teaching content, arrangement of courses as well as teaching methods. After reflecting on the previous class, it is possible for teachers to do things differently in future lessons.

B. Building good relationships with students

There is an old Chinese adage, 'if students are close to the teacher, they would love the teachers' lesson.' In other words, if students enjoy harmonious relationships with their teacher, they are likely to engage with the subject. This highlights the importance of establishing and maintaining good relationships with students. The participating teachers felt that if teachers could win dignity and respect from students, it would help in the learning and teaching of the subject. There was a consensus that one of the ways to achieve good relationships with students was to give praise and encouragement to students, which might increase their confidence and help them to put more effort in learning of the English language. The views of all the teachers were well articulated by Mrs Zhu who stated that: 'The communication between students and teachers is very important. Teachers are supposed to give students proper instruction and encourage them to study and not to disappoint them.'

C. Placing student into different levels based on their needs

It emerged from the interviews that recognising students' abilities was key in terms of meeting students' needs in class. Teachers indicated that they were having difficulties in working with students at different levels in the same class. Mrs Yang and Mrs Zhou pointed out that having different levels of students was one of the biggest problems in their classes. They felt that the school should consider establishing a multi-level English teaching system.

> In my teaching, I feel that different levels of students are one of the biggest challenges in my class. Therefore, I hope students will be divided into different levels such as the common level and the advanced level according to their English competence. In this way, students will be able to finish their English learning task earlier. (Mrs Yang)

D. Reforming English curriculum and the assessment system

One of the ideas proffered by teachers was the need to review the curriculum, including the testing system. One of the teachers, Mrs Zhou, suggested that it would be helpful to include speaking tasks in the examination. The teachers were currently putting more effort into improving students' grades instead of developing their comprehensive abilities. They expressed dissatisfaction about this and felt that the examination system needed to be changed. They considered that such teaching leaded to a phenomenon called 'deaf English' or 'dumb English.'

> If possible, I would like to add oral test in examination... English teaching cannot get separated from speaking. What I want is to establish a reasonable assessment and evaluation system that pays more attention to students' practical English competence. Therefore, it is quite necessary to reform secondary school English curriculum and the test system. (Mrs Zhou)

4.3.2.5 Regarding opportunities that exist for teachers to develop professionally in the school

Interview data reveal that there are many in-service professional development opportunities in all areas important for the effective teaching of English language, including reading and listening skills. For example, School B provides an opportunity for its English language teachers to visit a centre of good practice where they learn and develop teaching approaches. One teacher from the school reported that:

> The school provides us with opportunities to develop our reading and listening skills, among others. We are also provided with opportunities to improve our academic communication by working collaboratively with teachers from other schools. The school sends us to different schools to attend or give public lectures. (Mrs Yang)

The teachers demonstrated a lot of interest in participating in the in-service professional development programmes provided in the school and outside the school. The existence of these opportunities helps to enhance the learning and teaching of English language in the school.

4.3.2.6 Regarding the role that SDPD plays in the learning and teaching of English

In addition to enquiring about the existence of opportunities for professional development, I also want to find out how teachers engage in professional development, that is, whether they are intrinsically motivated to participate in further training or not. I found out that teachers appreciated the opportunities to communicate with teachers within the same school and from other schools, and also appreciated how other teachers presented knowledge, arranged activities and managed their students' engagement with activities. Teachers could learn from classroom observation, public lectures and review of other teachers' lesson plans. Mrs Yang was of the view that public lectures[1] gave her a lot of inspiration, helping her to identify the limitations of her own teaching and ways of improving her work. She kept a diary of all the lectures that she attended

---

[1] Public lectures are professional development opportunities organised at regional level by subject experts to give English language teachers from different schools a chance to share good practice.

and referred to the notes from time to time, which helped her to remember and apply new ideas and approaches to her teaching. The other two teachers were also positive about the opportunities for continuous professional development as indicated below.

> I went to another school to give a lecture, and had many opportunities to communicate with other teachers. I found out that teachers are concerned about the context of the word... When students do not know how to share their knowledge, teachers try to use simple words to enable students to bring out the message. They also pay much attention to students' oral expression. Regardless of the kind of questions they asked, the students had to answer with a sentence instead of simply 'yes' or 'no.' (Mrs Zhou)

> I attended a lot of training. For example, this year I attended secondary school elite teachers' training and went to other English language schools for two weeks of academic in-service training. I have been doing this every year since 2007. I found out that some of the teachers from other schools were excellent in classroom management and in the teaching of year 1 and year 2 students to imitate the pronunciation and tones. (Mrs Zhu)

I also asked teachers whether they had held discussions with other teachers concerning their teaching approach or not. The teaching approach can be a part of SDPD. Teachers indicated that they had many discussions with their peers around teaching approaches. For example, Mrs Zhu claimed that she used to ask for ideas from other teachers whenever she had difficulties in helping students to learn certain aspects of the English language. In addition, teachers expressed their willingness to discuss the effectiveness and limitations of different teaching approaches. From their discussions, they found that some teaching approaches were better than others; for example, they appreciated that task-based approaches were effective in helping students to learn, which could provide opportunities for students to practise English and greatly improve the students' interest. Teachers testified that they had many fruitful discussions with their peers.

> We have many discussions, for example, we discuss how to carry out a lesson review and how to present lectures. I learn many things from my peers since each one of them has got different experiences. (Mrs Zhou)

There are many discussions among ourselves regarding the application of task-based teaching in secondary schools. We think that students learn best if the learning atmosphere is stress-free and of fun. Students should not feel that learning is a burden. (Mrs Yang)

I also asked teachers about their perspectives regarding setting professional development goals to improve ELT. All the teachers were positive about the idea of setting clear goals for their professional development. They indicated that it was important to set goals to improve their teaching approaches in order to further develop the learning and teaching of ELT. Mrs Zhu indicated that:

Setting goals is very helpful in our teaching. Without it, it's easy to lose or forget our target and stay in the same place without going further. I like the phrase that says, 'Always dream and never give up.' (Mrs Zhu)

According to Mrs Yang, the importance of setting goals lies in the belief that finding an effective teaching approach is a challenge for many teachers particularly for the experienced teachers who may fall short of the knowledge and skills of teaching using modern approaches. This is because they were taught using traditional methods, for example, grammar-translation method as opposed to the current method like task-based approach. Most of them lack the confidence and skills to apply the CLT approach. Although the traditional approach helps to prepare students for examinations, it does not help to develop students' speaking and listening skills. It is hard to improve their teaching ability especially in listening and speaking area if they do not intend to improve speaking skills or set goals for themselves.

I also set out to find out how teachers felt about the importance of taking responsibility in their teaching. Teachers in School B showed their appreciation of the need to be responsible. For example, Mrs Zhou highlighted that she considered teaching responsibility to be an important virtue. She was very clear that students' communicative competence was more important than examination skills, as was excellent speaking competence. Therefore, she was very concerned about students' speaking ability. Similarly, Mrs Zhu pointed out that responsibility was a significant virtue, which had great influence on students' development. She considered it unhealthy for many students to get high scores in examinations while being short of communicative skills. As a teacher, she not only gives students knowledge, but also transmits a 'human' concept to them. She cares very much for students' physical and psychological development. In the same vein, Mrs Yang also agreed that it was important to be responsible.

> The teacher is expected to foster healthy, socially responsible behaviour among students on their way to adulthood. We should not only be concerned about the examinations, but also about the students' physical and psychological development. (Mrs Yang)

> A responsible teacher is one who is concerned about their student's comprehensive development, not just the success in examinations. This means that the teacher would teach students content and skills that are not necessarily beneficial in the examination but beneficial in life development. (Mrs Zhou)

It was encouraging to note that all teachers in the school were clear about the need to contribute not only to students' success in examinations but also to students' overall development.

4.3.2.7　Summary of the interviews with teachers from School B

Interviewing teachers in School B generated many interesting ideas, which capture the perspectives of teachers on a number of themes around ELT. Like teachers in School A, I found that teachers in School B also felt that the new course book was comprehensive enough and offered sufficient activities to train students in terms of developing listening, writing, reading and speaking skills. The teachers planned lessons as a team and also placed value on individual input. So although at first planning is done cooperatively, the teachers can also select activities to add to their own lessons. One key sub-theme that emerged in my conversations with teachers was their readiness to listen to students' feedback. All the teachers indicated that students' reflections on the course are taken seriously and each teacher responds to the feedback with a view to improving the teaching and learning of English language. The interview data showed that currently ELT is being affected by a number of factors, including the role of examinations, which is identified by teachers in School A as well. In addition, the teachers felt that although the course book provided activities in all the four areas, there was a mismatch with the focus of the examination. The course book emphasises listening and speaking skills whereas examinations focus more on grammar and vocabulary. Students are only motivated to learn because of examinations. Teachers felt that they themselves are agents of change and highlighted the need to reflect on practice, build good relationships with students, and reform the curriculum and the assessment of English language in order to improve the teaching and learning of English language. Similar to teachers in School A, teachers in School B indicated that they had good opportunities to engage in professional staff development opportunities, citing that they could visit other schools and centres of good practice to learn and share experiences. The teachers were intrinsically motivated and understood the value of setting their own professional development goals. Overall, the interviews helped to generate relevant data, which will be discussed in the next chapter. The following section presents data obtained from interviews with teachers in School C.

4.3.3   Interview data from teachers in School C

Between 12th March and 26th March 2012, I carried out interviews with Miss Zou, Miss Li and Miss Fang in School C. Similar questions raised with teachers in Schools A and B were discussed. These are described in the following paragraphs.

4.3.3.1   Teachers' perspectives regarding the content of the ELT curriculum
According to the three teachers, the aim of English teaching is to develop students' capacity to use English in an all-round way. They use both the textbook and their own teacher-made resources. The school pays much attention to developing listening abilities. Each lesson has listening practice and it requires students to speak out loud as much as possible.

> Every lesson plan relates to some particular skill but with different emphasis. We have listening practice in every class and we put the listening materials in the PowerPoint. In every class, students need to read loudly and follow the tape to repeat words and sentences. (Miss Fang)

Teachers in School C meet and discuss the content and the approaches for the teaching and learning of each unit. After the group discussion, each teacher will then proceed to design the lesson plan including activities for their classes. This was explained by one of the teachers:

> We need to design the lesson plan and guidance case study individually. However, we normally get together to discuss the direction of the teaching purpose first, following which we then take care of the details such as the design of PowerPoint or the arrangement of classroom activities. (Miss Zou)

4.3.3.2   Teachers' perspectives regarding how they design and teach the ELT curriculum

Based on my understanding of the importance of having a good lesson plan to be able to deliver an effective lesson, I decided to ask teachers about their experience of designing lesson plans for the delivery of the ELT curriculum. All the teachers appreciated the importance of designing a good lesson plan and indicated that in their school they worked together to discuss the structure of each lesson plan including identifying relevant activities for each lesson.

> Our school considers the designing of lesson plans very seriously, therefore, we all design lesson plans together. One unit will typically have four lessons. After planning together, we then ask one teacher to be in charge and design the PowerPoint for one unit. (Miss Li)

Although teachers plan together, each teacher has the responsibility to adapt the lesson plan to mirror the needs of the students in their classes. Miss Li claimed that 'classrooms are the main place for most students to learn English language, therefore, lesson plans should be very purposeful.' Teachers highlighted that it is important to see that students are not merely knowledge receivers in the classroom, emphasising that they should participate actively in the knowledge construction process. When teachers design the lesson plan, they need to consider its flexibility and ensure that students' individual differences are catered for, which means that teachers need to estimate the activities' difficulty according to students' acknowledge and learning characteristics. Teachers confirmed that they made the lesson plans before class. However, they would transform or change the details according to students' feedback and the classroom atmosphere. If students seem tired of one point of knowledge or feel it is boring, the teacher would make change accordingly.

> Normally, our class follows the lesson plan. However, if I feel the activity is not going well, I will change it to something different according to the need of the students. I think every teacher would do that. (Miss Fang)

In designing their lessons, teachers tend to focus more on grammar. It was evident during the interviews that teachers repeated grammatical activities in each lesson plan. Miss Fang believed that reinforcement and imitation was the way to build up a good habit of grammar. The idea of including many activities on grammar was supported by Miss Li, who agreed that basic grammar knowledge was the foundation of learning a language. Miss Li explained that she could not speak or write English properly without grammar. In order to engage the language knowledge in an effective and appropriate way, it is necessary to consider acquiring grammar in a proper way. Learning grammar is very complicated, containing categories such as word order, hierarchical structure, empty categories, lexical and functional categories. While acknowledging the importance of grammar, Miss Li does not want to teach grammar separately; instead, she prefers to teach grammar in a language environment through speaking and listening practice. She explained:

> I think grammar is very important. I cannot speak or write English without a good understanding of grammar... What we are trying to do is to teach grammar in a language environment; we not only ask students to memorise grammar, but hope they can understand it through their speaking and listening practice. (Miss Li)

Similarly, Miss Zou indicated that she made use of the communicative approach, which involves teaching grammar as well as other skills including speaking and listening. She reiterated the need to teach grammar, adding that 'without grammar, there is no sense for a language.' The teachers indicated that the emphasis on the teaching of grammar was due to the examination system's putting more weight on grammar. It is therefore important for teachers to find creative ways to teach grammar and this explains why teachers need to spend more time in designing their lesson plans.

4.3.3.3   Teachers' perspectives regarding the current situation of ELT in the school

I asked teachers to comment on their current experience of teaching English language, in particular the main problems that they were facing in the delivery of the

ELT curriculum. Teachers narrated the developments and changes that were taking place in ELT. Some notable developments were the new course book, new teaching approach and the structure of the examination. As indicated earlier on, teachers highlighted that they were now using a new course book, which was designed to facilitate more communication.

> The course book has really changed. Currently, the new course book added more pair work and group work in order to cultivate students' listening and speaking ability. Each lesson focuses on a particular ability: speaking, listening, reading or writing; personally, I think the new materials have many advantages. (Miss Li)

On the other hand, teachers in this school adopted a new teaching approach called 'guidance case study.' This approach is learner-centred, providing students with opportunities to participate actively in their learning. For instance, students have to engage in activities in preparation for lessons in the classroom, that is, they have more homework or independent work. Unlike in the past, the examination now includes more vocabulary and listening activities, the latter increased by five points from 20 to 25 in the examination.

Teachers highlighted some of the problems bedevilling the effective delivery of the ELT curriculum. In the first place, each teacher discussed the general problems they faced. I then asked them to comment on specific issues in line with my research questions. Each teacher expressed their personal views, with Miss Zou and Miss Li having similar thoughts, both of whom felt that the most difficult aspect to their teaching was the different levels of students. Some of the students start learning English when they were around 4—5 years old. Therefore, they have several years' learning experience and have built up a solid foundation before they enter secondary school. On the contrary, some of the students have never been taught English before entering secondary school. Thus, it is hard to give proper instructions and lesson plans to various students.

> I think the problem is that the students' level is quite different... So it is hard for me to make a two-sided lesson plan to take care of different-levelled students. I cannot only look out for every individual student; I need to consider the class. (Miss Zou)

However, Miss Fang had a different view from the other two teachers. To her, the most difficult point is that she does not know how to address the key issues for examination purposes and help students reach high achievements as well.

> To me, the most challenging thing is that I do not know how to deal with students' problems. I do not know their need and I am not always sure whether I manage to cover all the key points in time for the examinations or not. (Miss Fang)

This was not surprising because Miss Fang is a new teacher and is less experienced compared to the other teachers, being a recent graduate in her first year of teaching. In the following section, I will discuss the views of teachers on the specific questions I gave them regarding problems they faced in teaching English language. The questions focused on examinations, learning and teaching materials, teaching approach, learning motivation and classroom facilities.

A. Examinations

The teaching of English language is influenced by examinations. Teachers indicated that they worked under pressure as they were expected to prepare students for the examinations. The teaching of non-examinable aspects of English is made difficult as both teachers and students feel the need to prioritise the examinable material. Miss Fang pointed out an important contradiction between the examinations and the teaching approach. The teaching and learning materials tend to encourage students to have more speaking practice, claiming to promote communicative skills and learner-centred approaches. However, the examinations still focus on grammar. The main challenge is that the course book focuses on listening and speaking activities, yet, the examinations focus on grammar. Teachers feel that the course book does not provide enough activities to prepare students for the examination.

> We spend much time on speaking practice in the classroom; however, examinations still focus on the grammar... As a teacher, I'd like to train students to improve their speaking and listening ability; however, if the class focuses on the speaking and the examination focuses on grammar I feel it is very hard to have a balance on the teaching... Normally, we only teach the points related to the examinations. (Miss Fang)

The teachers felt that there should be a match between the course book and the examination as this would make it easy for them and the students to teach and learn the English language more effectively.

B. Learning materials

The students were making use of the course book and other practice books. Regarding the course book, teachers appreciated that there were many activities for students; however, they complained that the activities were not structured in a logical sequence. Teachers also felt that the book contained too much unnecessary vocabulary that could confuse students. However, one teacher, Miss Zou, argued that course books were ancillary material in teaching, and the key was how teachers dealt with it. If a teacher can utilise materials in a proper way, it will bring more benefit to students.

C. Teaching method: Guidance case study

There were mixed feelings among teachers regarding the approach they were using in teaching English language. Some teachers were positive about the approach while others were negative about it. Those who were positive cited that they enjoyed being facilitators in their students' learning and also celebrated the fact that students were provided with clear guidance thereby reducing the amount of work they had to do. Some of the advantages of the approach are indicated below:

> Guidance case is good at implementation of the writing work. It asked us to use some guidance words, which are easy to lead students in importing the context... There is a lot of group work, pair work and students are given more opportunities to speak. (Miss Li)

Miss Zou also holds a very positive attitude towards guidance case study. She declares that now she felt she had the chance to do something different with that by guidance case teaching method.

> I admired what the teachers in other countries implement in their school. I can make my students active while raising their interest in study, which I always pursued. And I got really surprised by the enthusiasm of my students. Most of them like English songs and speeches. This gave me encouragement and responsibility to improve their speaking skills. (Miss Zou)

While there appeared to be more advantages of using the guidance case study approach, it was also clear that teachers also felt that the approach created more work for themselves and for the students. Teachers needed more time to prepare on their own materials that students could use. Similarly, students had to dedicate more time to do the independent study. There was also a feeling that the approach tended to disadvantage top students as they had to spend some of their time helping less advanced students in their groups. It appears that the new approach has posed a challenge to teachers who found it difficult to create differentiated activities for students.

D. Learning motivation

Examinations were identified as the main factor motivating students to study English language. However, it was also highlighted that emphasis on passing examinations was not helpful in the overall learning of the language. Students focused their attention on learning examinable aspects of the language, ignoring other important elements and skills. For example, Miss Fang thought that exam-oriented motivation was negative for the learning of English language, citing that 'learning English is mainly for communication and development; however, it seems students do not realise it.' It is possible for students to miss the other important aspects of learning the language because of their concentration on passing the examinations.

On the contrary, Miss Zou considered that examinations were helpful in terms of motivating students to learn the language; however, she also indicated that it was hard to learn excellent English without an inner interest in learning English.

> Regardless of the learning motivation, if it can help students to learn English, it is a good motivation. However, those who get excellent achievement in English normally have a high interest in studying. They are autonomous students; they have high self-directed and self-managed ability. (Miss Zou)

Indeed, autonomous learners who have high self-directed and self-managed capacity find it easier to achieve advanced English level.

E. Large class sizes

I asked the teachers for their opinion on the ideal class size for the effective learning and teaching of the English language. The teachers unanimously agreed that small class sizes were more effective than large ones. For instance, teachers including Miss Fang and Miss Zou felt that their classes were too big and if given the opportunity they would reduce the number of students in each classroom from the current number of 45 to about 15 to 20.

My hope is for every class to have only 15 students, no more than 20. I know it is very difficult for China since we have such a large population. However, teaching refers to individuals; it's not like producing potatoes. I think it would be very helpful to teaching if we can reduce the number of the class size. (Miss Zou)

F. Teachers' perspectives on their role as agents of change in ELT

One of the issues discussed with teachers during the interviews is how they perceived their role as agents of change in ELT. It emerged that teachers understood that they had a role to bring about change; however, it was also clear that teachers could not change everything in the teaching of English language. It is difficult for teachers to change the course book, the structure of the examination as well as the class size. From the interviews held with three teachers, I generated three points regarding what teachers could do to bring changes to the current learning and teaching of English language. These are discussed in the following paragraphs.

Teachers in School C stated that they needed to carry out a review of lessons for every class, as one of the requirements at the school. This shows that the school puts reflective practice in a very important position. In the school, each teacher has to teach lessons to two different classes at the same level. Even though they have the same context and target, they will design different lesson plans and present the lessons in different ways according to the characteristics of the students in the classes.

Sometimes, I write down my reflections immediately after a class if I feel the need to; otherwise, I write them down later. Normally, my lesson plans are amended or improved immediately after the class. (Miss Zou)

I find it easy to find out the limitations immediately after a class session and will think about how to improve my teaching for the next class. I think it is a good way to improve our teaching. (Miss Li)

The teachers stated that it was a helpful practice for them to reflect on the effectiveness of their lessons and to implement changes to suit the needs of their students.

Teachers in the school have got freedom to organise classroom activities in ways that suit their students. However, the teachers do not have the flexibility to change the format of the lessons; for example, they cannot make decisions such as moving students from the classroom to engage in outdoor activities without the permission of the school authorities. One of the teachers, Miss Zou expressed her desire to have more freedom regarding the way she taught the subject. The same feelings were shared by her two colleagues who did not like the rigidity imposed by the current system in the school.

> I wish to have more authority and freedom to arrange my classroom activities, for example, carrying out practical dialogues outside classrooms or showing students some movies which will improve students' interest in learning the subject. (Miss Zou)

G. Improve students' interest in learning the subject

Teachers also shared their experience of how to motivate students to develop more interest in learning of English language. Miss Zou suggested that excellent classroom designs helped to stimulate students' interest in participation. Teachers need to consider how to stimulate students' learning interest and arouse their curiosity when they are designing a lesson plan. For instance, Miss Zou adds some pictures to her class and includes interesting activities to stir up students' learning interest.

> Firstly, I try to create an excellent classroom design to encourage students to speak. I give them some English stories or magazines to read and teach them how to sing English songs. If students like it, they will start to learn by themselves. In fact, today two boys came to me to say they want to sing an English song to me. It is good for them to practise and I am happy to note that they like it. (Miss Zou)

In addition, Miss Li pointed out that encouragement and positive evaluation was very important for learning English. It is unavoidable for students to make mistakes but teachers need to realise that this is part of the learning process.

> I always encourage students not to be worried or afraid of not speaking well or not being understood by others. (Miss Li)

Miss Fang stated that teachers' personalities constitute an important factor in students' learning of the English language. It is possible that if students find the teachers' personality attractive they can be motivated to learn. On the other hand, if students are not satisfied with the teachers' personality, they may not engage effectively with the subject. The impact of the teacher's personality on students' learning was articulated by Miss Fang.

> To a great extent, it depends on whether students like the teacher or not... If the students like you, then they will listen carefully and be interested in the study. (Miss Fang)

4.3.3.4   *Regarding opportunities that exist for teachers to develop professionally in the school*

School C provides opportunities for teachers to develop professionally. From the interviews with the three English teachers, it was indicated that there were many teaching research activities. For example, teachers have opportunities to engage in cross-school classroom presentation, which helps them to learn from each other and to improve their practice. Furthermore, teachers engage in competitions, for example, competition of teaching reading skills. The competitions are held at school level first and then the best teachers in the school are selected to compete with teachers from other schools. These competitions serve as incentives for the English teachers to work hard and provide excellent learning experience for their students. The school also provides opportunities for teachers to attend relevant academic conferences, including the chance to go through short-term and long-term in-service training programmes. Recently, the school started to appoint teachers to travel to England for them to enhance their teaching skills and knowledge of the English language. These opportunities are limited and competitive; hence, teachers work hard to earn such awards.

> Compared to the past, teacher development activities have been improved. Last summer, we had some teachers going to England for academic communication. However, you need to pass examinations and then the school will recommend you to go abroad. (Miss Li)

This school is providing opportunities for the teachers to engage in professional development and as a result, the teachers expressed that the teaching of English language in the school was very good.

4.3.3.5 Regarding the role that SDPD plays in the learning and teaching of English

I asked teachers about how they engaged in professional development activities at personal level, that is, to find out the extent to which individual teachers were committed to their professional development. It was encouraging to see that all the teachers were committed to their own professional development.

Teachers are taking advantage of the opportunities in the school to upgrade themselves. For example, Miss Li encouraged herself to attend 'the excellent reading' competition. During the period of preparation, she learned how to present to the class and discuss lesson plans with other teachers.

> This year I encouraged myself to attend 'the excellent reading' competition... I think I learnt many things from it. It also helped me to realise that practice is very important, 'Practice makes perfect.' (Miss Li)

Miss Li stated that it was necessary for her and other teachers to continue to engage in professional development activities citing that, 'Rome was not built in a day. What I need is much more practice.' What Miss Li is saying is important; professional development opportunities need to be organised systematically if teachers are to draw maximum benefits from them. The other teachers also commented on the opportunities they have for professional development:

> For me, there are many open classes. We have the 'excellent class' competition. Whoever's willing to attend is free to do so... Our school invited many scholars from other cities to give us many lectures which were very beneficial. The attitude of each teacher is important because one might not take advantage of these opportunities and remain the same. I feel self-consciousness is very important. (Miss Zou)

> As a new teacher, I need to be observed by other teachers at least once every term, that is, giving a public lesson. The school trains us through practice. Other teachers give me useful feedback. I feel I need to improve my speaking and listening abilities. (Miss Fang)

I also asked teachers if they discussed the teaching approaches with their colleagues, in particular, the guidance case study approach used in the school. It was noticeable that teachers held different views regarding the effectiveness of the teaching approach they were using in the school. According to Miss Fang, guidance case study added extra work for teachers and students. The guidance case study emphasises preparation; however, students normally do not have sufficient time to do it. If the teachers leave the preview of the guidance case to the class, it will be hard to complete the lesson. Both teachers and students feel much pressure from using this teaching method. However, Miss Zou held a different view, explaining that the guidance case study approach increased the workload for teachers but saved time for students. Guidance case study indicates the definite learning target of each lesson to students. It helps students to realise the learning purpose and head towards the right direction. In particular, it suits the context of large class teaching where students have diverse abilities and needs. This is because it divides students into smaller study groups, which are easier to manage for the teacher and students. In addition, it allows for individual participation and accountability, and improves positive attitudes towards learning.

Using a new teaching approach is always full of challenges, so it is recommended that teachers with an interest in guidance case study build up a co-operative teaching team to support each other. Therefore, it is necessary for teachers to work together to plan lessons, design tasks, observe each other teaching, share good ideas and help each other to sort out problems. The discussion and support among colleagues will make the experience more positive and productive. From the interview data, I found that teachers in School C have regular discussions with each other. They get together every Wednesday afternoon to discuss teaching purposes, progress and teaching approach. During the meetings, they exchange their teaching experience and think about how to be more effective in teaching. The teachers were positive about the idea of meeting to discuss issues related to teaching and learning. For example, Miss Fang who was a new teacher in the school felt it was a good idea to talk with other experienced teachers about lesson plans and teaching approach.

Teachers were also asked about their views regarding the setting of personal goals in order to improve English teaching. All the teachers agreed that setting personal goals was a useful way to improve their teaching. There are various reasons why teachers need to set personal goals. For example, Miss Zou mentioned that some teachers felt that they lack classroom experience and found it hard to build harmonious relationships with students. This frustration might lead them to be exhausted and discourage them from teaching. Setting a personal goal might help such teachers to understand that the frustrations and complications of teaching are not unsolvable problems. Setting achievable goals can also help keep teachers fresh and motivate them to improve their practice.

> I believe that learning how to teach is a lifelong proposition. So, having clear professional development goals in mind can help the teacher to improve their teaching skills. (Miss Zou)

In the same vein, Miss Li asserted that a good teacher always sets goals for themselves and work hard to achieve those goals.

> A good teacher must always improve by setting goals for themselves and work towards achieving those goals. I found that setting long-term learning goals for myself can help me grow into the best teacher I can be. As a teacher, I used to set learning goals for my students but neglect myself. Recently, I have realised that setting goals for myself is very important as well. (Miss Li)

I wanted to find out how teachers felt about the idea to improve themselves in their teaching. The development of teaching requires teachers' willingness to improve their capacity; otherwise, they cannot persist in what they want under the high pressure of the systemic constraints. Teachers in School C expressed their positive attitude towards self-awareness. For example, Miss Fang stated that teachers should exercise self-awareness and set personal development goals, adding that teaching could become a passive job if teachers were not willing to undertake personal development.

Miss Li is keen on becoming an effective teacher and the onus is on her to pursue higher goals of teaching. She always encourages herself to be a teacher who focuses on self-improvement and to build up a unique personal teaching identity.

> Personally, I appreciate teacher willingness very much. I asked myself, 'how can I become a more effective teacher?' This question always reminds me that no matter how good I am, I can become better. (Miss Li)

Finally, I asked the teachers for their perspectives on taking responsibility in their teaching. They were of the view that teaching was a conscious work and responsibility to a teacher was very important. Miss Li believed that learning and teaching English was not only for examinations or excellent teaching achievement, but also for students' further development. It is significant to help students to build a solid foundation for them to learn English at higher levels in future. If the teachers feel it is boring, how can students find interest in it? Therefore, teachers need to take responsibility to preserve the positive aspects while reducing the negative impact of guidance case study approach. From the discussions with the teachers during lesson observations, the teachers revealed that they were implementing the guidance case study approach reluctantly.

> Responsibility is very important for a teacher... Our teaching purpose is for student to experience, not merely to grasp knowledge. If study processes become a mechanised practice, students will lose their interest. (Miss Li)

As argued by teachers in the school, it is of paramount importance for teachers to contribute to the overall development of their students. This, together with other issues highlighted in this chapter will be discussed further in Chapter 5.

4.3.3.6   *Summary of the interviews with teachers in School C*

The interviews with teachers in School C yielded data on a number of issues relevant to the study's main research questions. Regarding teachers' perspectives on the content of the ELT curriculum, there was a consensus that the school was interested in developing students with all-round skills. The teachers talked about the importance of planning a lesson carefully in order to ensure effective teaching and learning of English language. Similar to teachers from Schools A and B, the teachers in School C valued feedback from students and indicated that they used this feedback to prepare new lesson plans. Planning is done cooperatively and individually. As a team, planning helps to ensure the course is run in the right direction and at individual level; the teacher then adapts the lesson plan to meet the needs of their students. The school emphasises the teaching of grammar and this reveals the impact of examinations on the teaching and learning of English language. The teachers felt they were compelled to adhere to the expectations of the examinations as it was important to ensure their students pass the examinations. The examinations constrained the teachers' freedom in the teaching and learning of English language. The teachers, for instance, appreciated the need to cultivate students' all-round language skills; however, in practice they had to pay more attention to the aspects of the language that dominated the examination. The teachers reflected on the situation around ELT and highlighted a number of factors affecting ELT, including the new course book, but a mismatch between the focus of the book and the examinations could be seen, as the book was said to focus more on listening and speaking skills while the examination placed a lot of emphasis on grammatical constructions and vocabulary. Large class sizes appeared to be one of the factors affecting ELT. The teachers felt that they were change agents and similarly, teachers reported that they had opportunities to engage in professional development activities. They also appreciated the need to take initiative in terms of engagement with SDPD with a view to improving the teaching of English language.

4.4 Summary

It can be seen that the interviews with teachers from different schools raised similar themes and sub-themes. These themes, along with those identified during lesson observations and document analysis, will now be brought together and discussed in the next chapter on discussion of findings.

CHAPTER 5

Discussion of Findings

In this chapter, I am going to outline the responses to the research questions drawing on the data presented in Chapter 4, linking to the literature review which is presented in Chapter 2. In Chapter 4, I presented data obtained from each school separately; however, in this chapter I will discuss the emerging themes across different schools under specific research questions.

From the lesson observation data the following themes were discussed: teaching methods being used in ELT, teaching and learning materials and the role of the teacher in ELT classrooms. In addition, the general characteristics of the schools were looked at to give the researcher a good sense of the context in which ELT was taking place. In the interviews, teachers were asked to reflect on a number of issues and in some cases similar themes and/or sub-themes to those raised during lesson observations were mentioned. In summary, themes covered during interviews include teachers' perspectives on the content of the ELT curriculum, teachers' perspectives on the design and teaching of the ELT curriculum, teachers' perspectives on the current situation of ELT in the schools, teachers' perspectives on their role as agents of change in ELT, opportunities that exist for teachers to develop professionally in the school and last but not least, teachers' perspectives regarding the role of SDPD in the teaching of the English language. These themes are closely linked to the main research questions. In this chapter, responses to each research question will be discussed, drawing from the themes that emerged during lesson observations and interviews with teachers. As highlighted earlier, the themes and sub-themes will now be discussed across schools. As you will notice, for each main research question, the findings from all the three schools will be synthesised first, then will be linked with literature to demonstrate where findings are in confirmation and/or where findings are different from the existing literature. Focus will also be placed on critical reflection on the findings and their implications for the Chinese context related to the teaching and learning of English language. Given that my study is only a case study, no attempt will be made to generalise findings; however, important insights into the teaching and learning of English language in Chinese schools will be commented on appropriately. In the next section, the response to research question 1 is discussed.

5.1　Response to research question 1

What are the teachers' perspectives on the content of the ELT curriculum?

English language is a compulsory course in Chinese secondary schools. Although the teachers in my research were working in three different schools (one private school and two public schools), they were using the same course book called *Go for It* which was published by the Ministry of Education and edited by both foreign teachers and local Chinese English language scholars. In the following section I will discuss what teachers feel about the content in the course book they are using to teach English language.

Findings from the study, based on interviews conducted with teachers as well as observations made in classrooms, reveal that teachers from all the schools were positive about the course book for ELT. All the three schools were using the same course book and it was clear during the study that for the teachers anything to do with content for the ELT curriculum was exclusive to the course book. No reference was made to any other sources of content for ELT in all the schools. My study found out that teachers felt that the content of the book was relevant and helpful in terms of developing students' skills including reading, speaking, listening and writing. The teachers from the three schools agreed that the book had been contextualized, containing many pictures and topics related to students' daily life, which makes it user friendly. The teachers were happy with the course book and indicated that it helped them to deliver their course effectively.

Ning (2011) claims that teaching methods in China primarily pay attention to linguistic accuracy and rote learning but with little emphasis on communicative skills and the actual use of English. However, this observation is different from what I found from these schools in my study, where the teachers stated that the purpose of the new course book *Go for It* is to improve students' overall competence in listening, speaking, reading and writing. The book includes more listening activities compared to the previous one. Each class has listening practice and it requires students to speak loudly as much as possible. The aim is to cultivate students' listening and speaking abilities. Most of the teachers agreed that students' learning skills had improved after using the course book *Go for It*. Each school is expected to encourage the development of each student's particular interests and talents, whether academic, artistic or athletic, whatever interests the students may have. I found that many research projects have identified the problem of learning and teaching of English in China (Xie, 2010, Hu, 2005; Liao, 2004; Li, 2003; Nunan, 1989, 1999). However, very few of them discuss the recent changes and developments of ELT in China.

There was, however, an overt feeling that the course book in use in schools did not match with the requirements of the English language examinations. There is an overwhelming consensus among teachers in the study that the current course book places more emphasis on speaking and listening skills compared to those used in the past. This simply means teachers have got the content they need to develop all the language skills. However, although there is scope for teachers to develop speaking and listening skills using the current textbook, it is also worth noting that the examination focuses more on the grammatical constructions and vocabulary. There is a mismatch between the content of the new book and the examination; what is happening is that teachers tend to focus more on developing skills that are prioritised in the examinations. There appears to be an issue around the impact of examinations on the teaching of English language. It was quite evident when talking to teachers that they had to place emphasis on teaching grammatical aspects of English language to prepare their students for the examinations. As expected, emphasis on grammar and vocabulary would take away time for doing other things like practicing speaking skills. Interestingly, although teachers from all schools pointed out the mismatch between the course book and the current examination system, all the schools chose to use it across all the levels of study. For teachers, their perspectives on the content for the ELT curriculum were the course book. What the teachers were alluding to when they talked of mismatch was that the book provides opportunities for the development of all skills; however, the examinations were not comprehensive, with more emphasis on grammatical skills and vocabulary. There were a few more concerns raised regarding the course book. For instance, some of the teachers felt that the vocabulary was complicated; and in some cases, the complexity of the listening activities did not always match the students' level of study; the organisation of the contents of the books is not user-friendly, that is, the content is not organised in a logical sequence. These issues came from all the teachers in all the participating schools are universal challenges in schools and therefore, need attention. Given the scope of my study, it is impossible to generalise this finding; however, this provides a useful insight into what is happening in the teaching and learning of English language in schools. I do not find any study that evaluated the course book in use in Chinese schools so this finding provides an important contribution to further studies in the field.

5.2　Response to research question 2

What are the teachers' perspectives regarding how they design and teach the ELT curriculum?

Teachers shared their views about how they design lesson plans and teach each lesson plan to different groups they were working with. In the following paragraph, I will discuss how the teachers involved in the study designed and taught their lessons. The first part will focus on the teachers' perspectives on how they design the curriculum and this will be followed by teachers' perspectives on how they teach the curriculum.

5.2.1　Teachers' perspectives on how they design the ELT curriculum

My study established that the designing of lesson plans was considered important in all the schools involved in the study. There was evidence of collaboration among teachers when it came to preparing lesson plans. Various sub-themes that emerged in the analysis of data are to be discussed below.

5.2.1.1　Collaborative approach to lesson planning

Teaching teams from all the three schools in my study would come together to define the overall direction of the lessons or, rather, to come up with the standard structure for the lessons. However, there was variation in the way this collaborative planning was organised. One of the schools actually highlighted that they identified a day for the teachers to come together to plan the lessons and after that, individual teachers selected relevant activities for their own classes. The other two schools did not mention anything like setting aside a day for planning, while stating that they actually had collaborative planning opportunities. Instead of setting a whole day dedicated for planning only, in the other two schools they have meetings of up to two hours which run concurrently with other school activities where teachers meet to discuss curriculum design issues for each topic. The common practice in all schools is that teachers teaching the same level come together and define the standard structure for their lessons. Individual teachers will add activities in their lessons according to the needs of their students. It is noticeable that teachers teaching at the same level would have different numbers of activities in a lesson. This approach, that is, the collaborative approach to lesson planning, has been considered to be very useful given that it facilitates an exchange of ideas between experienced teachers and new teachers. The discussions form an opportunity for teachers to develop themselves and become experts in teaching their subject.

5.2.1.2   *The role of the individual teacher in lesson planning*

As indicated earlier, there was still room for teachers to make independent decisions in lesson planning, despite working together initially to brainstorm the general guidelines for each lesson; teachers have the opportunity to exercise their autonomy when they select activities that suit the needs of students in their classes.

The study established that there is a difference between experienced and new teachers regarding the way they view the relevance of general guidance provided by the school to inform lesson delivery. For instance, one of the experienced teachers from School A, Mr Chen, explained that he did not need to use the general guidance provided by the school, but preferred to use his own plan based on his experience. He prepares the lesson plan, considers students' reflection according to students' level and thinks about how to respond to them. In contrast, one of the new teachers, Miss Fang, indicated that she relied more on the general guidance provided by the school as she struggled to know the key points that students should learn, particularly in order to pass examinations. She also finds it difficult to address the students' individual differences in the design of the lesson plan.

It was unanimously agreed that lesson plans should be purposeful and deliberate to facilitate students' learning. Teachers felt that an effective lesson plan takes time, needs diligence and an understanding of students' abilities. Teachers need to select activities according to students' acknowledge and learning characteristics. In addition, Mrs Zhu in School B stated that the lesson plan was a systematic way of going about planning instructions. For example, she stated that before she started to design a lesson plan, she asked herself: 'Why do we want an effective curriculum? How to help students to learn more than they learn now? How much more? How to increase their interest?' Knowing the different tasks and problems at each step is significant in making the lesson plan.

Furthermore, teachers highlighted that it was necessary to consider students' feedback and think about how to guide them to develop classroom practice. This issue was agreed by the teachers from all the three schools. Listening to the learners' voice is important; however, given other forces, for example, the need to ensure students pass the national examinations, it is doubtful to what extent students' feedback could be incorporated in the planning of lessons. The purpose of teaching is to motivate students to take in what the teacher is teaching and retain as much as possible. Some teachers pointed out that class activities should include a short and stimulating task to prompt or attract students' attention and stimulate their interest before the actual lesson begins. This highlights the importance of ensuring that students are intrinsically motivated. Ushioda (2011) argues that there is a close link between intrinsic motivation and learner autonomy. As argued earlier, teachers in the study did not appear to have time to focus on the development of learner autonomy though as they prioritised the passing of examinations rather than anything else.

5.2.1.3 The role of examinations

The selection of activities in the design of lesson plans is heavily influenced by the structure of the examination. The study reveals that while teachers have the freedom to choose activities to use in the class, they have to ensure that they focus on activities that develop students' skills that are tested in the examination. For example, Mrs Lu in School A mentioned that it was noticeable that each teacher placed emphasis on what they considered important for students' success in examinations. This means, speaking activities which are not included in examinations will be less than other activities like listening activities which are tested in examinations. It does appear that examinations tend to shape the teachers' selection of content to be developed in the English language classrooms. Earlier, teachers mentioned a mismatch between the content of the course book and the focus of the examinations. What happens is, the course book is comprehensive, providing content for the development of all the basic language skills, and yet, examinations focus more on grammatical skills and vocabulary. Teachers therefore felt that the textbook should contain more content on grammar.

My study has confirmed elements of existing literature which show that examinations have great power in driving teaching and learning (Hughes, 1989). The impact of examinations on the attitudes, behaviours and motivation of teachers and students is quite evident in my study. For instance, all the teachers in my study have concurred with the notion that they have to select activities that help them to ensure that students perform well in the examinations. The course book being used in all schools has activities that cover all the different language skills but it emerges that teachers tend to select activities that develop only those skills tested in the examinations. The findings from my study echo the findings in a study conducted in China by Kong (2009) which find that communicative skills are not likely to be developed in Chinese schools because teachers focus on grammatical skills and grammar that are tested in the examinations. Even students in Chinese schools are more interested in passing the examinations only, as indicated in a study by Yong (2015), finding out that Chinese students are motivated to study just to pass the examinations when they are learning English language in schools. At a time when there is a lot of discussion about developing learner autonomy, that is, ensuring that students take more responsibility in their learning which might include involving students in selecting learning materials and the way they want to learn, but the current situation which is dominated by examinations makes it difficult for teachers to focus on developing learner autonomy. This is again discussed by Yong (2015) who argues that examinations reinforce a more teacher-centred approach in the teaching and learning of English language.

5.2.2　How teachers teach the ELT curriculum

Teachers in the study discussed the different activities and procedures they engaged in to deliver the ELT curriculum, including the use of group work, selection of teaching materials, use of students' feedback, teaching approach and teacher autonomy. Each of these activities and procedures will be discussed in the subsequent paragraphs.

5.2.2.1 *Use of group work and pair work*

The study findings showed that in the majority of cases, students were engaged in their learning, working either in pairs or in small groups of up to five students in class. Due to the large class sizes, teachers agreed that group work gave learners more opportunities to use the language for themselves. The aim of group work is to offer students more opportunities for language development, thus enhancing their fluency and effectiveness in communication (Liao, 2004). It has been argued that group work and pair work increase peer interaction and collaboration, fostering collaborative autonomy where learners exercise a high level of control over their learning (Little, 2001). The peers can provide valuable sources of scaffold help and feedback to support language learning, which means teachers are no longer being the sole preserve of knowledge or 'expert' speakers of the target language, particularly in contexts where learners are able to work more autonomously (Legenhausen, 2001). What has emerged in my study does not align with the observations made by Little (2001) and Legenhausen (2001). In practice, even though the students were provided with opportunities for group work, there was no evidence of them controlling their own learning (being autonomous). According to the teachers in the study, they selected what the students were to work on in the groups and this was modeled around the structure of examinations. Students had to learn what was needed for them to pass the examinations and so, in this case, the system was very much teacher-centric. Learner autonomy involves students taking more responsibility for their own learning (Lamb, 2009), yet, what is happening in the schools under study reveals teacher domination in the system. There was no opportunity for learners to develop autonomy, and according to the teachers in the study, students were basically being drilled to pass examinations.

Teachers have indicated that it is a challenging task to use group work with Chinese learners because they have been continuously exposed to teacher-dominated classrooms. It is important for teachers to make it clear at the very beginning of a course that the main purpose of team tasks is to offer students chances to practise English with peers in authentic situations. Furthermore, teachers should realise that it is hard for students to benefit from activities by simply getting into groups and asking them to work together. Hence, activities must be well structured and integrated as an essential part of daily classroom teaching and course assessment. In other words, teachers should clearly inform students the specific procedures to follow in activities and get them ready to communicate with their group-mates in English in order to achieve the desired learning goals.

5.2.2.2　Selecting teaching materials

One of the important tasks for teachers is to stimulate interest among students to encourage them to learn the English language. One way of achieving this is to select the learning materials carefully. The study established that each teacher selected learning resources that appealed to students to keep the lesson interesting and relevant to students' needs. For example, to enable students to practise the use of the grammatical structures, Mrs Cao in School A showed a picture of Jackie Chan who was famous among students and asked them to give different answers to the questions she raised in class. I observed that students found this activity very interesting and they engaged very well throughout the lesson because Jackie Chan was a famous actor. In addition, teachers in School B made use of other materials such as *21st Century*, an English newspaper and resources in order to widen students' horizons and enhance their reading skills. The teachers differentiated the tasks taking into account the students' abilities. Articles which contain well-known characters like Harry Potter can encourage students to do more independent reading. Furthermore, teachers in School C created other learning materials that students used for preparatory work. For each lesson, teachers had to get together to discuss the key activities, including the aims of the session, the intended learning outcomes, the methods of delivery, content and tasks for students. After the meeting, one of the teachers would put together all the ideas for a single unit and distribute to all the teachers. They took turns to produce materials for each unit.

5.2.2.3　Using students' feedback

Feedback plays an important role in the learning and teaching process. Both students and teachers benefit from feedback, using it to improve their learning and teaching respectively. My study found that teachers could use student feedback to change lesson plans. For instance, Mr Chen from School A pointed out that 'a lesson plan is dead, but students and teachers are living.' If teachers find students are stuck, they will change the content or slow down the teaching speed to give more instructions and explanations concerning the particular point. Students' countenance and body language can tell what they are feeling in the class. There should be mutual communication between students and teachers. If teachers take care of students' needs and teach according to their level and standard, it will be very helpful. Making use of students' feedback is a classroom skill for a teacher. One of the prominent education professionals in China, Professor Ye Ran, argues that one does not become a famous teacher by merely writing lesson plans even if they do that for their whole life; however, it is possible to become a good teacher by constantly reflecting on each lesson over a three-year period. What the professor is saying is a way to emphasise the importance of reflective practice, which also involves the use of students' feedback.

5.2.2.4   Teaching methods

Although the schools were using the same course book for teaching English language, it was interesting to note that different methods were being used to teach the ELT curriculum. Each school placed emphasis on its own teaching approach. For example, School A used a CLT approach, School B used a task-based language teaching approach and School C used a guidance case study approach. It was also clear that variation did not only appear among the schools, in some cases teachers from the same school used the approaches differently. For instance, in School A, one of the three teachers used primarily the traditional grammar teaching approach while the other two placed emphasis on the CLT approach. Beside this, it was interesting to note that in all the approaches the teachers tried to engage students as much as possible to ensure that they take responsibility for their own learning. In all three schools, teachers used group work activities and pair work activities to enable the students to have opportunities to practise and develop speaking skills. Some of the teachers still felt obliged to place more emphasis on teaching grammar and vocabulary because of the impact of examinations. It emerged from the study that while the book focused on the development of four skills, that is, reading, listening, writing and speaking, the examination did not have a speaking component and placed emphasis on grammar and vocabulary.

As highlighted above, various approaches are being used in the schools to teach the English language. Each approach enabled the teachers to focus on the development of the relevant skills for student's success in examinations. Two teachers in School A were using the CLT approach in their classes and the other teacher chose the traditional grammar teaching approach. CLT was celebrated for enabling students to have more opportunities to speak English rather than concentrating on grammar. However, the approach presented a challenge to teachers especially when working with large class sizes where it was difficult to keep track of what every student was doing. But the traditional grammar teaching approach placed emphasis on the teaching of grammar and was considered to be more aligned to examinations. The teachers in my study indicated that students found it boring to spend most of the time just working on different grammar activities. The atmosphere in the classroom where the CLT approach was used was more lively and dynamic compared to the classroom where the traditional grammar approach was being used.

The choice of teaching approach in School A appeared to depend on the teacher. Teachers who were confident in their speaking ability used the CLT approach while the other teachers who could not speak English very well opted to use the traditional grammar approach. Teachers' background influenced their teaching. For instance, two of the teachers were trained using traditional grammar approach, but one of the two teachers, Mr Chen, went to Australia to improve his speaking and when he returned he realised the importance of communication skills. As a result, he started using the communication language teaching approach. The other teacher continued to use the traditional grammar approach, which she was familiar with from her training. Mr Chen serves as an example of the role that reflective practice can play in enhancing one's practice. Reflection is the process of critical examination of experiences and leads teachers to have a better understanding of other's teaching practices. Gün (2011) echoes that it is important for teachers to interpret data from their own teaching practice and use it as a basis for changes in their classrooms in future.

Unlike teachers in School A, I observed that teachers in School B were using the TBLT approach in their classes. As explained in Chapter 2, task-based language learning and teaching approach consists of giving students multiple tasks during the lesson. One key feature about TBLT is that teachers tend to focus on the use of authentic learning materials in the tasks that they give to students. Most of the tasks are taken from the course book and include individual work as well as group one. However, teachers also create their own learning materials, for example, use of local newspapers. The teachers select different activities to promote the development of all skills including reading, writing, speaking and listening. From my observations, students were quite positive with the approach.

School C requires the teachers to integrate guidance case study teaching techniques into second language learning classrooms. The goal of guidance case study approach is to stimulate students' self-awareness and group cooperation abilities. The principle of guidance case study is to let students do preparatory work first and then come to class to have discussions and other activities based on the preparatory work. This approach is relatively new as it has not been discussed in literature. However, teachers felt that the advantage of this approach is that it allows advanced students to help the less advanced students with their studies and there is a lot of collaborative learning inside and outside the classroom. Moreover, it was considered that guidance case study approach is likely to facilitate the learners' capacity to communicate in the class.

The guidance case study approach is a radical shift from teacher-centred to a learner-centred approach in the learning and teaching of English language. The approach makes the language learning process more transparent to learners, and thus enables students to improve their capacity for reflection and self-management, and helps them to increase their responsibility gradually and foster their interest in their own learning. As indicated earlier, the approach requires students to learn before class and cooperate with teachers' activities in class. Students are encouraged to get meaning across instead of simply focus on accuracy of language forms.

Teachers reflected on the effectiveness of the guidance case study approach in the learning and teaching of English language. There were mixed feelings towards the use of the approach. For example, Miss Zhou reported positive effects of using the guidance case study approach in her classroom, and commented that a good guidance case design could save students' time. It clarifies students' homework given that the teacher provides clear guidelines and instructions for students to follow. However, Miss Fang felt that the approach created more pressure and extra work for both students and teachers. Her feelings where shared by many other teachers. For instance, I observed a public class which was attended by around 50 teachers from five different

164

schools to observe and discuss how to use the guidance case study approach in English language learning. During the discussions, I found out that many teachers were negative about the approach. Teachers expressed that they experienced difficulties in adapting the new teaching method. They found that designing learning activities was time consuming where the teacher had to provide detailed guidelines and instructions. Furthermore, in-class activities were also time consuming and teachers felt that the approach was not convenient for their students who did not have a high comprehensive ability of English language.

Like any new approach, for the guidance case study approach to take root in the schools there is a need to provide opportunities for professional development. I noticed that effort was being made by schools to promote the use of the approach. For example, School C conducted many public class observations where the guidance case study approach was being used. In addition, the school organised a seminar with a group of English language teachers so that they could discuss and develop an experiential understanding of the guidance case study approach, helping teachers to understand the fundamental principles of the guidance case study approach.

As can be appreciated from the synthesis made above, there is use of different methods in the English language classrooms. However, teachers dominate the way they are using the methods. As observed by Oxford (1990) the teaching of English language in Chinese schools continues to be teacher-centred and book-centred. My study findings, therefore, resonate with previous findings where it is shown that there is rote learning in English language by the Chinese students (Ning, 2011). Book has also been shown to be the main source of language learning material as observed by Arndt et al. (2000). Surely, if students are being taught to pass the examinations only, it can be explained why they continue to struggle with speaking skills even when they reach college or university level as observed by Jin and Cortazzi (2002).

5.2.2.5　Autonomy in teaching

My study reveals that teachers enjoy autonomy in their teaching to some extent. For instance, they are able to design the lesson plan and arrange classroom activities by themselves; however, what they do has to be under the guidelines of national syllabuses. In addition, most activities are only allowed in the classroom. It is hard for the school to give permission to teachers to have outdoor activities. Many authors agree that schools should give teachers the freedom to select materials and ideas from outside the course and give teachers more freedom and authority to select their teaching objectives and classroom activities (Lamb, 1998; Lamb and Simpson, 2003). Understandably, this will help teachers to deliver the teaching/learning package successfully and also encourage them to make plans within the classroom setting. Teachers should have some degree of freedom to teach what they feel is necessary in a class (Varanoglulari et al., 2008). Despite the already known advantages of giving teachers autonomy in their work as stated by different authorities cited here, my study has found that the English language teachers have got limited autonomy in the teaching and learning of English language. As discussed earlier, teacher autonomy is constrained by a number of factors including examinations and the underlying educational theories of China (Rao, 2002a). In his study, Rao (2002a) argues that China does not need to westernise but to modernise its approaches to teaching in English language classrooms. He talks of making use of the old Chinese methods of teachings together with the new methods being advocated from the western countries. In the same vein, Burnaby and Sun (1989) indicate that there are some constraints for Chinese teachers to implement western-language teaching methods, including the context of the wider curriculum, traditional teaching methods, class sizes and schedules, resources and equipment which are so different from western countries. The point being made here is that autonomy cannot be achieved overnight, but has to be developed gradually and hence it needs to avoid radical changes in the classroom. Western approaches to teaching and learning are different from what goes on in Chinese context. In a study conducted in Hong Kong which may shed light on the situation in China as a whole, Pierson (1996) argues that compared to their western peers, Chinese students from Hong Kong are often perceived as syllabus dependent, passive and lacking in initiative. Similarly, Evans (1996) states that schools in Hong Kong by western standards are seen as traditional, rule-bond institutions, where independence, individuality and creativity are far less valued than obedience, conformity, discipline and diligence which are actively encouraged. It is therefore important to view Chinese schools and the teaching and learning of English language in light of the wider curriculum context.

5.3   Response to research question 3

What are the teachers' perspectives on the key problems being faced in the teaching and learning of English language in schools?

Teachers highlighted a number of factors and problems affecting the delivery of ELT in schools and these are to be discussed below.

5.3.1   Examination-oriented system

Teachers from all schools involved in the study expressed that examinations are the most important factor in the teaching and learning of English language particularly for students in the third year of their secondary education. What I have found in my study is consistent with findings from previous studies. For instance, Hughes (1989) claims that testing has a significant impact on the individual teaching approach, curriculum plan and syllabuses. Teachers feel that they are often compelled to implement controlling strategies because of the impact of external pressures such as national examinations (Deci and Ryan, 2002). A number of other interesting findings related to the impact of examinations on the delivery of the ELT curriculum emerged and these are to be discussed in the following section.

5.3.1.1   *Increasing the difficulty of writing and reading*

One of the aspects associated with examinations that emerged from my study is that due to the format of examinations (mainly multiple-choice questions) students do not have the opportunity to develop deeper understanding of the language. In particular, the limited opportunities to practise reading and writing. Teachers prepare students mechanically to pass the examinations and they expressed frustration about this. As teachers in my study have reported, examinations reduce the grammar in the multiple-choice questions and add more language trap in the context of the word.

5.3.1.2   *Increasing listening practice*

Following the increase of the listening score in examinations from 20 to 25 there have been some changes in the teaching and learning of English language. Teachers indicated that the current course book had more listening exercises and this had resulted in teachers putting more emphasis on the teaching of listening skills. Given that the listening examination is based on American accent, the current course book now includes videos produced by American native speakers. Students are now having more opportunities to develop listening skills not only for the examination but also for effective communication. Teachers commented that the format of the listening test was more reliable and applicable. For example, students have two opportunities to attend the listening test for high-school entrance examination and the higher score will be recorded as a final one.

5.3.1.3   Lack of speaking test

In my study, I have found there is no speaking test, and this affects the way teachers conduct the teaching of speaking skills in the class. Some teachers feel that they are not obliged to place emphasis on the teaching of speaking skills because they are not examined. It is interesting to note that, despite the lack of speaking tests, some of the teachers, in particular the new teachers, tend to teach these skills, while some of the experienced teachers do not bother to teach the skills. This shows a difference between new and experienced teachers. The experienced teachers appear to focus on what is asked in the examinations whereas the new teachers bring a new dimension to English language learning by adopting a more comprehensive approach to teaching. However, Mrs Yang in School B argued that there was communicative English in the written format. For example, in the multiple-choice questions, it may say 'would you like to...,' which is a spoken language format but appears in the written examination.

In addition, I have found that teachers make an effort to develop their students' pronunciation. They give students tape scripts which enable them to listen and imitate the accent in the recorded tapes. Students will then be given opportunities to recite in the class and get feedback from both their peers and teachers. It was reported that this practice helped to motivate students to improve their speaking skills.

5.3.1.4   The impact of examination-oriented system on students' learning

All the teachers in my study have agreed that examination is the main factor that motivates students to learn the English language. There is a consensus among teachers that teaching is carried out in line with the examinations standards, and students are subjected to great pressure by examinations. Interestingly, teachers feel they experience more pressure than their students. New teachers reported that it was challenging for them to know exactly what to be focused on to prepare their students adequately compared to more experienced teachers.

My study showed that different teachers hold different views towards the impact of examination on students' learning. Some teachers considered examinations to be a positive factor while others felt that it was negative. Miss Fang from School C believes that examinations have a negative impact on the learning and teaching of English citing that students learning under the pressure of examination may lack the personal interest in learning the language. This view is supported by Reeve (2002) who states that students are more likely to understand and utilise the newly acquired information more flexibly when they are free from the pressures of intensive exam-based learning. In addition, since syllabuses are usually controlled by high school entrance examinations, many teachers are not likely to devote much time to teaching communicative skills that have no bearing on the examination requirement in Chinese secondary schools. Vernon (1956) states that 'teachers tend to ignore topics and activities which do not refer directly to passing the examination' (cited in Alderson and Wall, 1993: 115).

However, Mrs Cao thinks that to most students, the examination plays a positive role in their learning of English, as it may stir up students' learning interests and foster their learning of the language. Many educationalists believe that examinations influence teaching and learning in a powerful way (Hughes, 1989; Davies, 1968; Vernon, 1956). In addition, Mrs Lu and Mr Chen from School A say that examinations can have both negative and positive impact on students' learning. Nonetheless, for students who are willing to study, the examination is a good motivation to them. It helps students to be guided in their study and to aim to achieve high scores which enable them to learn the language very well. But, to those who are not good at studies, examinations can be daunting.

5.3.1.5   The difficulty of changing the examination-oriented system

As mentioned above, many Chinese students learning the English language are primarily motivated by examinations. English, as one of three core subjects along with Mathematics and Chinese, is tested for students to enter senior high school and is a compulsory subject in the National College Entrance Examinations for all types of universities and colleges. Students strive to achieve excellence in their examinations as it guarantees that they can be selected for admission into top schools, which will direct them to institutions on a higher rank of the educational ladder in China (Eckstein and Noah, 1993). Also in order to obtain a bachelor's degree, Chinese students need to pass the CET4 (Cheng, 2008). Therefore, it is difficult for teachers to change the structure of the examination.

5.3.2 Learning materials

The students make use of the course book and other practice books. Regarding the course book *Go for It*, teachers appreciated that there were many activities for students. The course book contains many pictures and different topics to enhance students' understanding. All the teachers interviewed highlighted that the new course book *Go for It* not only emphasized students' reading abilities, but also paid attention to their comprehensive competence in the four skills (reading, writing, listening and speaking). It was stated that more emphasis was placed on the development of listening and speaking skills. However, the teachers complained that the activities were not structured in a logical sequence, also the book contained too much unnecessary vocabulary that could confuse students. However, one teacher, Miss Zou argued that course books were ancillary material in teaching; the key was how teachers dealt with it. If a teacher can utilise materials in a proper way, it will bring more benefit to students.

There is a mismatch between the focus of the course book and the examination. The course book *Go for It* aims to improve the learner's speaking and listening abilities while the examination focuses on grammar and vocabulary. Teachers expressed concern about how to find a good balance between teaching students to pass the examination with a good score while at the same time, maintaining a high level of motivation during class activities. For example, students find it boring to concentrate on the grammar and yet, teachers are afraid of spending too much time on speaking practice which is not examinable. This makes it difficult for teachers to manage the class.

5.3.3 Learning motivation

Teachers in my study have agreed that motivation is very important in the learning and teaching of English language. This is consistent with Gardner's (1985: 85) observation that 'the prime determining factor in language learning success is motivation.' Motivation, along with attitudes, determines the extent of active personal engagement in language learning. Although my study has not explored this, it is said that students who are highly motivated use more strategies than poorly motivated students (Oxford and Nyikos, 1989). For example, if a learner recognises that it is worthwhile to learn a second language, they tend to be motivated to study harder. The teachers in my study unanimously agreed that examinations formed the main factor that motivated students to work hard in the learning of English language at the secondary school. 'Most of the students aim to pass the examination and then go to a bright high school which can assist them to enter a celebrated university' (Mrs Zhu). However, Mrs Yang suggested that the influence of such motivation was very negative to students' learning of the language. This is because students focus on aspects of the language that are examinable (Alderson and Wall, 1993; Vernon, 1956). Studies have shown that this examination-oriented system develops passive, unmotivated learners whose primary interest is only in passing the examination. 'Students learn not because they want to, but because they feel they should' (Zhou et al., 2009). Students who experience such motivation which involves being compelled or guided by external and internal pressures, tend to be instilled with a sense of pressure, obligation and resistance. They work hard to pass the examination; however, they do not feel that everything they are asked in the examination is relevant to their real lives. For example, although the examination focuses on grammar, many students do not think they need to learn the complicated grammar, stating that, 'if they become a taxi driver, what they need is the simple communicative language' (Mrs Yang).

My study found that teachers believed that it was important for students to be intrinsically motivated to learn the English language effectively. This was reflected in the views of the teachers. For example, Mrs Zhou and Mrs Yang in School B suggested that improving students' interest in learning of English language was an important issue to help them to engage effectively in the learning of the subject. In the same vein, Mrs Zhu believed that students' interest in the subject played a pivotal role in their learning. Interest can simulate motivation to push students to study. In this case, interest can be either externally or internally motivated. The teachers' views are supported by Zhou et al. (2009) who maintain that autonomous motivation is an important factor in learning English language, citing that autonomous motivation leads to higher levels of interest, perceived competence and perceived choice. The teachers in my study indicated that there was a need to ensure that students were supported to develop interest in the subject because without interest it could be hard for students to learn. I observed that in the schools a number of strategies were being used to arouse students' interest in the subject. For example, teachers selected interesting topics to keep students motivated and also organised speaking competitions and other activities including singing English songs and reading popular English novels. Without interest, it is hard for students to achieve good results in English language. The view of Einstein, 'interest is the best teacher,' was supported by the teachers in my study.

5.3.4 Large class sizes and students with different levels of proficiency in English language

My study has established that large class sizes and working with students of mixed abilities are two factors that teachers are grappling with in the schools. Teachers unanimously agreed that when teaching English language small class sizes were more effective than large class sizes. This is because large class sizes make it difficult for the teachers to provide effective one to one support for each student. Teachers felt that working with small numbers of students would reduce the amount of work and enable them to give each student more time to work on activities. Given the large numbers they were working with, there was a feeling that teachers did not have enough time to conduct long conversations with students during sessions. Miss Fang and Miss Zou in School C felt that their classes were too big and if given the opportunity they would reduce the number of students in each classroom from the current number 45 to about 15 to 20. Teachers believe that they can manage and promote effective learning and teaching of the language if they work with smaller class sizes. 'My hope is for every class to have only 15 students, no more than 20... I think it would be very helpful to teaching if we can reduce the class size' (Miss Zou).

Some teachers indicated that they were having difficulties in working with students at different levels in the same class. For example, Mrs Yang and Mrs Zhou in School B pointed out that having different levels of students was one of the biggest challenges in their classes. It is hard to give proper guidance and lesson for students at different levels of proficiency in the language. They felt that the school should consider establishing a multi-level English teaching system, placing students in different groups based on their abilities. Alternatively, teachers were suggesting the use of differentiated tasks or activities when working with students of mixed levels. The idea of categorising students can be problematic especially if one considers principles of inclusive practice in education; however, this can be of great help if done in the spirit of recognising and supporting each student's individual needs. The factors discussed in this section including large class sizes and working with students with mixed attainment levels in the same class were cited by Burnaby and Sun (1989) as some of the areas where the Chinese language learning context differs from the western countries and as they say, this can be a constraint in the implementation of western language teaching methods in China.

5.4   Response to research question 4

From the teachers' perspectives, what can be done to ensure effective teaching of the English language in schools?

My study sought to find out how teachers felt about the way English language was being taught in the schools with a view to exploring ways to improve the system. Reflections made by the teachers presented a mixed picture. On the one hand, teachers were contented with some aspects of the learning and teaching of English language. For example, they expressed satisfaction with the course book, in particular, the opportunities it provided for students to develop communication skills. On the other hand, they identified a number of issues that they felt need to be improved. In this section, I will discuss the ideas highlighted by teachers that can be considered to improve the learning and teaching of English language.

5.4.1   Collaborative and reflective approach in designing of the lesson plan

A considerable majority of teachers in the schools in my study expressed satisfaction with the idea of working collaboratively in the designing of the lesson plans. They felt that this practice was helpful as it enabled teachers to learn from each other and swap ideas to enrich their lessons. As a result, the teachers felt that schools should promote both collaborative and individual ways of working among teachers. They also stated that schools should work together to reinforce collaboration between teachers, highlighting that there should be competitions among schools to encourage effective designing of the lesson plans. Although teachers plan together, there was a feeling that each teacher should continue to have the freedom to adapt the lesson plan to suit the needs of their students. In other words, teachers need to be able to add or remove some activities in the general lesson plan. For instance, Mrs Zhu mentioned that she might amend or change some details in class according to students' reaction. She teaches two classes and after delivering the first lesson she makes changes to the lesson for the next group in light of the feedback drawn from the first group. Similarly, Miss Zou in School C suggested that excellent classroom designs helped to stimulate students' interest in participation. Teachers need to consider how to stimulate students' learning interest and arouse their curiosity when making a lesson plan. For instance, Miss Zou adds some pictures to her class and includes interesting activities to stir up students' learning interest. It is this kind of flexibility that teachers would want to see maintains in line with teacher autonomy.

5.4.2　Effective classroom management

My study found that teachers in the school have the freedom to organise classroom activities in ways that suit their students. However, the teachers do not have the flexibility to change either the structure of the lessons or the venue where the lesson should take place; for example, they cannot make decisions such as moving students from the classroom to engage in outdoor activities without the permission of the school authorities. One of the teachers, Miss Zou, expressed her desire to have more freedom regarding the way of her teaching the subject, for example, to carry out practical dialogues outside classrooms or show students some movies which could improve students' interest in learning the subject. This view is supported by Willis and Willis (2007) who state that real-world activities give opportunities to learners to engage in developing meanings. Teachers can help students to develop vocabulary by engaging them with some authentic learning materials and activities.

5.4.3　Reflective practice

All teachers in my study indicated that reflective practice was very important for effective learning and teaching of English language. They argued that through reflection they could identify areas in need of improvement as well as to reinforce good

174

practice. Many studies support the idea that teachers learn from experience through reflection on the nature and meaning of the teaching experience (Richards and Lockhart, 1994; Schon, 1983). Teachers indicated that after reflecting on the previous class, it was possible for them to do things differently in future lessons. It is essential to give teachers opportunities to consider their teaching practice so that they can become more aware of their own beliefs and how they are influenced by those beliefs to foster learners' second language acquisition (Raya, 2006). Reflection is a process of critical examination of experiences and leads teachers to gain a better understanding of other teaching practices. In line with this view, Mrs Cao in School B stated that reflective approach helped her to consider how to re-organise classroom materials and tasks for use in the classroom and how to restructure individual knowledge. Furthermore, Mr Chen in School A said, reflection helped him to think about the following questions: 'What have I learnt this week? How can I integrate what I have learnt in my teaching? If there is a problem, how can I solve it?' Mr Chen mentioned that schools required teachers to complete the teaching reflection form and he believed that reflection was a way to perfect a teacher's role. The purpose of completing reflection forms consistently is to help teachers to be aware of their strengths and weaknesses and thus to improve their practical teaching ability.

Furthermore, all schools in my study required teachers to complete checklists for self-assessment. The completion of checklist and self-assessment forms is believed to have an important influence on teacher professional development. When teachers achieve one of their goals stated in the checklist, they would look ahead for another target and think about the way to achieve it. Ross and Bruce (2007) consider that self-assessment involves bringing together three different processes, namely (a) self-observation, (b) self-judgements, and (c) self-reactions. These three processes help to encourage teachers to derive important insights which can be used to develop their professional career. Braun and Crumpler (2004) emphasise the need for teachers to take note of their own experiences as a source of ideas for enhancing their practice and working with students in the classrooms. This is another example of how teachers can be autonomous: setting up personal goals for their own professional development.

5.4.4   Building good relationships with students

Teachers indicated that building a good relationship with students is important for the learning and teaching of the English language. This is consistent with Bullough's (2008) observation that teacher–student relationship is at the core of any quality learning experience. The nature of the relationship influences interactions between teachers and students both inside and outside the class. There is an old Chinese adage which states that 'if students are close to the teacher, they would love the teachers' lesson.' In other words, if students enjoy harmonious relationships with their teacher, they are likely to engage with the subject. This highlights the importance of establishing and maintaining good relationships with students. If teachers could win dignity and respect from their students, it will help in the learning and teaching of the subject. For example, in my study, Miss Fang in School C stated that teachers' personalities constituted an important factor in students' learning of the English language. On the one hand, it is possible that if students find the teachers' personality attractive they can be motivated to learn. On the other hand, if students are not satisfied with the teachers' personality, they may not engage effectively with the subject.

One of the ways to achieve good relationships with students is to give praise and encouragement, which might increase their confidence and help them to put more effort in the learning of the English language. As Isenbarger and Zembylas (2006: 123) state, 'taking the time to listen to students' problems or worries, giving advice or guidance to them, and showing warmth and love are all examples of emotional work in teaching.' Teachers need to take the lead in encouraging, motivating and showing sensitivity towards their students' learning. Apart from giving praise and encouragement, students like teachers who show them love, care, respect and who are accessible when students need help. For example, teachers in School C were readily available for their students even during lunch hour break. The communication between students and teachers is very important. Teachers are supposed to give students proper guidance and encourage them to study and not to disappoint them (Mrs Zhu). Similarly, Miss Li pointed out that encouragement and positive evaluation were very important for learning English. It is unavoidable for students to make mistakes but caring teachers need to realise that this is part of the learning process and give the necessary support to their students.

5.5   Response to research question 5

What opportunities exist for teachers to develop professionally in schools?

My study sought to find out whether teachers had opportunities to develop them-selves professionally or not. Through interviews, it was revealed that a number of opportunities for continuous professional development were available for the teachers. Interview data reveal that there are many in-service teacher training opportunities in all areas important for the effective teaching of English language including reading and listening skills, as well as opportunities for lesson observations, attending seminars and specific training programmes. Good professional development opportunities for teachers help to promote the quality of teaching in English language classrooms. In order for language teachers to stimulate learning processes to help students achieve their study goals, it is essential for them to know what they believe about teaching and learning. The data collected by Trebbi (2008) show that provision of in-service education opportunities can change teachers' views or beliefs about teaching and learning. Some examples of this are to be discussed below.

School A provides a conducive environment for teachers to improve their practice. The teachers in the study stated that it was good practice to offer a place for teachers to share their teaching experiences, expertise and offer opportunities for them to learn from each other. The importance of creating an enabling environment for teachers to develop themselves cannot be overemphasised.

The teachers in School B demonstrate a lot of interest in participating in the in-service professional development programmes organised at school level and by some external organisations, with other schools in the region participating in. The existence of these opportunities helps to enhance the learning and teaching of English language in the schools. In-service training helps to develop teachers' understanding of collaboration and creates more opportunities for exploiting the advances offered by technology. Teachers tend to teach in the same way they were taught. Therefore, in order for teachers to adopt new ways of teaching and thinking about how students learn, schools need to offer more opportunities for teachers to experience autonomous learning. If they lack personal experience of autonomous learning, even if they are interested in the ideas of autonomy, it is very hard to implement it in their teaching

(Miliander, 2008). It is further argued that it is unrealistic to expect teachers to facilitate the growth of autonomy in their learners if they do not know how to be autonomous learners themselves (Little, 1999). Therefore, in-service training and other forms of professional development are crucial if the learning and teaching of English language is to be improved.

School C provides opportunities for teachers to engage in cross-school classroom presentation. This helps them to learn from each other and to improve their practice. Furthermore, teachers engage in competitions, for example, competition of how to teach reading skills. The competitions are held at school level first and the best teachers in the school are selected to compete with teachers from other schools. These competitions serve as incentives for the English teachers to work hard and provide excellent learning experience for their students. The school also provides opportunities for teachers to attend relevant academic conferences as well as the chance of short-term and long-term in-service training programmes. Recently, the school started to appoint teachers to travel to England for them to enhance their teaching skills and knowledge of the English language. These opportunities are limited and competitive, for which teachers work hard. What is being done in this school should be replicated in other schools to enhance the quality of teachers' professional development.

5.6 Response to research question 6

From the teachers' perspectives, what role does SDPD play in the learning and teaching of the English language?

One of the key issues I wanted to establish was the role of SDPD in the learning and teaching of English language in the schools. Teachers articulated their views during interviews. McGrath (2000) asserts that autonomous teachers are those who have control over their own lives by engaging in SDPD. Bearing this in mind, I sought to find out whether teachers in my study were in control and taking responsibility to develop themselves or not. Teacher development is not related to years of experience but to the extent to which teachers engage in self-directed, collaborative and reflective inquiry. This view is further buttressed by Tort-Moloney (1997: 51) who says that 'the autonomous teacher is one who is aware of why, when, where and how pedagogical skills can be acquired in the self-conscious awareness of the teaching practice itself.' In the following sections, a discussion of the teachers' views will be considered.

5.6.1   Engagement with in-service training programmes

My study has shown that self-engagement is very important for teachers' professional development, that is, whether they are intrinsically motivated to participate in further training or not. This is because without engagement, without genuine interest, there can be no focus on meaning or outcome. Teachers have to pursue a clearly defined outcome, as well as the engagement in further training, that is, on the job training. As Bailey (1992) says, a sense of ownership of ideas and innovations in teacher development programmes is a prerequisite for change to take effect. In this way, it is assumed that teachers feel they are not only part of innovation, but innovation is part of them (Bailey, 1992). It is important for teachers to take ownership of their development rather than being compelled by authorities in the school.

My study revealed that teachers were motivated and eager to take advantage of the existing opportunities to improve themselves through swapping ideas with their peers within the same school and from other schools, reflecting that the English teachers were deeply interested in their job and as a result they were looking for ways to improve their practice to enhance students' learning experience. For example, teachers in School A mentioned that they had on-going discussions with other teachers regarding teaching approaches. It must be noted that the school authorities facilitate the organisation and implementation of such development-oriented activities. It is necessary for teachers to have the support of their authorities, otherwise their own motivation may not produce substantial results if the school does not provide an enabling environment. Given the opportunity, teachers are able to exchange different views, agree or disagree, explain, and develop the ability to organise their arguments. The importance of understanding how teachers work together and share practices with their colleagues is reflected in the interview data. Mr Chen shared his experience of the discussions held with other teachers. He stated that he 'likes to discuss with other teachers on how to present a class, how to attract students' attention and stir up their interest.' Sometimes he felt his colleagues were mirrors for him to view his own practice in the discussions. These kinds of in-service training impact on teaching by stimulating teachers to alter or strengthen their teaching practice. When teachers become more aware of themselves, they will recognise their weaknesses and thus can investigate and overcome their problems or limitations. For example, Mrs Lu in School A stated that staff development opportunities helped them to reflect on their practice, including the selection of appropriate teaching methods. She stated, 'There exist different teaching methods; however, it is not advisable to apply everything in the class without thinking.' Every class has students at different levels and it is important for teachers to under-stand how to respond to the needs of each student. Mrs Cao in School A stated that she would prepare for opportunities to be observed by her peers, referring to how she made use of 'public lessons,' that is, lessons open to other teachers to come in, observe and provide constructive criticism. She believed that the feedback from other teachers was very useful. In addition, Mr Chen stated that he never stopped learning from his colleagues and books. Hence, it is important to discuss with others. Learning should be an on-going process which is particularly helpful for teachers who need to refresh their knowledge and keep on top of the situation in terms of acquiring new teaching approaches.

Similarly, the English teachers in School B were positive about the idea of learning how their peers were presenting knowledge, arranging activities and managing their students' engagement with activities. Teachers learn from classroom observations, public lectures and reviews of other teachers' lesson plans. Mrs Yang was of the view that public lectures helped her to identify the limitations of her own teaching and ways of improving her work. She kept a diary of all the lectures that she attended and referred to the notes from time to time. This would help her to remember and apply new ideas and approaches to her teaching. In addition, teachers indicated that they had many discussions with their peers around teaching approaches. Peer support appears to be a significantly important aspect of professional development among the teachers in my study. Teachers indicated the importance of sharing ideas among themselves as a way to improve their practice. For example, Mrs Zhu highlighted that she used to ask for ideas from other teachers whenever she had difficulties in helping students to learn certain aspects of the English language.

Teachers from School C shared similar experiences to those in School A and School B. They indicated that they were committed to their professional development. For example, Miss Li encouraged herself to attend 'the excellent reading competition.' During the period of preparation, she learnt how to present to the class and discuss lesson plans with other teachers. Miss Li stated that it was necessary for her and other teachers to continue to engage in professional development activities citing that 'Rome was not built in a day. What I need to do is much more practice.' This echoes the idea discussed earlier which emphasises the importance of constant engagement in professional development activities.

5.6.2   Setting personal professional development goals

All the teachers agreed that setting personal professional development goals was a useful way to improve their teaching. To illustrate this, Mr Chen in School A pointed out that setting a goal was important for a teacher to develop professionally. It is hard for a teacher to develop speaking and listening capacity without setting goals regarding the development of these skills. In particular, for teachers who have been teaching for many years and who focus only on preparing students to pass examinations, it is important to realise and set professional development goals aimed at developing speaking skills. Mrs Zhu in School B indicated that, 'setting goals is very helpful in our teaching. Without clearly defined professional development goals, it is easy to lose or forget our target and stay in the same place without going further.' In addition, Mrs Lu in School A emphasised the importance of setting goals, highlighting that, 'setting a goal has an important impact on our teaching. However, how to carry out and reach the goal is another separate challenge.'

There are various reasons why teachers need to set personal professional development goals. For example, Miss Zou in School C mentioned that some teachers felt that they lacked classroom experience and found it hard to build harmonious relationships with students. This frustration might lead them to be exhausted and discourage them from teaching. Setting a personal professional development goal might help such teachers to understand that the frustrations and complications of teaching are not unquenchable problems. Setting achievable goals can also help keep teachers fresh and motivate them to improve their practice. Miss Li echoed the above views, adding that 'a good teacher always sets goals for themselves and work to achieve those goals.'

5.6.3   Teachers' willingness to manage constraints

One key aspect explored in my study was the teachers' willingness to manage constraints in the teaching and learning of English language. There was a consensus that the development of teaching requires teachers to be willing to improve themselves; otherwise, they cannot persist in what they want under the high pressure of the systemic constraints. Vieira (2003: 219) explains teacher autonomy as the willingness and ability to manage constraints within a vision of education as liberation and empowerment. The key issue is to emphasise teachers' development of autonomy as learners. It is important for teachers to find out who they are in relation to others, how they teach, how their ideas and skills change over time, and why they think, act, learn and interact as they do. If teachers lack willingness to engage in in-service training, it will be hard for them to develop professionally. My study indicated that teachers participated in in-service training activities but did not explore whether teachers were engaging in these activities willingly or as a matter of compliance. However, the crucial factor is the teacher's willingness to recognise the need for change and to try new teaching approaches. For example, at the moment, the main focus in School C is to increase the teachers' willingness to adopt the guidance case study approach in their teaching. Arguably, if teachers are not willing to adopt this teaching method, it is hard to perceive the benefits of the approach no matter how beneficial it is. However, teachers in this particular school might be resisting the prescription of teaching methods that they do not consider to be important in their work. Teacher autonomy is about being able to make choices at personal level that help to improve or enhance one's practice though informed by reflection and evidence. Therefore it is necessary to encourage teachers to participate in activities aimed at developing themselves. Interview data demonstrated that teachers were willing to be involved in professional development activities. For example, all the teachers in School C expressed their positive attitude towards self-awareness. The views of all the teachers were well articulated by Miss Fang who stated that teachers should exercise self-awareness and set personal professional development goals, adding that teaching could become a passive job for teachers unwilling to undertake personal development. Teachers felt that the development of teaching skills depended very much on self-awareness. To Miss Fang, self-management is about setting and working towards teaching goals with reflective self-awareness. Similarly, the rest of the teachers in my study were keen on becoming effective teachers and the onus was on them to pursue higher goals of teaching. The teachers encourage themselves to focus on self-improvement and to build up a unique personal teaching identity.

5.6.4   Being responsible

One of the key aspects of an autonomous teacher is the capacity to take responsibility for the practice of teaching. This means taking care of students and ensuring that students develop comprehensively. As Farrell (2010) states that all teachers must fulfill a wide range of roles and responsibilities which include motivating students to learn and keeping their lessons interesting. Teachers in my study agreed that being a responsible teacher was very important in the teaching and learning of English language. The work of English language teachers is not only to teach language but also to develop learners as individuals. The teachers understood that their role was not only to prepare students to pass examinations but to contribute to their overall development to succeed in life. To substantiate this, Mrs Lu in School A said that 'a responsible teacher is a self-motivated, self-developed and self-managed person.' Furthermore, she added that if a teacher was responsible, they would respect students and encourage them to improve their learning approaches and not just criticise them. In addition, Mrs Cao in School A pointed out that, 'teaching is not an easy job, thus it takes time to set one's mind on teaching. A teacher needs to think about the best way to present knowledge and to prepare students for life.' A responsible teacher does not simply accept, without critically reviewing what curriculum specialists give them (Raya et al., 2007). They think about whether they agree or disagree with what is suggested. Another teacher, Mr Chen from school, highlighted that teachers should take respon-sibility for the education offering to students. Teaching is a lifelong job, a teacher is like a 'farmer' and a student is like a 'plant.' Mr Chen also emphasised the amount of time that students spend in school. Teachers need to help students to build up good learning habits and to consider students' lifelong development in addition to their academic achievement.

I also noted that teachers in the other two schools were positive about the need to be responsible. For example, in School B, Mrs Zhou highlighted that she considered teaching responsibility to be an important virtue. She was very clear that students' communicative competence was more important than examination skills, as well as speaking competence. As can be gleaned from the above, the teacher was very con-cerned about students' speaking ability, a skill going beyond passing examinations. Similarly, Mrs Zhu pointed out that responsibility had great influence on students' development. She considered it unhealthy for many students to get high scores in examinations but be short of communicative skills, which were relevant in life. As a teacher, she tries not to give students knowledge only, but also transmits a 'human' concept to them. She cares very much for students' physical and psychological development. Furthermore, teachers in School C held a view that teaching was a conscious work and responsibility to a teacher was very important. For example, Miss Li believed that learning and teaching English was not only for examination or excellent teaching achievement, but also for students' further development, citing that, 'it is significant to help students to build a solid foundation for them to learn English language at higher levels in future.' It was encouraging to note that all teachers in the three schools were clear about the need to contribute not only to students' success in examinations but to students' overall development.

5.7   A summary of data about the three schools

The three schools in my study presented some similarities as well as differences in the way they organised and implemented the teaching and learning of English language. Table 4 is a summary the main features of each participating school.

As can be seen from Table 4, the three schools in the study presented a diversity of features including differences in the experience of teaching staff in English classrooms, with School C having teachers with the least experience. One notable similarity is the class size here being of between 40 and 50 students. This confirms Evans's (1996) comment that Chinese schools have larger class sizes compared to western schools and constitutes a constraint in the teaching of English language. It is worth noting that each school has put in place some strategies and initiatives to enhance the teaching and learning of English language and this is contrary to the observations made by Pierson (1996) who comments that Chinese schools are passive and lack in initiative. Compared with public schools, School A places more emphasis on the teaching and learning of English language. Although each school provides a standard lesson structure, it can be seen that there is scope for teacher autonomy given that each teacher can select their own learning activities in each lesson. As shown by the interview data, there is variation in the amount of activities that each teacher gives students in the development of the different language skills in the classroom. Each

Table 4　A summary of the main features of each participating school

School	A	B	C
Type of school	private school; established in 1995; comprehensive school	public school; established in 1954; comprehensive school	public school; established in 2000; comprehensive school
Average class size	40–50 students/class	40–50 students/class	40–50 students/class
Teacher experience	all three teachers had more than 10 years of teaching experience ranged from 12 to 22 years	teacher experience ranged from 15 to 20 years	work experience for the three teachers ranged from less than 1 to 5 years
Teaching methods	CLT; traditional grammatical approach	task-based learning	guidance case study
Preparing and design of lessons	standard lesson structure used; planning done collaboratively; individual input valid	standard lesson structure; collaborative planning including individual input	standard lesson structure; collaborative planning including individual input
Teaching & learning materials	core textbook: *Go for It* & teachers' own created resources	core textbook: *Go for It* & teachers' own created resources	core textbook: *Go for It* & teachers' own created resources
Teacher professional development opportunities	lesson observations; seminars; training programmes including public lessons organised by the school; travelling to native English speaking countries	visit to other schools (centres of good practice) to learn and share experiences in teaching and learning of English language	cross school lesson presentation; teachers engage in competitions at school and out of school level; attendance at conferences; travels to native English speaking countries
Focus of teaching	whole school curriculum offered (all subjects) but with emphasis on the teaching of English language	whole school curriculum offered (all subjects taught)	whole school curriculum offered (all subjects taught)
Other distinctive features	more emphasis on English activities, e.g. English saloons, English speech contests and Cambridge English lessons	students given more tasks to do in English classrooms compared to the other two schools; use of authentic learning materials, e.g. newspapers & students bring materials of their choice, e.g. videos and songs	placing emphasis on the teaching of speaking and grammar skills

school is providing opportunities for professional development, which is an important incentive for teachers to engage in their own development. Teachers are challenged to identify their needs and pursue relevant training needs which can make them more autonomous in the teaching and learning of the English language. The following section provides a summary of the discussions in this chapter.

5.8 Summary

This chapter discusses a number of key findings that emerged from the study. Each research question has been discussed under the themes and sub-themes that emerged from the analysis of findings. The first research question focuses on teachers' perspectives on the content of the ELT curriculum. The main finding is that teachers in all participating schools think of the course book as the content of the ELT curriculum. In general, the teachers are satisfied with the new course book *Go for It*, citing that the book is comprehensive with activities to develop students' speaking, writing, listening and reading skills. The role of examinations is evident in teachers' thinking about the design of lessons and selection of learning activities and teaching methods. The teaching of English language in the schools is very much examination-oriented. With regards to the design of the ELT curriculum, teachers make use of collaborative approach to lesson planning and at the same time individual teachers can select activities for their own lessons depending on the needs of the students. The chapter discusses the various teaching methods/approaches used by teachers. In addition, teachers share ideas about ways of improving the teaching and learning of English language and the opportunities made available in schools for teachers' professional development. Last but not least, the chapter has discussed the teachers' perspectives on the role of SDPD in the teaching of English language. Each theme has been discussed in light of the data and the existing literature, making explicit the sub-themes that emerged in the analysis of data.

The next chapter will present the conclusion and recommendations emerging from my study.

CHAPTER 6

Conclusion and Recommendations

6.1   Introduction

This chapter provides a summary of the important findings I drew from my study. An effort is made to highlight how the findings from my study contribute to the existing body of knowledge in English language learning. In addition, I will highlight the limitations of the study as well as the implications of the research findings. Furthermore, I will discuss some recommendations for further research. The key issues from the study are framed in terms of areas corresponding to the main research questions. The study sought to generate answers to the research questions highlighted below:

- What are the teachers' perspectives on the content of the ELT curriculum?
- What are the teachers' perspectives regarding how they design and teach the ELT curriculum?
- What are the teachers' perspectives on the key problems being faced in the teaching and learning of English language in schools?
- From the teachers' perspectives, what can be done to ensure effective teaching of the English language in schools?
- What opportunities exist for teachers to develop professionally in schools?
- From the teachers' perspectives, what role does SDPD play in the learning and teaching of the English language?

6.2   The content of the ELT curriculum

My study found out that the English language teachers were contented with the content of the ELT curriculum, that is, the ELT textbook, addressed the core issues in their students' learning experience of the English language. Teachers felt that the content of the curriculum enabled students to improve overall competence in listening, speaking, reading and writing. Comparing the current course book with the previous one, there was a feeling that the current book was better as it contained more activities for students. For instance, teachers felt that the course book had more listening activities compared to the previous one. Furthermore, the language included in the content was presented in contexts which relate to students' daily lives. The book contains many pictures and topics that students can understand and help them to develop relevant language skills. All teachers in my research indicated that the new course book helped them to teach their course effectively and agreed that students' learning skills had improved after using the course book. Negative views about the current course book focused on the following issues:

1. Complicated vocabulary used in the books;

2. The complexity of the listening activities not always matching the students' level of study;

3. The organisation of the contents not in a logical sequence.

Most of the teachers, eight out of nine, complained that the current course book contained many difficult words for the students. While it could be appreciated that students had an opportunity to expand their vocabulary, teachers felt that it was too much hard work for the students to learn all the complex words over a short period of time. In some cases, the teachers indicated that they also found that some of the words used in the book were not familiar to the teachers themselves. The other problem cited by teachers was the mismatch between the complexity of the learning activities and students' level of study. For example, it was observed that in some cases the listening activities for level 2 students were easier than those for level 1 students. Teachers indicated that the speed of listening activities was faster for level 1 students compared to those for level 2 students, which defied the logical sequence of progression in students' learning. There was also a feeling that the way the activities were organised could be improved. Significant for me also was the meaning of the ELT curriculum content to the teachers in my study. Although in some cases teachers made use of their own created resources, when asked to comment on the ELT curriculum content, all the teachers thought about the content of the ELT curriculum in terms of the course book only. I felt that this was a rather limited way of thinking about the ELT curriculum; however, in practice, they actually made use of other sources to supplement the content from the textbook.

6.3　The design and implementation of the lesson plan

My study has found that the way teachers design and deliver the lesson plan is very important in the learning and teaching of English language. In general, teachers plan their lessons both collaboratively and individually. Each school identified a convenient time for the teachers to come together to plan the lessons and after that, individual teachers selected relevant activities for their specific classes. For instance, in School C, they actually set aside a whole day for designing the lesson structures. This approach is useful given that it facilitates exchange of ideas between experienced teachers and new teachers. In a way, this is an excellent continuous professional development opportunity. It is evident that experienced and new teachers have different views on how to design and deliver a lesson plan. The experienced teachers prefer to use their own plan which is based on their teaching experience while new teachers tend to rely more on the general guidance provided by the school as they struggle to know the key points that students should learn, particularly in order to pass examinations. However, whether being experienced or not, teachers unanimously agreed that lesson plans should be purposeful and deliberate to facilitate students' learning. Teachers felt that an effective lesson plan might take time, diligence and need an understanding of the characteristics of the students. Teachers need to select activities according to students' knowledge and learning characteristics. In designing the lesson plans, teachers aim to motivate students to learn as much as they can by carefully selecting topics that are both relevant and interesting to students.

The study has established that each teacher selects learning resources that appeal to students to keep the lesson interesting and easy to understand. For example, teachers used some famous characters as illustrations in their class. The use of characters like Jackie Chan and Harry Potter enlivened the atmosphere in the classrooms. As discussed in Chapter 5, I observed that students found this kind of activity very interesting and they engaged very well throughout the lesson. In addition, my study showed that the selection of activities in the design of lesson plans was heavily influenced by the structure of the examination. Teachers have to ensure that they focus on activities which develop students' skills that are tested in the examination.

In terms of the way teachers taught their lessons, group work activities might be a popular one. Lesson observations showed that students were engaged in their learning working either in pairs or in small groups of up to five students in class. Due to the large class sizes, teachers agreed that group work gave learners more opportunities to use the language for themselves. The aim of group work is to offer students more opportunities for language development and thus enhancing their fluency and effectiveness in communication (Liao, 2004). It has been argued that group work and pair work increase peer interaction and collaboration and foster collaborative autonomy where learners exercise a high level of control over their learning (Little, 2001). The peers can provide valuable sources of scaffolding help and feedback to support language learning, which means that teachers are no longer being the sole preserve of knowledge or 'expert' speakers of the target language, particularly in contexts where learners are able to work more autonomously (Legenhausen, 2001).

The use of group work still has its problems. Teachers indicated that it was a challenging task to use group work with Chinese learners because they had been continuously exposed to teacher-dominated classrooms. In addition, there was a difficult point in that some students use Chinese instead of English in group work in order to understand and express ideas clearly and complete tasks quickly, adding another layer of difficulty to teachers' efforts to develop students' English speaking skills.

My study found that teachers made use of students' classroom feedback. Reflection on student feedback helps teachers to identify areas of difficulty that need emphasis in teaching as well as what they need to reinforce in students' practice. If teachers find students are stuck, they will change the content or slow down the teaching speed to give more instructions and explanations concerning the particular point. Understandably, there should be mutual communication between students and teachers. It can be argued that every teacher should be able to use student feedback in the classroom. Teachers in my study indicated that both students and teachers benefitted from feedback as they could use it to improve their learning and teaching respectively.

My study highlighted that there were various approaches being used in the schools to teach the English language. As discussed in Chapter 5, each school used a different teaching approach. In some cases, teachers in the same school used different approaches. For example, two teachers in School A were using the CLT approach in their classes and the other teacher chose the traditional grammar teaching approach. CLT is celebrated for enabling students to have more opportunities to speak English rather than concentrating on grammar. However, the approach presents a challenge to teachers, especially when working with classes of large size where it is difficult to keep track of what each student is doing. The traditional grammar teaching approach places emphasis on the teaching of grammar and is considered to be more aligned to the examinations. Nevertheless, students found it boring to spend most of time just working on different grammar activities. It is important to strike a balance as to how to apply these two approaches. There is an overlap between the different teaching approaches and I think it will be helpful if teachers can take advantage of the strengths of each method in their classrooms. Teachers in School B were using the TBLT approach in their classes. This approach consists of giving students multiple tasks during the lesson. The tasks are taken from the course book and include individual as well as group work. From my observations, students were quite positive with the approach.

Unlike teachers in School A and School B, teachers from School C used an approach called 'guidance case study.' As highlighted in Chapter 5, this approach was relatively new as it had not been discussed in literature. Teachers felt that one of the advantages of this approach was that it allowed advanced students to help the less advanced students with their studies and it fostered a lot of collaborative learning outside and inside the classroom. The guidance case study approach is a radical shift from a teacher-centred to a learner-centred approach in the learning and teaching of English language. The approach makes the language learning process more trans-parent to learners, and thus enables students to improve their capacity for reflection and self-management, and helps them to increase their responsibility gradually, fostering interest in their own learning. There were mixed feelings about the use of the approach. A minority of teachers who were positive commented that a good guidance case design might save students' time. It could clarify students' homework given that the teacher provides clear guidelines and instructions for students to follow. However, most of the teachers who were negative about the approach cited that it created more pressure and extra work for both students and teachers. They found that designing learning activities was time consuming given that the teacher had to provide detailed guidelines and instructions. Furthermore, class activities were also time consuming and teachers felt that the approach was not convenient for their students who did not have a high comprehensive aptitude in English language. Like any new approach, for the guidance case study approach to take root in schools there should be a need to provide opportunities for professional development. I noticed that effort was being made by schools to promote the use of the approach. For example, School C conducted many public class observations where the guidance case study approach was used. In addition, the school organised a seminar with a group of English language teachers so that they could discuss and develop an experiential understanding of the guidance case study approach.

My study revealed that teachers enjoyed autonomy in their teaching to some extent. For instance, they are able to design the lesson plan and arrange classroom activities by themselves; however, what they do has to be under the guidelines of national syllabuses. One of the constraints cited by teachers is that most of the activities are only allowed to be done in the classrooms. School authorities do not allow teachers to conduct outdoor activities whenever they want. Yet, teachers expressed that at times they preferred to teach some of their lessons outside of class-room settings. Many authors agreed that schools should give teachers the freedom to select materials and ideas from outside the course and give teachers more freedom and authority to select their teaching objectives and classroom activities (Lamb, 1998; Lamb and Simpson, 2003). Understandably, this will help teachers to facilitate the teaching and learning package successfully.

6.4 The challenges and problems being faced in the delivery of the ELT curriculum in schools

Teachers from all schools involved in the study indicated several improvements in the learning and teaching of English language in schools including the use of a new course book, the new structure of the examination and the emphasis on development of communication skills. In line with the changes in the examination where, for instance, listening scores increased from 20 to 25, the course book now contains more listening activities.

The delivery of the ELT curriculum is facing some problems. Firstly, teachers have expressed that examinations are the most important factor in the teaching and learning of English. As identified in a number of studies, teachers feel that their decisions are often impacted by the national examinations (Deci and Ryan, 2002). Some teachers feel that they are not obliged to place an emphasis on the teaching of speaking skills because they are not examined.

Secondly, regarding the course book, teachers have appreciated the many activities for students. As discussed earlier in this chapter, some of the teachers complained that the activities were not structured in a logical sequence. They felt that the book contained too much unnecessary vocabulary that might confuse students. In addition, there is a mismatch between the focus of the course book and the examination. The course book aims to improve the learner's speaking and listening ability while the examination focuses on grammar and vocabulary. Teachers expressed concern about how to find a good balance between teaching students to pass the examination with a good score while at the same time, maintaining high levels of motivation during class activities.

Thirdly, my study has found that from the teachers' perspectives the examination is the main factor that motivates students to work hard in the learning of English language at the secondary school. Studies have shown that this examination-oriented system develops passive, unmotivated learners whose primary interest is only in passing the examinations (Alderson and Wall, 1993; Vernon, 1956). As argued by Zhou et al. (2009) there has been a feeling that 'students learn not because they want to, but because they feel they should.' Teachers in my study expressed that it was important for students to be intrinsically motivated to learn the English language effectively. The teachers' views are supported by Zhou et al. (2009) who maintain that autonomous motivation is an important factor in learning English language citing that autonomous motivation leads to higher levels of interest, perceived competence and perceived choice.

Finally, my study has shown that large class size and working with students of mixed abilities are areas of concern for the teachers in the schools. There has been an overwhelming consensus that when teaching English language small class sizes are more effective than large class sizes. Teachers indicated that it was easier for them to give effective support to students when working with small groups than large ones. In addition, some teachers indicated that they were having difficulties in working with students at different levels in the same class. It is hard to design a lesson for students at different levels of proficiency in the language. Teachers felt that the school should consider establishing a multi-level English teaching strategy, placing students in different groups based on their attainment levels. Alternatively, teachers were suggesting the use of differentiated tasks or activities when working with students of mixed abilities. The idea of categorising students can be problematic especially if one considers principles of inclusive practice in education; however, this can be of great help if done in the spirit of recognising and supporting each student's individual needs.

6.5 What teachers can do to ensure the effective learning and teaching of the English language

My study indicated a number of strategies and procedures that teachers felt they should apply in the learning and teaching of English language. Regarding the designing of the lesson plan, teachers felt that schools should promote both collaborative and individual ways of working among teachers. Furthermore, teachers expressed their desire to have more freedom regarding the way they might teach the subject; for example, the freedom to carry out practical dialogues outside classrooms or to show students some movies, which would improve their interest in learning the subject. This view is supported by Willis and Willis (2007) who state that real-world activities give opportunities to learners to engage in developing meanings.

In addition, teachers considered reflective practice as one of the effective ways of improving the learning and teaching of English language. Many studies support the idea that teachers learn from experience through reflection (Richards and Lockhart, 1994; Schon, 1983).

Furthermore, teachers reflected on the importance of building a good relationship with students, citing that this was important for effective learning and teaching of English language. This seems to be in consonance with an old Chinese adage which states that 'if students are close to the teacher, they would love the teacher's lesson.'

194

6.6   The existing opportunities for teachers to develop professionally in schools

A number of opportunities for teachers to develop themselves in the teaching of English language exist in the schools, including opportunities for lesson observations, attending seminars and other specific in-service training programmes. My study showed that teachers understood the importance of engaging in continuous professional development to improve their practice. Trebbi (2008) suggests that provision of in-service education opportunities can change teachers' views of teaching and learning. It is helpful for teachers to have a platform to share their teaching experience and expertise and to offer opportunities for them to learn from each other.

6.7   The role of SDPD in the learning and teaching of English language

My study provided more evidence reflected in teachers' views about the role of SDPD on the effective learning and teaching of English language.

Firstly, self-engagement is very important for teachers' professional development, that is, whether they are intrinsically motivated to participate in further training or not. This is because without engagement or genuine interest, there can be no focus on meaning or outcome. Teachers in my study demonstrated that they were taking initiatives to engage in professional development activities. For example, teachers encouraged themselves to attend seminars within and outside their schools, they participated in competitions aimed at enhancing their teaching skills, and where possible they visited other countries to expand their knowledge and teaching skills. It is important to note that in each case the teachers are making personal decisions to participate in these professional development opportunities. Teachers have to pursue a clearly defined outcome, as well as engagement in further training, that is, on the job training. As Bailey (1992) says, a sense of ownership of ideas and innovations in teacher development programmes is a prerequisite for change to take effect. In this way, it is assumed that teachers feel they are not only a part of innovation, but innovation is part of them (Bailey, 1992). It is important for teachers to take owner-ship of their development rather than being compelled by authorities in the school.

Secondly, all the teachers agreed that setting personal professional development goals was a useful way to improve their teaching. This practice could help each teacher to be honest with themselves and to identify their strengths and weaknesses. The importance of setting personal goals was clearly articulated by one of the teachers who stated that 'a good teacher must always improve by setting goals for themselves and work towards achieving those goals' (Miss Li). This suggests, for example, that it can be difficult for a teacher to develop speaking and listening skills without setting goals regarding the development of these specific skills.

Finally, the need for teachers to take responsibility and be willing to develop themselves has been reflected in my study. Teaching requires teachers to be willing to improve themselves; otherwise, they cannot persist in what they want under the high pressure of the systemic constraints. All teachers in my study agreed that being a responsible teacher was very important in the teaching and learning of English language. The teachers understood that their role was not only to prepare students to pass examinations but also to contribute to their overall development to succeed in life.

6.8   Contributions made by my study

It is necessary to see China as a country in the process of progressing when it comes to the teaching and learning of English language. Before I started my research, I thought that English teachers in China still focused on grammar and examinations. However, after the interviews and lesson observations, I found that the situation had undergone some significant changes. Most of the teachers expressed the desire to help students improve their communication skills. They realised learning language was for communication and not only for passing examinations. All the language test and training should be undertaken with the goal of helping students to develop com- munication skills. Therefore, they tried to apply more materials, thinking carefully on their lesson plan and adopting new teaching approaches. This has been done with a view to creating more opportunities for students to speak. I am glad to see this change, and I think the world also needs to know the current situation of teaching and learning of English in China. The schools also provide some opportunities for teachers to further develop their professional skills through various initiatives such as going to English speaking countries to study, having open classes, organising the teachers' discussion groups and teaching competitions. Most of the teachers are actually willing to attend all these different kinds of activities and it is important to create more opportunities for change to help them to improve themselves. I believe if more teachers have this ideology and pursue the improvement of English language speaking ability, in the near future, English language learning will experience a massive change in China.

In addition, as argued in Chapter 2, although considerable research has been conducted in the field of ELT in China, most of the studies sought to identify the existing problems rather than to describe and explore the situation through accessing the voices of teachers in their working contexts. My study engages teachers in sharing their experiences regarding different aspects of English language learning. In addition, the study findings are contextually rooted. This is a valuable addition to literature on the teaching and learning of English language in Chinese secondary schools. It is difficult to find literature that discusses about the perspectives of Chinese teachers on various aspects of English language teaching and learning; hence, this study can make a significant contribution. The concept of teacher autonomy which has been addressed in this research is also a relatively new concept, so researchers in this field might find it an interesting and useful addition to the field. There exist conflicting views on the role of teacher autonomy in language learning, but this study helps to confirm the case for teacher autonomy, as the findings help demonstrate its significance in improving the quality of students' learning experience as well as teachers' own professional development. In a nutshell, the work of English language teachers is not only to teach English but also to develop learners as individuals. My study findings reinforce the view that if teachers are to help learners to be successful individuals, it is imperative that they should also be independent learners (Little, 2007; Chan, 2003).

In particular, the study has involved working with teachers from two public schools and one private school. The study findings show the factors affecting the teaching and learning of English language, including the role played by teachers in enhancing student learning experience of the English language. Through my study, it has been possible to gain important insights into the needs of English language teachers working in both public and private schools. The study provides important insights into the kind of support that schools should provide to enable teachers to perform their duties effectively. Some of the key contributions from my study are listed below:

- Providing new knowledge of the current ELT in China (the changes of teachers' ideology and their effect to improve students' communication skills).
- Showing teacher autonomy is important to ensure the development of learner autonomy.
- Indicating examinations, among other factors, can be a constraint in the development of both teacher and learner autonomy.
- Illuminating teacher willingness to engage in professional development is key to the development of teacher autonomy.
- Providing an opportunity to hear the voice of teachers. Teachers are struggling with examinations (outward pressure) and the communication skills (inward desire).
- Helping schools to understand the importance of teacher development. Schools will create more opportunities and activities for teachers to improve their ability and willingness.

Although some of the findings from my study are not necessarily new, they do confirm the existing literature, for instance, the impact of examinations on the teachers' ability to foster learner autonomy. Arguably, the findings form an important addition to the existing body of knowledge in the area of second language learning as well as in the areas of teacher autonomy and learner autonomy. Based on my study, researchers in the field can design and conduct more studies on scale within the Chinese context. In addition, researchers can find the findings from my study useful for comparative studies in ELT.

6.9 Limitations

This study is a multiple case study, which focuses on providing thick descriptions of how English language is being taught in three Chinese secondary schools. As a result, it is not possible to make any wider generalisations about the teaching and learning of English in all Chinese schools. Due to limited time and other resources, the study has been limited to three schools and only nine teachers in total involved. Understandably, the findings cannot represent the current situation regarding the learning and teaching of English language in the whole China. However, the findings provide useful insights into the learning and teaching of English in schools. In addition, this study reflects the views of teachers only, for it being impossible for me to engage students as this would require more time and resources. Teachers have been notified in advance about lesson observations so it is possible that they prepared special lesson for my visits. My presence might have influenced the way teachers behaved in the classroom. During data collection, I have to use Chinese language (Mandarin), which must be translated to English. It is possible that some meaning might have been lost in translation.

6.10   Implications of the study findings

In this section I will consider ways in which the findings from my study can impact on the work of different stakeholders including English language teachers, school authorities and researchers in the field of English language teaching and learning. My study focuses on a very important topic in the field of second language teaching and learning. The study challenges assumptions about teaching and learning of English language in China. It looks at the way for English language being taught not only in public schools but also in a private school setting which helps to bring to light issues being faced in the sector. It gives opportunities to teachers to talk freely and share their experiences of teaching English language. The findings of my study have potential to make contributions to different stakeholders as well as to further research in the same field as discussed below.

6.10.1   Implications of study findings to English language teachers
It is my hope that my analysis and interpretation of findings from the study could inspire English language teachers in schools in China to reflect upon their teaching and be encouraged to improve their practice. One of the key ways of improving practice is by engaging in continuous in-service professional development activities.

6.10.2   Implications for school authorities
It is possible that findings from my study can be useful to school authorities. My study has shown that teachers have the desire to have more freedom and authority in

the arrangement of class activities. In addition, the study has indicated the importance and the need for teachers to engage in continuous professional development. On the basis of these findings, school authorities can identify areas for future investments aimed at increasing more opportunities for teachers to develop professionally.

6.10.3 Implications for further research

As highlighted earlier on, findings from my study cannot be generalised to other schools not involved in the study. This makes it necessary for future research in the same area to be broadened, that is, to be conducted on a large scale to allow for generalisation of findings. One area worth exploring is the views of students, which have not been reflected in this study.

6.11 Final note

Conducting this study has been a massive learning curve for me as an emerging researcher in the field of English language learning and learner autonomy as well as teacher autonomy. The study offers me an opportunity to develop relevant research skills, which can be further developed as I continue to engage in more research activities.

The study was conducted using a systematic approach and an effort was made to ensure that the research process was underpinned by a sound theoretical framework. For instance, this was a qualitative study and, as can be appreciated, all the procedures were informed by qualitative research paradigmatic assumptions. My background was disclosed in Chapter 1 to help the readers to be aware of any potential biases in the study. For example, the bias of this is a study conducted in China by a Chinese student. I must say that, in the whole process, I maintained a professional stance as a researcher and avoided allowing my personal beliefs, values and perceptions to influence the research process. Every effort was made to ensure that the data generated in the study was credible and helpful in terms of responding to the main research questions.

The study discussed the teachers' perspectives on a number of issues related to the teaching and learning of English language. Perhaps it can be argued that the study could have been more comprehensive if it had included students' voice. This remains a possibility and can be a good starting point for further research.

In its current shape, the study has explored the teaching and learning of English language and has helped to bring out the teachers' perspectives on the content of the ELT curriculum, the design of the curriculum and the way to teach it, among other things as discussed earlier. Important key concepts have been addressed in my study including learner autonomy and teacher autonomy. There are a lot of debate and discussion regarding the role of teacher autonomy and learner autonomy in language learning. As indicated earlier, the findings of my study have added something new to the existing body of knowledge.

REFERENCES

Alderson, J., and Wall, D. Does wash back exists?. *Applied Linguistics Journal*, 1993, 14(2): 115-129.

Anderson, G., and Arsenault, N. *Fundamentals of Educational Research*. London: Falmer Press, 1998.

Anderson, J. Is a communicative approach practical for teaching English in China, pros and cons. *System*, 1993, 21(4): 471-480.

Aoki, N. Aspects of teacher autonomy: Capacity, freedom and responsibility. Hong Kong University of Science and Technology Language Centre Conference, 2000.

Arndt, V., Harvey, P., and Nuttall, J. *Alive to Language: Perspectives on Language Awareness for English Language Teachers*. Cambridge: Cambridge University Press, 2000.

Babbie, E. *Paradigms, Theory and Social Research in the Practice of Social Research*. 11th ed. Belmont, CA: Thomson Wadsworth, 2007.

Bailey, K. M. The processes of innovation in language teacher development: What, why and how teachers change. In J. Flowerdew, M. Brock, and S. Hsia (eds.). *Perspectives on Second Language Teacher Education*. Hong Kong: City University of Hong Kong, 1992: 253-282.

---. Reflective teaching: Situating our stories. *Asian Journal of English Language Teaching*, 1997, 7(1): 1-19.

Bartlett, L. Teacher development through reflective teaching. In J. C. Richards and D. Nunan (eds.). *Second Language Teacher Education*. Cambridge: Cambridge University Press, 1997: 202-214.

Bax, S. The end of CLT: A context approach to language teaching. *ELT Journal*, 2003, 57(3): 278-287.

Bell, J. *Doing Your Research Project: A Guide for First-time Researchers in Education and Social Science*. 3rd ed. Buckingham: Open University Press, 1999.

---. *Doing Your Research Project: A Guide for First-time Researchers in Education and*

Social Science. 4th ed. Buckingham: Open University Press, 2005.

Benson, P. *Teaching and Researching Autonomy in Language Learning*. London: Longman, 2001.

Biggs, J. B. Western misperceptions of the Confucian-heritage learning culture. In D. A. Watkins and J. B. Biggs (eds.). *The Chinese Learner: Cultural, Psychological, and Contextual Influences*. Hong Kong: Comparative Education Research Center; Melbourne: Australian Council for Educational Research, 1996: 45-68.

Billing, D. E. The nature and scope of staff development in institutions of higher education. In L. Elton and K. Simmonds (eds.). *Staff Development in Higher Education*. Guildford, Surrey: Society for Research into Higher Education, 1977.

Black, A. E., and Deci, E. L. The effects of instructors' autonomy support and students' autonomous motivation on learning organic chemistry: A self-determination theory perspective. *Science Education*, 2000, 84(6): 740-756.

Black, J., and Butzkamm, W. Classroom language: Materials for communicative language teaching. *ELT Journal*, 1978, 32(4): 270-274.

Borko, H., Elliot, R., and Uchiyama, K. Professional development: A key to Kentucky's educational reform effort. *Teaching and Teacher Education*, 2002, 18(8): 969-987.

Brandt, C. Integrating feedback and reflection in teacher preparation. *ELT Journal*, 2008, 62(1): 37-46.

Braun, J. A., and Crumpler, T. P. The social memoir: An analysis of developing reflective ability in a pre-service methods course. *Teaching and Teacher Education*, 2004, 20(1): 59-75.

Braun, V., and Clarke, V. Using thematic analysis in psychology. *Qualitative Research in Psychology*, 2006, 3(2): 72-101.

Breen, M., and Candlin, C. The essentials of a communicative curriculum in language teaching. *Applied Linguistics*, 1980, 1(2): 89-112.

Brown, H. D. *Teaching by Principles: An Interactive Approach to Language Pedagogy*. Englewood Cliffs, NJ: Prentice Hall, 1994.

Bryman, A. *Social Research Methods*. 2nd ed. Oxford: Oxford University Press, 2004.

Bullough, R. V. The writing of teachers' lives: Where personal troubles and social issues meet. *Teacher Education Quarterly*, 2008: 35(4), 7-26.

Burbank, M. D., and Kauchak, D. An alternative model for professional development: Investigations into effective collaboration. *Teaching and Teacher Education*, 2003, 19(5): 499-514.

Burgess, R. G. *In the Field: An Introduction to Field Research*. London: George Allen and Unwin, 1994.

Burnaby, B., and Sun, Y. Chinese teachers' views of western language teaching: Context informs paradigms. *TESOL Quarterly*, June 1989. https://doi.org/10.2307/3587334.

Burrell, G., and Morgan, G. *Sociological Paradigms and Organizational Analysis*. London: Heinemann, 1979.

Campbell, K., and Zhao, Y. The dilemma of English language instruction in the People's Republic of China. *TESOL Journal*, 1993, 2(4): 4-6.

Canale, M., and Swain, M. Theoretical bases communicative approaches to second language teaching and testing. *Applied Linguistics*, 1980, 1(1): 1-47.

Carey, K. The teacher autonomy paradox. *The American Prospect*, 2008-09-17. https://prospect.org/online-extras/teacher-autonomy-paradox/.

Carr, W., and Kemmis, S. *Becoming Critical: Education, Knowledge and Action Research*. London and New York: Falmer, 1986.

Carter, K. The place of story in the study of teaching and teacher education. *Educational Researcher*, 1993, 22(1): 5-12, 18.

Castle, K. Autonomy through pedagogical research. *Teaching and Teacher Education*, 2006, 22(8): 1094-1103.

Chan, V. Autonomous language learning: The teachers' perspectives. *Teaching in Higher Education*, 2003, 8(1): 33-54.

Charmaz, K. *Constructing Grounded Theory: A Practical Guide through Qualitative Analysis*. London: Sage Publications, 2006.

Cheng, L. Y. The key to success: English language testing in China. *Language Testing*, 2008, 25(1): 15-37.

Chikwa, G. An investigation into the introduction and use of new technologies in secondary science teaching. Doctoral Dissertation. Sheffield: University of Sheffield, 2012.

Chirkov, V. I., Ryan, R. M., Kim, Y., and Kaplan, U. Differentiating autonomy from individualism and independence: A self-determination theory perspective on internalization of cultural orientations and well-being. *Journal of Personality and Social Psychology*, 2003, 84(1): 97-110.

Cicourel, A. V. *Method and Measurement in Sociology*. New York: Free Press, 1964.

Clough, P., and Nutbrown, C. *A Student's Guide to Methodology: Justifying Enquiry*. London: Sage Publications, 2006.

Cohen, L., and Manion, L. *Research Methods in Education*. 4th ed. London: Routledge, 1994.

Cohen, L., Manion, L., and Morrison, K. *Research Methods in Education*. 5th ed. London: Routledge, 2000.

Coleman, H. (ed.). *Society and the Language Classroom*. Cambridge: Cambridge University Press, 1997.

Connelly, M., and Clandinin, J. Stories of experience and narrative inquiry. *Educational Researcher*, 1990, 19(5): 2-14.

Cook, V. Learners as individuals. In V. Cook. *Second Language Learning and Teaching*. New York: Arnold, 1996: 95-117.

Cotterall, S., and Crabbe, L. (eds.). *Learner Autonomy in Language Learning: Defining the Field and Effecting Change*. Frankfurt: Peter Lang, 1999.

Creswell, J. W. *Qualitative Inquiry and Research Design: Choosing among Five Approaches*. 3rd ed. Thousand Oaks: Sage Publications, 2007.

---. *Research Design: Qualitative, Quantitative, and Mixed Methods Approaches*. 3rd ed. Thousand Oaks: Sage Publications, 2009.

Crystal, D. *English as a Global Language*. Cambridge: Cambridge University Press, 2003.

Davies, A. *Language Testing Symposium: A Psycholinguistic Approach*. Oxford: Oxford University Press, 1968.

Day, C. Reflection: A necessary but not sufficient condition for teacher development. *British Educational Research Journal*, 1993, 19(1): 83-93.

Deci, E. L., and Ryan, R. M. *Intrinsic Motivation and Self-determination in Human Behaviour*. New York: Plenum Press, 1985.

---. The "what" and "why" of goal pursuits: Human needs and the self-determination of behavior. *Psychological Inquiry*, 2000, 11(4): 227-268.

---. Self-determination research: Reflections and future directions. In E. L. Deci and R. M. Ryan (eds.). *Handbook on Self-determination Research*. Rochester, NY: University of Rochester Press, 2002: 431-441.

Denscombe, M. *The Good Research Guider*. Buckingham: Open University Press, 1998.

Denzin, N. K., and Lincoln, Y. S. *Handbook of Qualitative Research*. 2nd ed. Thousand Oaks: Sage Publications, 2000.

---. Introduction: The discipline and practice of qualitative research. In N. K. Denzin and Y. S. Lincoln (eds.). *The Landscape of Qualitative Research*. Thousand Oaks: Sage Publications, 2008: 1-44.

DeVries, R., and Kohlberg, L. *Programs of Early Education*. New York: Longman, 1987.

DeVries, R., and Zan, B. *Moral Classrooms, Moral Children*. New York: Teachers College Press, 1994.

Dewey, J. *How We Think: A Restatement of the Relation of Reflective Thinking to the Education*

Process. Boston: D.C. Heath and Company, 1933.

Dickinson, L. *Self-instruction in Language Learning*. Cambridge: Cambridge University Press, 1987.

Eckstein, M. A., and Noah, H. J. *Secondary School Examinations: International Perspectives on Policies and Practice*. New Haven: Yale University Press, 1993.

Ellis, R. *Task-based Language Learning and Teaching*. Oxford: Oxford University Press, 2003.

ESRC. Developing a framework for social science research ethics. (2005-12-15)[2021-05-10]. http://www.york.ac.uk/res/ref.

Evans, S. The context of English language education: The case of Hong Kong. *RELC*, 1996, 27(2): 30-55.

Fantilli, R. D., and McDougall, D. E. A study of novice teachers: Challenges and supports in the first years. *Teaching and Teacher Education*, 2009, 25(6): 814-825.

Farrell, T. S. C. *Reflective Practice in Action: 80 Reflection Breaks for Busy Teachers*. Thousand Oaks: Sage Publications, 2003.

---. Critical incidents in ELT initial teacher training. *ELT Journal*, 2008, 62(1): 3-10.

---. *Reflecting on Teacher-student Relations in TESOL*. Oxford: Oxford University Press, 2010.

Fendler, L. Teacher reflection in a hall of mirrors: Historical influence sand political reverberations. *Educational Researcher*, 2003, 32(3): 16-25.

Feryok, A. Teaching for learner autonomy: The teachers' role and sociocultural theory. *Innovation in Language Learning and Teaching*, 2013, 7(3): 213-225.

Fishman, B. J., Marx, R. W., Best, S., and Tal, R. T. Linking teacher and student learning to improve professional development in systemic reform. *Teaching and Teacher Education*, 2003, 19(6): 643-658.

Flick, U. *Managing Quality in Qualitative Research*. London: Sage Publications, 2007.

---. *An Introduction to Qualitative Research*. 5th ed. London: Sage Publications, 2014.

Flowerdew, L. A cultural perspective on group work. *ELT Journal*, 1998, 52(4): 323-329.

Flynn, L. R., and Goldsmith, R. E. *Case Studies for Ethics in Academic Research in the Social Sciences*. London: Sage Publications, 2013.

Ford, M. E. *Motivating Humans: Goals, Emotions, and Personal Agency Belief*. Thousand Oaks: Sage Publications, 1992.

Fullan, M., and Hargreaves, A. *What's Worth Fighting for? Working Together for Your School*. Toronto: Ontario Public School Teachers Federation; Andover, MA: The Network, North East Laboratory; Buckingham: Open University Press; Melbourne: Australian Council for

Educational Administration, 1991.

Ganze, W. L. *Learner Autonomy-teacher Autonomy: Interrelating and the Will to Empower*. Amsterdam: John Benjamins, 2008.

Gardner, R. C. *Social Psychology and Second Language Learning: The Role of Attitudes and Motivation*. London: Edward Arnold, 1985.

Gay, L. R. *Educational Research: Competencies for Analysis and Application*. Columbus: Merrill Publishing, 1987.

Ginsberg, E. Not just a matter of English. *HERDSA News*, 1992, 14(1): 6-8.

Glaser, B., and Strauss, A. *The Discovery of Grounded Theory: Strategies for Qualitative Research*. New York: Aldine de Gruyter, 1967.

Goldman, A. I., and Olsson, E. J. Reliabilism and the value of knowledge. In A. Haddock, A. Millar, and D. Pritchard (eds.). *Epistemic Value*. Oxford: Oxford University Press, 2009: 19-41.

Gower, R., Phillips, D., and Walters, S. *Teaching Practice*. Oxford: Macmillan, 2005.

Graves, K. *Designing Language Courses: A Guide for Teachers*. Beijing: Foreign Language Teaching and Research Press, 2005.

Griffiths, V. The reflective dimension in teacher education. *International Journal of Educational Research*, 2000, 33(5): 539-555.

Grolnick, W. S., and Ryan, R. M. Autonomy in children's learning: An experimental and individual difference investigation. *Journal of Personality and Social Psychology*, 1987, 52(5): 890-898.

Groundwater-Smith, S. Introducing dilemmas into the practicum curriculum. The 5th National Practicum Conference, Macquarie University, Australia, May 5, 1993.

Guba, E. G. The alternative paradigm dialog. In E. G. Guba (ed.). *The Paradigm Dialog*. Thousand Oaks: Sage Publications, 1990: 17-30.

Guba, E. G., and Lincoln, Y. S. *Fourth Generation Evaluation*. Thousand Oaks: Sage Publications, 1989.

Gün, B. Quality self-reflection through reflection training. *ELT Journal*, 2011, 65(2): 126-135.

Hansen, D. T. The moral is in the practice. *Teaching and Teacher Education*, 1998, 14(6): 653-655.

Hargreaves, A. Mixed emotions: Teachers' perceptions of their interactions with students. *Teaching and Teacher Education*, 2000, 16(8): 811-826.

Hatch, J. A. *Doing Qualitative Research in Education Settings*. New York: State University of New York Press, 2002.

Hennink, M., Hutter, I., and Bailey, A. *Qualitative Research Methods*. London: Sage Publications, 2011.

Hepple, E. Questioning pedagogies: Hong Kong pre-service teachers' dialogic reflections on a transnational school experience. *Journal of Education for Teaching*, 2012, 38(3): 309-322.

Hess, R. D., and Azuma, M. Cultural support for schooling: Contrasts between Japan and the United States. *Educational Researcher*, 1991, 20(9): 2-8.

Hird, B. How communicative can English language teaching be in China?. *Prospects*, 1995, 10(3): 21-27.

Hoekstra, A., Brekelmans, M., Beijaard, D., and Korthagen, F. Experienced teachers' informal learning: Learning activities and changes in behaviour and cognition. *Teaching and Teacher Education*, 2009, 25(5): 663-673.

Hu, G. Cultural resistance to pedagogical imports: The case of communicative language teaching in China language. *Culture and Curriculum*, 2002, 15(2): 93-105.

---. English language teaching in China: Regional differences and contributing factors. *Journal of Multilingual and Multicultural Development*, 2003, 4(4): 290-318.

---. CLT is best for China: An untenable absolutist claim. *ELT Journal*, 2005, 59(1): 65-68.

Hughes, A. *Testing for Language Teachers*. Cambridge: Cambridge University Press, 1989.

Isenbarger, L., and Zembylas, M. The emotional labour of caring in teaching. *Teaching and Teacher Education*, 2006, 22(1): 120-134.

Israel, M., and Hay, I. *Research Ethics for Social Scientists*. London: Sage Publications, 2006.

Jackson, J. Reticence in second language case discussions: Anxiety and aspirations. *System* 2002, 30(1): 65-84.

James, M., and McCormick, R. Teachers learning how to learn. *Teaching and Teacher Education*, 2009, 25(7): 973-982.

Jan, W. *Ontological Categories, Their Nature and Significance*. Oxford: Clarendon Press, 2005.

Jay, J. K., and Johnson, K. L. Capturing complexity: A typology of reflective practice for teacher education. *Teaching and Teacher Education*, 2002, 18(1): 73-85.

Jin, L., and Cortazzi, M. English language teaching in China: A bridge to the future. *Asia Pacific Journal of Education*, 2002, 22(2): 53-64.

Jones, M. The guest from England: Exploring issues of positionality in a foreign and yet familiar setting. *European Societies*, 2006, 8(1): 169-187.

Jones, P. Mind in the classroom. In J. Hammond (ed.). *Scaffolding: Teaching and Learning in Language and Literacy*. Newtown, NSW: (Australia) Primary English Teaching Association, 2001: 69-90.

Jurasaite-Harbison, E., and Rex, L.A. School cultures as contexts for informal teacher learning. *Teaching and Teacher Education*, 2010, 26(2): 267-277.

Kage, M. Effects of evaluation-subject and evaluation standard on intrinsic motivation. *The Japanese Journal of Educational Psychology*, 1990, 38(4): 428-437.

King, M. B. Professional development to promote school wide inquiry. *Teaching and Teacher Education*, 2002, 18(3): 243-257.

Knight, P. A systemic approach to professional development. *Teaching and Teacher Education*, 2002, 18(3): 229-241.

Kohonen, V. Towards experiential foreign language education. In V. Kohonen, R. Jaatinen, P. Kaikkonen, and J. Lehtovaara (eds.). *Experiential Learning in Foreign Language Education*. London: Routledge, 2000: 8-60.

Kong, P. P. An analysis of the problem of how to apply the communicative language teaching approach to the teaching of English as a second language through the research of secondary schools in China. Master Dissertation. Hull: University of Hull, 2009.

Krashen, S. *The Input Hypothesis: Issues and Implications*. London: Longman, 1988.

Krashen, S., and Terrell, T. *The Natural Approach: Language Acquisition in the Classroom*. Oxford: Prentice Hall, 1983.

Lakomski, G. Unity over diversity: Coherence and realism in educational research. *Curriculum Inquiry*, 1992, 22(2): 191-203.

Lamb, T. Now you are on your own! Developing independent language learning strategies. In W. Gewehr (ed.). *Aspects of Modern Language Teaching in Europe*. London: Routledge, 1998: 30-47.

---. Finding a voice: Learner autonomy and teacher education in an urban context. In B. Sinclair, I. McGrath, and T. Lamb (eds.). *Learner Autonomy, Teacher Autonomy: Future Directions*. London: Longman, 2000: 118-127.

---. Learner autonomy in eight European countries: Opportunities and tensions in education reform and language teaching policy. In M. Raya and T. Lamb (eds.). *Pedagogy for Autonomy in Language Education: Theory, Practice and Teacher Education*. Dublin: Authentik, 2008: 36-57.

---. Controlling learning: Learners' voices and relationships between motivation and learner autonomy. In R. Pemberton, S. Toogood, A. Barfield (eds.). *Maintaining Control: Autonomy and Language Learning*. Hong Kong: Hong Kong University Press, 2009: 67-86.

Lamb, T., and Reinders, H. *Learner and Teacher Autonomy: Concepts, Realities and Responses*. Amsterdam: John Benjamins, 2008.

Lamb, T., and Simpson, M. Escaping from the treadmill: Practitioner research and professional autonomy. *Language Learning Journal*, 2003, 28(1): 55-63.

Larsen-Freeman, D., and Freeman, D. Language moves: The place of 'foreign' languages in classroom teaching and learning. *Review of Research in Education*, 2008, 32: 147-186.

Larsen-Freeman, D., and Long, H. M. *An Introduction to Second Language Acquisition Research*. London: Longman, 1991.

Lau, K. L., and Lee, J. C. K. Validation of a Chinese achievement goal orientation questionnaire. *British Journal of Educational Psychology*, 2008, 78(2): 331.

Lee, I. Preparing pre-service English teachers for reflective practice. *ELT Journal*, 2007, 61(4), 321-329.

Legenhausen, L. Discourse behaviour in an autonomous learning environment. In L. Dam (ed.). *Learner Autonomy: New Insights*. Huddersfield, West Yorkshire: AILA Review, 2001: 56-69.

Li, L. *A Study on Communicative Approach to the Teaching of English Reading*. Changchun: Jilin University Press, 2003.

Li, X. In defence of the communicative approach. *ELT Journal*, 1984, 38(9): 2-13.

Liamputtong, P., and Ezzy, D. *Qualitative Research Method*. 2nd ed. Melbourne: Oxford University Press, 2005.

Liao, X. Q. The need for communicative language teaching in China. *ELT Journal*, 2004, 58(3): 270-273.

Lim, H. W. Concept maps of Korean EFL student teachers' autobiographical reflections on their professional identity formation. *Teaching and Teacher Education*, 2011, 27(6): 969-981.

Lin, J. *Social Transformation and Private Education in China*. Westport, CT: Praeger Publishers, 1999.

Lincoln, Y. S., and Guba, E. G. *Naturalistic Inquiry*. Thousand Oaks: Sage Publications, 1985.

Little, D. Learning as dialogue: The dependence of learner autonomy on teacher autonomy. *System*, 1995, 23(2): 172-182.

---. *The European Language Portfolio and Self-assessment*. Strasbourg: Council of Europe, 1999.

---. How independent can independent language learning really be?. In J. A. Coleman, D. Fearney, D. Head, and R. Rix (eds.). *Language-learning Futures: Issues and Strategies for Modern Languages Provision in Higher Education*. London: CILT, 2001: 30-43.

---. Language learner autonomy: Some fundamental considerations revisited. *Journal of*

Innovation in Language Learning and Teaching, 2007, 1(1): 14-29.

Little, D., Hodel, H. P., Kohonen, V., Meijer, D., and Perclova, R. *Preparing Teachers to Use the European Language Portfolio-arguments, Materials and Resource*. Strasbourg: Council of Europe, 2007.

Littlewood, W. *Communicative Language Teaching an Introduction*. Cambridge: Cambridge University Press, 1981.

---. Defining and developing autonomy in East Asian contexts. *Applied Linguistics*, 1999, 20(1): 71-94.

---. Do Asian students really want to listen and obey?. *ELT Journal*, 2000, 54(1): 31-35.

---. The task-based approach: Some questions and suggestions. *ELT Journal*, 2004, 58(4): 319-326.

Liu, N. F., and Littlewood, W. Why do many students appear reluctant to participate in classroom learning discourse?. *System*, 1997, 25(3): 371-384.

Lovett, M. W., Lacerenza, L., de Palma, M., Benson, N. J., Steinbach, K. A., and Frijters, J. C. Preparing teachers to remediate reading disabilities in high school: What is needed for effective professional development?. *Teaching and Teacher Education*, 2008, 24(4): 1083-1097.

Luo, W. H. English language teaching in Chinese universities in the era of the world trade organization: A learner perspective. Doctoral Dissertation. Shanghai: Shanghai International Studies University, 2007.

Marcosa, J. M., Sancheza, E., and Tillema, H. H. Promoting teacher reflection: What is said to be done. *Journal of Education for Teaching*, 2011, 37(1): 21-36.

Markus, H. R., Kitayama, S., and Heiman, R. J. Culture and basic psychological principles. In E. T. Higgins and A. W. Kruglanski (eds.). *Social Psychology: Handbook of Basic Principles*. New York: Guilford, 1996: 857-913.

Martinez, H. *The Subjective Theories of Student Teachers: Implications for Teacher Education and Research of Learner Autonomy*. Amsterdam: John Benjamins, 2008.

May, T. *Social Research: Issues, Methods and Process*. Buckingham: Open University Press, 2001.

Mays, N., and Pope, C. Qualitative research: Observational methods in health care settings. *British Medical Journal*, 1995: 311(6998), 182-184.

McGrath, I. Teacher autonomy. In B. Sinclair, I. McGrath, and T. Lamb (eds.). *Learner Autonomy, Teacher Autonomy: Future Directions*. London: Longman, 2000: 100-110.

Mckenzie, G., Powell, J., and Usher, R. *Understanding Social Research: Perspectives on*

Methodology and Practice. London: Falmer Press, 1997.

Miliander, J. Portfolios in teacher education. In M. Raya and T. Lamb (eds.). *Pedagogy for Autonomy in Language Education: Theory, Practice and Teacher Education*. Dublin: Authentik, 2008: 143-157.

Morrison, K., and Lui, I. Ideology, linguistic capital and the medium of instruction in Hong Kong. *Journal of Multilingual and Multicultural Development*, 2000, 21(6): 471-486.

Mulhall, A. In the field: Notes on observation in qualitative research. *Journal of Advanced Nursing*, 2003, 41(3): 306-313.

Murphy, J. M. Reflective teaching in ELT. In M. Celce-Murcia (ed.). *Teaching English as a Second or Foreign Language*. Boston: Heinle and Heinle, 2001: 499-514.

Newby, P. *Research Methods for Education*. London: Longman, 2010.

Ng, C., and Tang, E. Teachers needs in the process of EFL reform in China: A report from Shanghai. *Perspectives*, 1997, 9(1): 63-85.

Nielsen, D. C., Barry, A. L., and Stab, P. T. Teachers' reflections of professional change during a literacy-reform initiative. *Teaching and Teacher Education*, 2008, 24(5): 1288-1303.

Ning, H. P. Adapting cooperative learning in tertiary ELT. *ELT Journal*, 2011, 65(1): 60-70.

Nir, A. E., and Bogler, R. The antecedents of teacher satisfaction with professional development programs. *Teaching and Teacher Education*, 2008, 24(2): 377-386.

Nunan, D. *Designing Tasks for the Communicative Classroom*. Cambridge: Cambridge University Press, 1989.

---. *Language Teaching Methodology*. London: Prentice Hall, 1991.

---. *Second Language Teaching and Learning*. Boston: Heinle and Heinle, 1999.

---. *Task-based Learning and Teaching*. Cambridge: Cambridge University Press, 2004.

---. *Go for It*. Beijing: People Education Press, 2007.

O'Connell, D., and Kowall, S. Basic principles of transcription. In J. A. Smith, R. Harré, and L. van Langenhove (eds.). *Rethinking Methods in Psychology*. London: Sage Publications, 1995: 93-104.

OECD. *Teachers Matter: Attracting, Developing and Retaining Effective Teachers*. Paris: OECD, 2005.

Oxford, R. L. *Language Strategies: What Every Teacher Should Know*. New York: Newbury House/Harper and Row, 1990.

Oxford, R. L., and Nyikos, M. Variables affecting choice of language learning strategies by university students. *The Modern Language Journal*, 1989, 73(3): 291-300.

Pierson, H. D. Learner culture and learner autonomy in the Hong Kong Chinese context. In R. Pemberton, E. Li, W. Or, and H. D. Pierson (eds.). *Taking Control: Autonomy in Language Learning*. Hong Kong: Hong Kong University Press, 1996: 48-58.

Ponte, P., Ax, J., Beijaard, D., and Wubbels, T. Teachers' development of professional knowledge through action research and the facilitation of this by teacher educators. *Teaching and Teacher Education*, 2004, 20(6): 571-588.

Posteguillo, S., and Palmer, J. C. Reflective teaching in EFL: Integrating theory and practice. *TESL-EJ*, 2000, 4(3): 1-15.

Prasad, P. *Crafting Qualitative Research: Working in the Postpositivist Traditions*. London: M. E. Sharpe, 2005.

Preus, B. Educational trends in China and the United States: Proverbial pendulum or potential for balance?. *Phi Delta Kappan*, 2007, 89(2): 115-118.

Qi, L. Is testing an efficient agent for pedagogical change? Examining the intended washback of the writing task in a high-stakes English test in China. *Assessment in Education*, 2007, 14(1): 51-74.

Rao, Z. Reconciling communicative approaches to the teaching of English with traditional Chinese methods. *Research in the Teaching of English*, 1996, 30(3): 458-471.

---. Chinese students' perceptions of communicative and non-communicative activities in EFL classroom. *System*, 2002a, 30(1): 85-10.

---. Bridging the gap between teaching and learning styles in East Asian context. *TESOL Journal*, 2002b, 11(2): 5-11.

Raya, M. Autonomy support through learning journals. In T. Lamb and H. Reinders (eds.). *Supporting Independent Learning: Issues and Interventions*. Frankfurt: Peter Lang, 2006: 123-140.

Raya, M., and Lamb, T. *Pedagogy for Autonomy in Language Education: Theory, Practice and Teacher Education*. Dublin: Authentik, 2008.

Raya, M., Lamb, T., and Vieira, F. *Pedagogy for Autonomy in Language Education in Europe: Towards a Framework for Learner and Teacher Development*. Dublin: Authentik, 2007.

Raya, M., and Vieira, F. Teacher development for learner autonomy: Images and issues from five projects. In M. Raya and T. Lamb (eds.). *Pedagogy for Autonomy in Language Education: Theory, Practice and Teacher Education*. Dublin: Authentik, 2008: 283-302.

Reeve, J. Self-determination theory applied to educational settings. In E. L. Deci and R. M. Ryan (eds.). *Handbook of Self-determination Research*. Rochester, NY: University of Rochester, 2002: 183-203.

---. Teachers as facilitators: What autonomy-supportive teachers do and why their students benefit. *Elementary School Journal*, 2006, 106(3): 225-236.

Reeve, J., Bolt, E., and Cai, Y. Autonomy-supportive teachers: How they teach and motivate students. *Journal of Educational Psychology*, 1999, 91(3): 537-548.

Richards, J. C., and Farrell, T. S. C. *Professional Development for Language Teachers: Strategies for Teacher Learning*. Cambridge: Cambridge University Press, 2005.

Richards, J. C., and Lockhart, C. *Reflective Teaching in Second Language Classrooms*. Cambridge: Cambridge University Press, 1994.

Ross, J. A., and Bruce, C. D. Teacher self-assessment: A mechanism for facilitating professional growth. *Teaching and Teacher Education*, 2007, 23(2): 146-159.

Roulston, K. Analysing interviews. In U. Flick (ed.). *The SAGE Handbook of Qualitative Data Analysis*. London: Sage Publications, 2014: 297-312.

Ruan, Y., Duan, X., and Du, X. Y. Tasks and learner motivation in learning Chinese as a foreign language. *Language, Culture and Curriculum*, 2015, 28(2): 170-190.

Sahinkarakas, S., Yumru, H., and Inozu, J. A case study: Two teachers' reflections on the ELP in practice. *ELT Journal*, 2010, 64(1): 65-74.

Samuda, V., and Bygate, M. *Tasks in Second Language Learning*. London: Palgrave Macmillan, 2007.

Sato, K., and Kleinsasser, R. C. Beliefs, practices and interactions in a Japanese high school English department. *Teaching and Teacher Education*, 2004, 20(8): 797-816.

Schon, D. A. *The Reflective Practitioner: How Professionals Think in Action*. New York: Basic Books, 1983.

---. *Educating the Reflective Practitioner*. New York: Basic Books, 1987.

Scott, J. *A Matter of Record: Documentary Sources in Social Research*. Cambridge: Polity Press, 1990.

Selinker, L. Interlanguage. *International Review of Applied Linguistics*, 1972, 10(3): 209-231.

Shaw, J. *Teacher Working Together*. Amsterdam: John Benjamins, 2008.

Shu, D. Towards a new model of classroom instruction in foreign language teaching. *Journal of the Foreign Language World*, 2006, 114(4): 21-29.

Sieber, J. The ethics and politics of sensitive research. In C. Renzetti and R. Lee (eds.). *Researching Sensitive Topics*. London: Sage Publications, 1993.

Sikes, P. Methodology, procedures and ethical considerations. In C. Opie (ed.). *Doing Educational Research: A Guide to First-time Researchers*. London: Sage Publications, 2004: 15-33.

Smith, J. A. Semi-structured interviewing and qualitative analysis. In J. A. Smith, R. Harré, and

L. van Langenhove (eds.). *Rethinking Methods in Psychology*. London: Sage Publications, 1995: 8-12.

Smith, R. C. Learner and teacher development: Connections and constraints. *The Language Teacher*, 2001, 25(6): 43-44.

Snape, D., and Spencer, L. The foundations of qualitative research. In J. Ritchie and J. Lewis (eds.). *Qualitative Research Practice: A Guide for Social Science Students and Researcher*. London: Sage Publications, 2003: 1-23.

Spratt, M., Humphreys, G., and Chan, V. Autonomy and motivation: Which comes first?. *Language Teaching Research*, 2002, 6(1): 245-266.

Stake, R. E. *The Art of Case Study Research*. Thousand Oaks: Sage Publications, 1995.

Stenhouse, L. A note on case study and educational practice. In R. G. Burgess (ed.). *Field Methods in the Study of Education*. London: Falmer Press, 1985: 263-271.

Stevick, E. *Humanism in Language Teaching*. Oxford: Oxford University Press, 1990.

Strauss, A. L. *Qualitative Analysis for Social Scientists*. Cambridge: Cambridge University Press, 1987.

Strauss, A. L., and Corbin, J. M. *Basics of Qualitative Research: Grounded Theory Procedures and Techniques*. 2nd ed. Thousand Oaks: Sage Publications, 1998.

Thavenius, C. Teacher autonomy for leaner autonomy. In S. Cotterall and D. Crabbe (eds.). *Learner Autonomy in Language Learning: Defining the Field and Effecting Change*. Frankfurt: Peter Lang, 1999: 159-163.

Tholin, J. Learner and teacher autonomy: Concepts, realities, and responses. *ELT Journal*, 2009, 63(2): 179-181.

Tomlinson, B. Testing to learn: A personal view of language testing. *ELT Journal*, 2005, 59(1): 39-44.

Tort-Moloney, D. Teacher autonomy: A Vygotskian theoretical framework. CLCS Occasional Paper, 48, Dublin: Trinity College, CLCS, 1997.

Trebbi, T. Language teacher education for learner autonomy in Norway: Focus on meta-cognition. In M. Raya and T. Lamb (eds.). *Pedagogy for Autonomy in Language Education: Theory, Practice and Teacher Education*. Dublin: Authentik, 2008: 234-248.

Tschirhart, C., and Rigler, E. LondonMet e-packs: A pragmatic approach to learner/teacher autonomy. *Language Learning Journal*, 2009, 37(1): 71-83.

Tudor, L. Teacher roles in the learner-centred classroom. *ELT Journal*, 1993, 47(1): 22-31.

Ushioda, E. Why autonomy? Insights from motivation theory and research. *Innovation in Language Learning and Teaching*, 2011, 5(2): 221-232.

216

Van Lier, L. *Interaction in the Language Curriculum: Awareness, Autonomy and Authenticity.* New York: Longman, 1996.

Varanoglulari, F., Lopez, C., Pessanha, L., and Williams, M. Secondary EFL courses. *ELT Journal*, 2008, 62(4): 401-419.

Vernon, P. E. *The Measurement of Abilities.* London: University of London Press, 1956.

Vescio, V., Ross, D., and Adams, A. A review of research on the impact of professional learning communities on teaching practice and student learning. *Teaching and Teacher Education*, 2008, 24(1): 80-91.

Vieira, F. Pedagogy for autonomy: Teacher development and pedagogical experimentation. AILA Conference, Finland, August 1996.

---. Addressing constraints on autonomy in school contexts-lessons from working with teachers. In R. Smith and D. Palfreyman (eds.). *Learner Autonomy across Cultures-language Education Perspective.* London: Palgrave Macmillan, 2003.

---. Introduction to section III. In M. Raya and T. Lamb (eds.). *Pedagogy for Autonomy in Language Education: Theory, Practice and Teacher Education.* Dublin: Authentik, 2008: 199-202.

Vieira, F., Barbosa, I., Paiva. M., and Fernandes, I. S. *Teacher Education towards Teacher and Learner Autonomy.* Amsterdam: John Benjamins, 2008.

Vieira, F., and Moreira, M. A. Reflective teacher education towards learner autonomy. In M. Raya and T. Lamb (eds.). *Pedagogy for Autonomy in Language Education: Theory, Practice and Teacher Education.* Dublin: Authentik, 2008: 266-282.

Voller, P. Introduction to part 2: Roles and relationships. In P. Voller (ed.). *Autonomy and Independence in Language Learning.* London: Longman, 1997.

Vrasidas, C., and Zembylas, M. *Technology and Teachers' Professional Development.* Dublin: Authentik, 2008.

Vygotsky, L. S. *Mind in Society: The Development of Higher Psychological Processes.* Cambridge, MA: Harvard University Press, 1978.

Wang, Q., and Ma, X. Educating for learner-centredness in Chinese pre-service teacher education. *Innovation in Language Learning and Teaching*, 2009, 3(3): 239-253.

Wang, Y. When teacher autonomy meets management autonomy to enhance learner autonomy. *Chinese Journal of Applied Linguistics*, 2017, 40(4): 392-409.

Ward, J. R., and McCotter, S. S. Reflection as a visible outcome for preservice teachers. *Teaching and Teacher Education*, 2004: 20(3): 243-257.

Wellington, J. *Educational Research: Contemporary Issues and Practical Approaches.* London:

Continuum, 2000.

---. *Making Supervision Work for You: A Student's Guide*. London: Sage Publications, 2010.

Wellington, J., Bathmaker, A., Hunt, C., McCulloch, G., and Sikes, P. *Succeeding with Your Doctorate*. London: Sage Publications, 2005.

Willis, D., and Wills, J. *Doing Task-based Teaching*. Oxford: Oxford University Press, 2007.

Winner, E. How can Chinese children draw so well?. *Journal of Aesthetic Education*, 1989, 23(1): 41-63.

Wolcott, H. T. *Ethnography: A Way of Seeing*. Walnut Greek, CA: AltaMira, 1999.

Xie, X. Y. Why are students quiet? Looking at the Chinese context and beyond. *ELT Journal*, 2010, 64(1): 10-20.

Yin, H. B., Lee J. C. K., and Zhang, Z. H. Examining Hong Kong students' motivational beliefs, strategy use and their relations with two relational factors in classrooms. *Educational Psychology*, 2009, 29(6): 685-700.

Yin, R. K. *Case Study Research: Design and Methods*. Thousand Oaks: Sage Publications, 2009.

Yong, Z. Pedagogical suggestions on boosting learner autonomy in China. *International Journal of English Language, Literature and Humanities*, 2015, 3(9): 216-224.

Zeichner, K. M., and Liston, D. P. *Reflective Teaching: An Introduction*. Mahwah, NJ: Lawrence Erlbaum Associates, 1996.

Zhang, X. Q., and Head, K. Dealing with learner reticence in the speaking class. *ELT Journal*, 2010, 64(1): 1-9.

Zhou, M. M., Ma, W. J., and Deci, E. The importance of autonomy for rural Chinese children's motivation for learning. *Learning and Individual Differences*, 2009, 19(4): 492-498.

APPENDIX

Teachers' Interview Guide

The following are the questions used during semi-structured interviews with English language teachers in schools.

- How long have you been teaching English language?
- What does the job of teaching English language involve?
- What do you think about the content of the ELT curriculum?
- What resources/books and any other materials do you use for teaching English language?
- What is your role in the designing and teaching of the English language curriculum in the school?
- How do you support students' learning of English language in the school?
- Do students have any role in your planning and teaching of English language? What role do they play?
- What is the current situation regarding ELT in Chinese secondary schools? What problems or challenges do you think exist in ELT?
- Describe how you would see yourself as an agent of change in ELT.
- Are there any opportunities for professional development in your school? Explain.
- What does self-directed professional development (SDPD) involve? Do you think this plays any important role in your job?

图书在版编目(CIP)数据

英语基础教育中教师自主性实证研究 = A Study of Teachers' Perspectives on the Role of Teacher Autonomy in English Classrooms in Chinese Secondary Schools: 英文 / 孔佩佩著. —杭州：浙江大学出版社，2022.1

（外语·文化·教学论丛）

ISBN 978-7-308-21950-1

I. ①英… II. ①孔… III. ①英语—师资培养—研究 IV. ①G633.317

中国版本图书馆 CIP 数据核字 (2021) 第 227748 号

英语基础教育中教师自主性实证研究

A Study of Teachers' Perspectives on the Role of Teacher Autonomy in English Classrooms in Chinese Secondary Schools

孔佩佩　著

责任编辑	张颖琪
责任校对	仝　林
封面设计	项梦怡
出版发行	浙江大学出版社
	（杭州天目山路 148 号　邮政编码 310007）
	（网址：http://www.zjupress.com）
排　　版	浙江时代出版服务有限公司
印　　刷	广东虎彩云印刷有限公司绍兴分公司
开　　本	710 mm×1000 mm　1/16
印　　张	14.5
字　　数	338 千
版 印 次	2022 年 1 月第 1 版　2022 年 1 月第 1 次印刷
书　　号	ISBN 978-7-308-21950-1
定　　价	52.00 元

版权所有　翻印必究　印装差错　负责调换

浙江大学出版社市场运营中心联系方式：0571-88925591；http://zjdxcbs.tmall.com